The Return of Nature

The Return of Nature asks you to critique your conception of nature and your approach to architectural sustainability and green design. What do the terms mean? Are they de facto design requirements? Or are they unintended design replacements? The book is divided into five parts giving you multiple viewpoints on the role of the relations between architecture, nature, technology, and culture. A detailed case study of a built project concludes each part to help you translate theory into practice. This holistic approach will allow you to formulate your own theory and to adjust your practice based on your findings. Will you provoke change, design architecture that responds to change, or both?

Coedited by an architect and a historian, the book features new essays by Robert Levit, Catherine Ingraham, Sylvia Lavin, Barry Bergdoll, K. Michael Hays, Diane Lewis, Andrew Payne, Mark Jarzombek, Jean-François Chevrier, Elizabeth Diller, Antoine Picon, and Jorge Silvetti. Five case studies document the work of MOS Architects, Michael Bell Architecture, Steven Holl Architects, George L. Legendre, and Preston Scott Cohen.

Preston Scott Cohen is Gerald M. McCue Professor at the Harvard University Graduate School of Design and Principal of Preston Scott Cohen, Inc., based in Cambridge, Massachusetts, USA.

Erika Naginski is Professor of Architectural History and Co-Director of the PhD Program in Architecture, Landscape Architecture, and Urban Planning at the Harvard University Graduate School of Design, Cambridge, Massachusetts, USA.

The Return of Nature

Sustaining Architecture in the Face of Sustainability

Edited by Preston Scott Cohen and Erika Naginski

Routledge
Taylor & Francis Group

NEW YORK AND LONDON

First published 2014
by Routledge
711 Third Avenue, New York, NY 10017

and by Routledge
2 Park Square, Milton Park, Abingdon, Oxon OX14 4RN

Routledge is an imprint of the Taylor & Francis Group, an informa business

Library of Congress Cataloging in Publication Data
The return of nature : sustaining architecture in the face of sustainability / edited by Preston Scott Cohen and Erika Naginski.
pages cm
Includes bibliographical references and index.
1. Sustainable design. 2. Sustainable architecture. I. Cohen, Preston Scott, editor of compilation. II. Naginski, Erika, editor of compilation.
NK1520.R534 2014
720'.47--dc23
2013038677

ISBN: 978-0-415-89788-4 (hbk)
ISBN: 978-0-415-89789-1 (pbk)
ISBN: 978-1-315-79618-5 (ebk)

Acquisition Editor: Wendy Fuller
Editorial Assistant: Grace Harrison
Production Editor: Alanna Donaldson

Typeset in Univers by
Servis Filmsetting Ltd, Stockport, Cheshire

Printed by Bell and Bain Ltd, Glasgow

Contents

Figures

Case Study I: MOS Architects, afterparty, PS 1 YAP Pavilion (2009)

Case Study II: Michael Bell Architecture, Gefter-Press House, Hudson Valley, NY (2007)

Case Study III: Steven Holl Architects, Sliced Porosity Block, Chengdu, China (2007–2012)

Case Study IV: George L. Legendre, Henderson Waves, Singapore (2004–2008)

Case Study V: Preston Scott Cohen, Inc., Fahmy House, Los Gatos, CA (2007–2014)

Contributors

Michael Bell is Professor of Architecture at Columbia University's Graduate School of Architecture, Planning, and Preservation, New York. He collaborates with the architect Eunjeong Seong, founder of the New York-based Visible Weather.

Barry Bergdoll is Meyer Schapiro Professor in the Department of Art History and Archaeology at Columbia University, New York. From 2007 to 2013, he served as the Philip Johnson Chief Curator of Architecture and Design at New York's Museum of Modern Art (MoMA).

Jean-François Chevrier is a critic, curator, and Professor of the History of Contemporary Art at the École nationale supérieure des beaux-arts, Paris.

Preston Scott Cohen is Gerald M. McCue Professor at the Harvard University Graduate School of Design, and Principal of Preston Scott Cohen, Inc., based in Cambridge, Massachusetts.

Elizabeth Diller is a founding Partner of the award-winning design studio Diller Scofidio + Renfro, New York, and Professor of Architectural Design at the Princeton University School of Architecture, Princeton, New Jersey.

K. Michael Hays is Eliot Noyes Professor of Architectural Theory and Associate Dean for Academic Affairs at the Harvard University Graduate School of Design, Cambridge, Massachusetts.

Steven Holl, an award-wining architect and educator, is Principal of Steven Holl Architects with offices in New York, Beijing, and San Francisco.

Catherine Ingraham is Professor of Architecture at the Pratt Institute, Brooklyn, NY, in the Graduate Architecture and Urban Design Program for which she served as Chair between 1999 and 2005.

Mark Jarzombek is Professor of the History and Theory of Architecture and Associate Dean of the School of Architecture and Planning, Massachusetts Institute of Technology, Cambridge, Massachusetts.

Sylvia Lavin is Professor of Architectural History and Theory as well as Director of Critical Studies in the Department of Architecture and Urban Design at the University of California, Los Angeles.

George L. Legendre, a founding Partner of the London-based practice IJP, is Associate Professor in Practice of Architecture at the Harvard University Graduate School of Design, Cambridge, Massachusetts.

Robert Levit, Principal of Khoury Levit Fong, Toronto, is Associate Professor and Director of the Master of Architecture Program of the University of Toronto's John H. Daniels Faculty of Architecture, Landscape, and Design.

Diane Lewis, Professor at Cooper Union's Irwin S. Chanin School of Architecture, New York, founded Diane Lewis Architects, New York, in 1983.

Michael Meredith is Assistant Professor of Architectural Design at the Princeton University School of Architecture, Princeton, New Jersey. Along with his partner Hilary Sample, he is principal of MOS Architects, New York.

Erika Naginski is Professor of Architectural History and Co-Director of the PhD Program in Architecture, Landscape Architecture, and Urban Planning at the Harvard University Graduate School of Design, Cambridge, Massachusetts.

Andrew Payne is Senior Lecturer on the University of Toronto's John H. Daniels Faculty of Architecture, Landscape, and Design.

Antoine Picon is G. Ware Travelstead Professor of the History of Architecture and Technology and Co-Director of Doctoral Programs (PhD & DDes) at the Harvard University Graduate School of Design, Cambridge, Massachusetts.

Jorge Silvetti is a founding Partner with Rodolfo Machado of the award-winning Machado and Silvetti Associates, Boston. He is the Nelson Robinson, Jr., Professor of Architecture at the Harvard University Graduate School of Design, Cambridge, Massachusetts.

Acknowledgments

- Beat Widmer
- Berlin/ Frankfurter Goethe-Haus / Art Resource, NY
- Bilyana Dimitrova
- Canadian Centre for Architecture, Montréal
- Chicago History Museum
- Collections of the Library of Congress Prints and Photographs Division
- David Turturo
- Diller Scofidio + Renfro
- Élia Pijollet
- Getty Images
- Iwan Baan
- James Corner Field Operations
- John Roloff
- Margherita Spiluttini
- MBEACH1, LLLP
- MHJT
- Michael Bell
- MOS
- Nathan Willock
- Piet Oudolf
- Richard Barnes
- Sir John Soane's Museum, London
- Steven Holl Architects
- Sue Palmer

- The New York Public Library for the Performing Arts, Astor, Lenox and Tilden Foundation
- The Snow Show
- Tom Wiscombe Design

Introduction

The Return of Nature

Preston Scott Cohen and Erika Naginski

> Our oaks no longer proffer oracles, and we no longer ask of them the
> sacred mistletoe; we must replace this cult by care . . .
> —Charles-Georges Le Roy, "Forêt," *Encyclopédie* (1751–1772)[1]

> American biopolitics sees in nature its same condition of existence:
> not only the genetic origin and the first material, but also the sole
> controlling reference. Politics is anything but able to dominate nature
> or "conform" *[formare]* to its ends and so itself emerges "informed" in
> such a way that it leaves no space for other constructive possibilities.
> —Roberto Esposito, *Bios: Biopolitics and Philosophy* (2008)[2]

That Nature has returned with a vengeance in architectural theory and practice
goes far beyond the transmutation of the Vitruvian qualities of *firmitas, utilitas*, and
venustas into sustainability's motto of equity, biodiversity, and wise development.
The relation of architecture and nature found in the abundant literature on
sustainability rests on a moral imperative provided by the current environmental
crisis, which sets, as in a Greek tragedy, the finitude of natural resources over and
against the dismal and infinite cycle of human production and consumption. From
this agon emerges the quest for a responsible architecture. The apocalyptic drama
is rehearsed in such movements as natural architecture, which reifies the presumed
mysteriousness and fragility of natural materials by disposing and exposing leaves,
branches, and rocks in ephemeral interventions. By the same token, hope is made
to reside, resolutely and problematically, in the promise of technology (this despite
the specter of historical modalities such as pollution and obsolescence); thus there
is biomimicry, to give but one example, in which the emulation of natural forms

and processes undergirds the creation of such materials as adhesives replicating the bonding materials found in mussels, ceramic tiles with the strength of abalone shells, or glass with the air purifying capacities of certain plants.

Yet to what degree such bioethical platforms potentially negate the project of architecture remains a fundamental question. At present, the trend to "naturalize" architectural form in the digital regime has made manifest two tendencies which, each in its own way, reject the social, political, and symbolic life of forms: the first involves a direct calculus attempting to translate the perceived conduct of natural systems, thereby imbuing form with a sort of naturalized behavioralism; the second, tied to a classical tradition aligning mathematics and nature, replaces the compositional authority of the designer with the computational generation of pattern. The result is all too often the production of a devitalized ornament, of rhetorical forms that, in the end, re-present nature and so return to mimicry as principle (the copy newly moralized). If modernist formalism veered too far towards the utopian purity of the autonomy of art, then sustainability has radically tilted the scales the other way—that is, towards the ontological primacy of the bio-environment, all the while finding refuge in an ethical agenda and so eschewing critique and denying that it, too, belongs to a formal and formalized system. Such tilting of the scales has not come without costs: namely it risks endorsing a critical terrain marked by neo-empiricism and ahistoricism.

Precisely because sustainability introduces new, complex, and inexorable constraints, it becomes necessary to shift gears—this to prevent subsuming the social, political, and cultural dimensions of the built environment under nature's primary status. We would need, first, to say something about the role of those constraints in contemporary interpretations of nature as they relate to matters of function and codes. Then, we would have to provide real comparison between the environmental limiting condition and other moments of "functional interference" with architectural form (such as the introduction of the elevator, which transformed the relationship of buildings to the city and thus the city itself; fire safety, which radically altered the social arrangements of interiors; or the adoption of ADA (Americans with Disabilities Act) standards for accessible design and newly requisite elements such as access ramps, which fundamentally altered the conception of thresholds, passages, and spatial sequences). For in all of those instances in which constraints did, in fact, operate on the corpus of architecture, spatial and institutional mutations of profound consequence occurred; there is, after all, a long tradition of architects redeploying that which intervenes in order to grant themselves experimental license.

More importantly, there is no one-way street here; architecture is just as likely to provoke change (transformative architecture) as it is to respond to it (responsive architecture). We could argue that despite the maelstrom of claims to newness and the moralistic rhetoric now swirling around the sustainable what-have-yous or what-have-you-nots, thinking about responsible design will necessarily contribute to the legacy of how externalities have imposed themselves on architecture in both recent and distant pasts, in both concrete and symbolic ways. Put differently: to demystify the ecological and the sustainable while acknowledging the reality of new necessities is to reveal conditions of possibility for architecture. Indeed, sustainability's call to arms belongs to a complex historical arc with crucial junctures: these range from the Italian jurist and political philosopher Giambattista Vico's primordial forest (as antipode to human civilization) to the French visionary architect Claude-Nicolas Ledoux's Royal Saltworks at Arc-et-Senans (as the exemplification of a philosophized exploitation of natural resources); or from twentieth-century analogies between ecological systems and political economies to more recent demonstrations of the ways in which fundamental forces and resonances accumulate into alternately inventive or conventionalized shapes and figures.

All this reveals that the problem of form in design continues to be vital, not ancillary—and, above all, that it cannot be deemed simply subservient to, or the passive recipient of, the claims of an ethical horizon as it is delimited by current environmental modalities. Consider, for a start, the purposeful search for the dissolution of boundaries: whether we think of the evaporation of the object engineered by filtered lake water shot through fog nozzles in Elizabeth Diller and Ricardo Scofidio's Blur Building (Chapter 10), or the photographer Andrew Moore's attention to the blooming green moss invading, in the form of a perfect rectangular carpet, the floor of the former executive offices of the Ford Model-T Headquarters, Highland Park, these are instances in which architecture seems poised at, yet refuses to push past, the edge of its own annihilation. It is as if architecture now seeks to be arrested on the edge of an ecological fantasy, whereas it used to be arrested on the edge of nature's presumed harmonic perfection (the Renaissance) or its reasoned mimeticism (Laugier's Enlightenment).

By means of the single continuous surface (OMA's 1992 project for the Jussieu Library is a founding example), the paradigm of dissolution emerges as a ruin and channels the architectural desire to replicate the erosion, corrosion, and slow death of human culture at the hands of nature. The great German sociologist Georg Simmel put it this way:

> Although architecture, too, uses and distributes the weight and carrying power of matter according to a plan conceivable only in the human soul, within this plan the matter works within its own nature, carrying out the plan, as it were, within its own forces. This unique balance . . . breaks, however, the instant a building crumbles. For this means nothing else than that merely natural forces begin to become master over the work of man: the balance between nature and spirit, which the building manifested, shifts in favor of nature.[3]

In addition to the sense that continuous surfaces and the flow of skins might represent this shift "in favor of nature" only to signal a confused authorial position, nature's return has likewise fueled a symptomatic interest in what might best be described as territorial transgression: what belongs outside goes inside where it shouldn't be and vice versa, and the resulting proposals benefit from a discrete and absolute differentiation from architecture. Thus projects such as MOS Architects' afterparty pavilion inverts outwards, externalizes the soft internal realities of architecture (see Case Study I). What is preserved, and ironically sexualized, is the dichotomy between the artifice of architecture (in strict and hard and masculine conical form) and a soft "naturalness" (of woolly, outside textures). And lastly, we might speak of the formalism embedded in precipitous interventions: how, for instance, Steven Holl's Sliced Porosity Block, as it is presented in this volume (Case Study III), investigates a different temporality of light, one that is decisive, instantaneous, dramatic, and incontrovertible. The orthogonal regularity of the vast architectural body is preserved through its violation, with a "sun-sliced geometry" performing the act of nature's return all the while maintaining architecture and nature as separate entities.

These new formal concerns, which invoke in turn contiguity, inversion, and transgression, prompt us to weigh the legacy of a posthuman(ist) framework in architecture against the a priori value ascribed to nature in bio-ethical ideologies. How might architectural form demarcate the shifting crossroads between ecology, society, and aesthetic philosophy? How might we clear the (ideological) air? The speculative essays and architectural case studies included in this book traverse a whole array of interpretive and creative answers to such questions and underscore how one of the defining themes of architecture today is not nature qua nature but, rather, its return. We've seen such returns many times before, and these returns have been definitive, critical, catalytic—producing ruptures alongside continuities in architecture's history.

The architects, theoreticians, and historians who contribute their insights here all in their own way take up the theme of return as transformative. Part I brings together essays by Robert Levit, Catherine Ingraham, and Sylvia Lavin under the rubric of "Organic Conceits" in order to foreground the various anthropological, ontological, and ideological stakes enmeshed in contemporary architecture's commitment to the "state of nature." Moving from present to precedents, Part II, entitled "The Sublime Past," includes contributions by Barry Bergdoll, K. Michael Hays, and Diane Lewis, which elicit those aesthetical and historical instances (from Kant to Schinkel to Mies) in which transcendence appears as an explicitly architectural operation securing the split of object and subject, of nature and culture. Meanwhile, the chapters by Andrew Payne, Mark Jarzombek, and Jean-François Chevrier in Part III, "Sustaining Nature," propose to gloss the conflation, as opposed to separation, of nature and architecture—a mutual encroachment whose outcome is either, depending on the author, disastrous or liberating. Next a shift of scale: the architectural encounter with nature turns into an infrastructural encounter in Part IV, "The Nature of Infrastructure," and Elizabeth Diller's rigorous account of the High Line's conceptualization extends, for Antoine Picon, into the poetic epitome of a situation in which nature, or that which had served as the technological and scenographic "support" for roads, bridges, and canals, now itself requires infrastructural support. The book concludes in Part V, "Nature, Unnaturally," with a consideration of pedagogical implications and Jorge Silvetti's advice to take heed of the metaphor that "Nature" risks becoming for new generations of architects. What serves throughout as a vivid and continuous intervention—as a visual response to the texts—is the series of case studies, architectural projects by MOS Architects, Michael Bell, Steven Holl, George L. Legendre and Preston Scott Cohen as well as Elizabeth Diller (Chapter 10) and Herzog & de Meuron (Chapter 9). These works render apparent the complex demands made on the architectural imagination by nature's return as well as the fact that limiting conditions are precisely what spawns architecture's most successful and inspired coming into being.

In closing, it is important to say that this work was generated out of the Harvard Symposia on Architecture, a lecture series held at the Harvard University Graduate School of Design over the course of 2009 and 2010. The series was spearheaded by Preston Scott Cohen, who was then Chair of the Department of Architecture, so as to explore with seriousness the question of architecture's autonomy in the face of the sustainability imperative. We would like to thank all the participants of the series as well as the colleagues, assistants, and departmental and technological staff who made this project possible, including Daniel Sherer, Faye Antonia Hays, Elizabeth MacWillie, Colin Hartness, Alienor de Chambrier, Abigail Stone, and Élia Pijollet. We would also thank Dean Mohsen Mostafavi, who continues to work tirelessly so as to ensure the intellectual and creative life of our school. Finally at Routledge, Wendy Fuller, Laura Williamson, Alanna Donaldson and Emma Gadsden deserve special recognition for their care and patience in seeing the project through.

Notes

1   Charles-Georges Le Roy, "Forêt," in Denis Diderot, Jean Le Rond d'Alembert, eds., *Encyclopédie ou Dictionnaire raisonné des sciences, des arts et des métiers, par une Société de Gens de lettres* (1751–1772), vol. 7 129: "Nos chênes ne rendent plus d'oracles, et nous ne leur demandons plus le gui sacré; il faut remplacer ce culte par l'attention . . ." See Robert Pogue Harrison, *Forests: The Shadow of Civilization* (Chicago, IL: University of Chicago Press, 1993), 113–124, for a discussion of Le Roy's entry.

2   Robert Esposito, *Bios: Biopolitics and Philosophy*, trans. Timothy Campbell (Minneapolis and London: University of Minnesota Press, 2008), 22.

3   Georg Simmel, "The Ruin," in Kurt H. Wolff, ed., *Essays in Sociology, Philosophy, and Aesthetics* (New York: Harper & Row, 1965), 259.

Part I

Organic Conceits

1

Design's New Catechism

Robert Levit

The ethical imperatives raised by ecological crisis have thrust landscape architecture to the center of design discourse, and architects, along with their big-scale brethren, urban designers, have desisted from their clichéd condescension and become converts to the environmental vocation.[1] Landscape architecture is no longer dismissed by architects who have imagined it as a background—figureless and ornamental—a passive ground waiting for building (terms of habitual condescension directed by architects towards landscape architecture, identified by Elizabeth Meyer).[2] Rather, now, it is *the* discipline, and, by their adaptation to it, architects and urban designers have recast their own position, joining landscape architects to attend to today's environmental crises and mitigate threats to our survival.

All this may be for the best, but it is worth asking what is being made of landscape architecture by architects and, in some cases, how it is being recast even by landscape architects. Mohsen Mostafavi raises this question in the introduction to his volume *Ecological Urbanism* (2010):

> Is it enough for architects, landscape architects, and urbanists to simply conceive of the future of their various disciplines in terms of engineering and constructing a more energy-efficient environment? As important as the question of energy is today, the emphasis on quantity—on energy reduction—obscures its relationship with the qualitative value of things.[3]

That is: what is the aesthetic vocation for ecologically oriented design practices— what Mostafavi calls, citing Guattari, a new "ethico-esthetic paradigm"? Continuing to draw on Guattari, Mostafavi promotes an aesthetic that will reveal the complementarity between us and the milieus that make us and that we make. But what city does not already reveal (or at least demonstrate to the inquisitive mind) the complementarities between ecological forces including those of human activity? To put it bluntly, the city has always been just such a system. It simply is an ecology in which people and built systems dynamically interact with each other and with the environment (non-human and inanimate). To see the city in such terms is but a matter of disposition, not a distinguishing mark by which to sort—according to a nonsensical distinction—the ecological from the non-ecological city. Thus, the question remains: What is the new thing that should become apprehensible to sensuous perception—that is, to aesthetic experience—under a new ecological regime?

To be clear, the question of what is to become perceivable is a different one from what instruments should be used and perhaps invented to face a mounting environmental crisis. Absent such a distinction there would be no need to raise the aesthetic question as Mostafavi does. He assumes not only that changes in technique for dealing with environmental challenges will have a sufficient impact on the physique of cities, but that these changes will (or should) demand, as it were, the invention of a new aesthetic regime through which to turn the brute fact of technique into aesthetic experience (as Le Corbusier's "five points" did for the technical innovations of ferroconcrete column and slab construction). However, it is no more possible today to account for the aesthetic commitments of environmentally oriented practices by seeking their derivation from technical or instrumental origins than it was in the case of Le Corbusier's fashioning of a new architectural idiom through his "five points."[4] Thus, in reference to the claims that Charles Waldheim makes, as we shall see, on behalf of an undisguised instrumentality in environmental design (landscape urbanism), something more is at stake than simply making visible the new means of managing the environment, and what this something is bears some consideration.

But, before coming to what this something is, let us consider a more prosaic question. It lies outside the nimbus cast by the moral imperatives of design's "ethico-esthetic" response to the challenges of sustainable design. This question, urgent to designers, is one in which disciplinary identity and professional prerogatives are at stake. Professionals in adjacent technical disciplines such as engineering, building technologies, and materials science increasingly compete against design professionals around issues of technical competence in an ever more complex field of design. Not to mention the growing competition between architects and landscape architects. Increasingly, sustainability is a key concern. How are designers to respond? The acquisition of new forms of technical mastery—or at least familiarity with the deployment and management of new technologies—can only be part of the response. Arguably as important, if not more so, has been the growing centrality of a rhetoric in design that overtly communicates design's new (renewed?) ethical dedications.[5]

Thus Waldheim remarks that while the canonical landscapes of Frederick

Law Olmsted—Central Park and the Emerald Necklace—were, in fact, designed as ecological infrastructures, they masqueraded as pastoral landscapes. (Masquerading or not, whatever Waldheim's reservations may be, for Olmsted and his peers the dual status of these landscapes as works of landscape rhetoric and infrastructure was not a contradiction to be overcome but a virtue.) By contrast, Waldheim continues,

> contemporary practices of landscape urbanism reject the camouflaging of ecological systems within pastoral images of "nature." Rather, contemporary landscape urbanism practices recommend the use of infrastructural systems and the public landscape they engender as the very ordering mechanisms of the urban field itself, shaping and shifting the organization of urban settlement.[6]

He insists that infrastructures should shape the urban field—arguably something they have always already done—but also, as if this were a separate effort, that the impact of infrastructures on the shape of urban settlement should be left undisguised.[7] The exception taken to Olmsted's work, according to this view, is not that it made a less perfect infrastructure (it did not) because it took on pastoral form. Rather, the problem is that this work did not present itself as infrastructure as such, unvarnished and naked to the eye.

Yet what, after all, is camouflage or disguise? The Fens of Olmsted's Emerald Necklace was both a working wetland (before the damming of the Charles River) *and* a polysemic allusion to other landscapes—Scottish fens, the marshlands of the New England shore, and more—suggesting an atavistic, fictive origin for the city of Boston.[8] Should these allusions or their forms count as a disguise? Especially given that the constitutive elements of the iconography of Olmsted's landscape design also happened to be the very elements of the landscape ecology that performed the remediating function constituting its infrastructural performance? The wetland planting was *both* the instrument and the form of literary and scenographic allusions. If, regardless of its performative success, the Fens is to be construed as camouflaged infrastructure, then what would it mean to be to be undisguised? What would or does uncamouflaged infrastructure look like?

From an ecological perspective, the city in its entirety has always already been an infrastructure—always caught up in shaping and being shaped by the dynamic interactions between living and nonliving matter. That is simply what the city is. Manuel De Landa's *A Thousand Years of Nonlinear History* (1997) serves as a guide here.[9] In what he describes as a "natural history" of the city, even the typological carapace of the city—its architecture, its stable (only slowly changing) urban typologies and morphologies—is viewed through a naturalist's vision.[10] Buildings—the calciferous shells of a living multi-species reef (i.e. the built form of the city) made by women and men but inhabited by much more—is by definition a system within a larger ecology, an infrastructure among infrastructures.[11] In other words, there is no city or settlement pattern that is ever anything but an urban ecology and, in that sense, an infrastructure for the living. Thus what is recognized as infrastructure depends, in some large measure, on one's perspective. From the naturalist's point of view, everything is infrastructure.

If everything is already infrastructure, as I believe it is, then there can be no dispensing of camouflage because, following the logic above, there is no such thing.[12] What, then, is at stake in Waldheim's call to do so? Perhaps it is better, for the moment, to put aside the finer points of definition and simply allow that what counts as infrastructure in ordinary conversation is simply systems: bridges, sewers, streets, power lines and a host of technical instruments that have today been supplemented by a wider view that includes organic and hydrological systems. To unveil infrastructure is to make these systems speak directly of themselves and to make their operations and dynamic interactions present themselves as such. In order to be uncamouflaged, they must present themselves without, paradoxically, representing themselves. They must simply be and, in so being, be present to our perception.

However, since the appearance of such systems—to the extent that they are even in part products of human ingenuity—are so inadequately determined by anything approaching an absolute performative logic, what comes to stand as the undisguised, unadorned, and visible system is a visual rhetoric. As such it must claim to present a naked instrument whose appearance is simply a given. For an instrument, according to this claim, need not be expressive, it need only work, yet all the while paradoxically relying on a choice of expression that is nothing less than a rhetorical expression of its instrumentality. Infrastructure is understood to be naked (uncamouflaged) to the extent that the idiom communicating its instrumental status remains unrecognized as a visual code. Instead, this code must appear to be no more than the unmediated ontology of instrumental necessity. Two false premises commingle in the fantasy of uncamouflaged landscapes: first, that there is a mode of perception which operates outside of symbolic codes and recognizes directly the performative logic of things, and second, that there are sufficiently objective conditions to determine environments free of symbolic codes and practices.[13]

Let us return to Mostafavi's summons to an aesthetic project. His call to attend to questions of quality in the face of quantitative demands addresses the distinction (which is not to say the conflict) between performative and aesthetic goals. He would like new aesthetic experiences to raise consciousness of the imbricated relationship between ourselves and the extended milieus in which we live, at the same time that new aesthetic experiences might simply be discovered through the experience of the new arrangements of environments responding to the challenges of sustainability. The first goal is epistemological and didactic in nature; the second is simply openness to new experience. He mentions seeing Paris, or at least one of its boulevards, from a new vantage point, elevated, on the Arts Viaduct as an example of the latter. Now, if, at first blush, Mostafavi's ruminations seem different from Waldheim's, with the former setting up a difference between quality and

Robert Levit

quantity and between engineering and something more, something aesthetic, and if these distinctions are seemingly incompatible with Waldheim's uncamouflaged landscapes, on second thought the differences between these two authors is quite minor. Waldheim may exclude aesthetic categories from his terminology and dedications, but the didactic nature of Mostafavi's "ethico-esthetic" goal seeks to foster consciousness of the same underlying (uncamouflaged) infrastructural realities. And because Mostafavi does not provide goals for his aesthetic notions beyond a didactic purpose (i.e. instilling a consciousness of milieu) and finding quality in the formation of new milieus, the aesthetic project is left without criteria. Thus, the new aesthetic project alludes to no more than an attunement of sensibilities to environments shaped by new infrastructural mechanisms, while relying on unexamined artistic commitments and the shared tastes of design communities. What is more, theories of affect and sensation which justify an aesthetics of pure effect provide the alibi which permits such theorizations to avoid articulating the symbolic discourses which design brings to bear on infrastructure and which shapes the reception of the designed environment.

So what is supposed to shape the appearance of the city and its constituent infrastructures? Today it is the demonstration of process, the succession of ecologies, the unpredictable flux of the metropolitan phenomenon, of ecologies taken in the broadest sense. The instruments of their management have become didactic media that show nature as a process and building as environmental apparatus. Where landscape is concerned, consider the arguments and diagrams that accompany such inaugural projects of the sustainable present as *Fresh Kills* by James Corner, *Downsview Park* by OMA and Bruce Mau, or, more recently, the many submissions to the Van Alen Institute's competition for *Envisioning Gateway: A Public Design Competition for Gateway National Park*, including Ashley Kelly and Rikako Wakabayashi's winning submission.[14] These projects are oriented toward the revelation of the processes of nature that they manage. Alongside these works, functional landscapes acquired an aesthetic caché in such collections as James Corner and Alex S. MacLean's *Taking Measures Across the American Landscape* (2000).[15] The documentation in this volume of essays both reflected and fostered the rising interest in design schools in the geographer's account of the economic and technical forces structuring regions. For Corner and MacLean, the appearance of the environment is both bound to and the consequence of performative arrangements; environments are shaped by forces and designed to shape forces. Such a stance may provide knowledge, as it were, of unselfconsciously constructed utilitarian landscapes—of farming, logging, wind farming, and parking (to name a few objects of their observation)—but the images provided by such landscapes are also fodder for a design idiom that chooses, with a self-consciousness absent in the original utilitarian vernaculars, an aesthetic vocation derived from infrastructural utility. Whatever the objects were in the first instance, once they are collected and made into environmental paradigms and points of reference, they are transmuted into the basis for a new landscape iconography.[16] As in landscape architecture so in architecture: new practices of eco-architecture focus on the performative arguments that structure both performance *and* appearance. Consider the green buildings of Behnisch, Foster, Jacques Ferrier, or, among young designers, Howeler + Yoon's *Eco-Pods* or Iwamoto + Scott's *Hydro-Net City* and *Jellyfish House.* Regardless of whether or not buildings by these architects perform in a newly sustainable manner, the presentation of performative goals is also a mode of *representation* in these works—a rhetorical flourish that discloses performative claims through representation. There are student works—those found, say, in the renewable building types explored in the Architectural Association's Diploma Unit 6, such as *Multiple Public Ground* by Minseok Kim—exhibiting entire urban morphologies that claim to be shaped by their response to hydrological phenomena during flooding.[17] Buildings evoking irregular versions of hydrodynamically shaped bridge piers, school-like fish or boats caught in currents or wind: these are settlements shaped by infrastructure, as Waldheim would have it. Yet such examples must also be taken to speak of their overdetermination by hydrodynamic forces. To make proper sense of such projects, in other words, it becomes necessary to recognize the implausibility of the technical argument and to recognize the centrality of the expression of hydrodynamic shaping (a cousin of the aerodynamics of 1950s car *styling*).

Whence this discursive centrality of the performative, the useful, and the environmentally ameliorative in the styling of design in the context of the sustainability-oriented, landscape-keyed present? Why does it represent such a broad swath of design practice today?[18] Why should we want instruments to make such efforts to announce their activities as instruments? The urge to reveal the conditions of production that we could find, nearly one hundred years ago, in the architectural work of Hannes Meyer or in the desire to reform the aesthetic content of industrial products among the functionalists of his generation arose from the more rarefied perspectives of the avant-garde rather than from a broader public interest in didactic and reformist gestures.[19] Yet today, environmentally oriented design draws on a widespread public sentiment: mediatized anxiety focused on ecological peril. Such danger creates an appetite for technical solutions and, in particular, for the comforting aura of expertise in an expert style.

None of this is to argue that environmental risks today are not real. They are more frightening than ever, particularly as they are now coupled with dangers that are eminently the products of our own making. But whereas in the past such threats may have been perceived as local, they are now global with catastrophe and human extinction as their horizon. Ulrich Beck, in *World at Risk* (2009), has described the unique impact of the ecological crisis upon contemporary experience. He makes two important points. First, risk is the consequence of human actions. Thus what were once the chance threats of nature, experienced fatalistically, are now brought about by our own actions and are only resolvable through our own further actions and technical know-how.[20] Whereas a historically significant event like the Lisbon earthquake of 1755 conjured punitive nature and divine providence, the devastating earthquake and tsunami that hit Japan in March 2011 initiated an additional crisis by unleashing sources of radiation not occurring in nature, which may be worse than the initial disaster. As important in Beck's characterization of the relationship of risk to the transformative impacts of technical modernization is the fact of a global scale. Risk is no longer limited to this or that group, class, or territory (even if risk is distributed unequally in the world). The contemporary horizon of risk is global; global warming and nuclear disaster (as we feared it in Japan) place the entirety of the human habitat at risk through not only the immediate consequences of catastrophic events but also the repercussions they are bound to have on global food supplies and economies (even for those areas outside of a given crisis zone). Extinction is the horizon of contemporary risk.

Beck's second important point is that circumstances in which risks put into motion through human activity have taken on a complexity of such scope that their management—which is to say, evaluating the likelihood of future events as well as devising precautionary measures—exceeds the predictive capabilities of technical experts. Combined with the global scope of risk, this increasing uncertainty in technical management has created both a political and cultural problem. Declining faith in technical expertise is accompanied by the migration of risk management to political arenas in which the forms of deliberation render more overt the cultural dimensions of judgment that always underlie the putatively technocratic means of risk management. In the play of anxieties that shape the cultural experience of risk, the persuasive representation of expert solutions becomes progressively more important as a balm for our anxieties. And while an aura of expertise or a rhetoric of instrumentality may very well coexist with actual technical expertise, it is important to bear in mind that these are not the same thing.

For what follows, it is important to distinguish between actual expertise— technical know-how—and the comfort derived from the aura of expertise. In his *Terrors and Experts* (1997), the British psychoanalyst Adam Phillips has described how the patient in analysis desires that the analyst possess an expertise that he or she cannot, in fact, possibly possess. The patient wishes for this in order that pronouncements might be made about what to do, how to proceed, and how to set right what is wrong.[21] Regardless of the fact that the analyst cannot possess such expertise (it does not exist), the patient is nevertheless tempted to believe, and sometimes decides, that the analyst possesses just such knowledge. Such a belief allows patients to make their own determinations about how to proceed under the illusion that they are gathering this direction from the analyst.

The appetite for expertise has a life of its own. It creates and enlists phantasms on behalf of a need that is in excess of the availability of expertise. That faith in expertise may decline, may not even matter. This is because, paradoxically, there may be faith in nothing else. In the deliberative realms of secular societies, the disrepute of the expert fuels the search for reliable expertise rather than dismissing the possibility of expertise as such. This is why disbelief in global warming is supported by its own body of experts.

And in the unique comfort provided by the balm of expertise lies design's new vocation. Since design deploys the infrastructures of the urban ecology (landscape infrastructures, buildings, roads, etc.), it must determine their appearance. The instrumentality of such infrastructures must become the very substance of design's new rhetoric.

The global character and terrifying potency of today's ecological threats lend a millenarian character to the ecological anxieties of the present, as if we were again in an age of eschatological fear when prayers have to be made and tributes offered. No longer believers in a religious faith that could read into the events of the world the workings of divine providence, we see in them only elements of a calamity brought on by our own meddling. Today's dispensation requires the articulation of new acts of faith made on behalf of those who imagine themselves beyond faith. No cathedrals this time, and while we may save ourselves through technological know-how, fears themselves—ecological in character—will be appeased by the *appearance* of functioning landscapes and green buildings. There will be no place for musty myths about Scotland or bucolic reverie but only didactic demonstrations of nature's repair. Like a catechism, landscape must teach us what is proper. Landscape emerges as a territorial system through which to create a sheltering milieu, a dynamic but safe harbor brought about by technique but revealed through what can only be the rhetoric of technique.

If these rhetorical offerings appeal to an emotional need for visible solutions, they also demonstrate the one remaining arena in which plural publics can come together and agree: that is, the desire for survival. Consensus on what constitutes the proper idiom for an architecture dedicated to collective life may not be easy to achieve. Yet to the extent appeals are directed to an instinct for survival they work broadly. The appeal has the quality of a neutral procedural apparatus, which requires adherence to no other ideal than naked survival. In view of this common denominator, the antagonisms of a plural public might just yield to consensus. Thus designers, as technocrats in their own right, not only can manage the threats posed to professional control by the technical disciplines, but also can bind diverse constituencies to their projects.

So today, when we look at technical diagrams of flow, and see highlighted in them the instruments of sustainability in all their technical detail, let us not forget that whatever successes our instruments have in creating a world in which we can survive, the sheer visibility of these instruments signals a mode of representation. In the contemporary idiom of landscape architecture as much as in the buildings and districts emblazoned with the insignia of sustainability concerns, we are seeing much more than a coming to terms with the simple and inexorable realities with which we are confronted. Such an approach to architecture and landscape also functions as a fearful tribute offered up with the same rhetorical verve that motivated generations of unrecognized confrères-in-fear of bygone ages.

Robert Levit

Notes

1   I would like to thank Evonne Levy and Andy Payne for their invaluable discussions with me on the themes of this essay. Among the many publications that point to this event, I refer the reader to Charles Waldheim, ed., *The Landscape Urbanism Reader* (New York: Princeton Architectural Press, 2006), and, more recent, Mohsen Mostafavi, ed., with Gareth Doherty, *Ecological Urbanism* (Cambridge, MA, and Basel: Harvard University Graduate School of Design/Lars Müller Publishers, 2010).

2   Elizabeth K. Meyer, "The Expanded Field of Landscape Architecture," in George F. Thompson, Frederick R. Steiner, eds., *Ecological Design and Planning* (New York: John Wiley, 1997), 45–47.

3   Mostafavi, *op. cit.*, 17. This book can be seen as a compendium of thought that reflects the reorientation of design discourse that Dean Mohsen Mostafavi is seeking to implement at the Harvard Graduate School of Design and that conforms to broader shifts in design discourse.

4   It is certainly possible to imagine subjectively rich appreciations arising from the experience of what might be taken as brute facts—think of the famous account by Richard Serra of his interstate journeys in New Jersey—but such heroic accounts of subjective attachments to things is a far cry from the fashioning of quality out of quantity that Mostafavi suggests or the invention of new syntaxes out of ferroconcrete construction that Le Corbusier fashions.

5   Admittedly many sophisticated arguments would do away with old-fashioned dichotomies that divide things into a functional and aesthetic binary. But this binary remains relevant to anyone who is able to recognize that no necessitarian logic is ever sufficient in determining the design of essentially all objects of architecture, landscape architecture, or city design.

6   Waldheim, *op. cit.*, 29.

7   After all, what has the field of cities been at least since the beginning of the nineteenth century? Consider that the New York City Commissioner's plan of 1810, Baron Haussmann's boulevards, Ildefons Cerdà's Barcelona, or the interstate-highway-dependent-suburb all are settlement forms shaped in significant ways by infrastructure. Rem Koolhaas ("Advancement versus Apocolypse," in Mostafavi, *op. cit.*, 57), points back to Vitruvius's concerns with the siting of cities in relationship to environmental conditions. Infrastructures come in a mix of registers, but the interplay between systems of movement, water treatment, and landscape all converged, for instance, in Second Empire Paris. However, the point here is not to belabor historical dating of complementarities between urban settlement and infrastructural concerns, but rather to underline what is new today: a concern with unveiling infrastructural logics.

8   See Walter Creese, *Crowning of the American Landscape: Eight Great Spaces and Their Buildings* (Princeton, NJ: Princeton University Press, 1985), 171–172. Creese writes: "Although the Fens was to deal boldly with water pollution through ingenious engineering, it was never to be entirely present or accountable, but rather was supposed to unlock memories of an 'untroubled horizon.' Those no longer easily reachable stretches of marsh along the open Atlantic Coast (now called 'wetlands' by conservationists), where the new inhabitants of Boston had roamed as children."

9   Manuel De Landa, *A Thousand Years of Nonlinear History* (New York: Zone Books, 1997).

10   Waldheim elsewhere characterizes typological thought as a cul-de-sac, as if there were parts of the city that were properly infrastructural as opposed to other parts that were not. In the long arc of time, they all are.

11   There are no cul-de-sacs in typology as Waldheim has stated, because typology is one of many infrastructures in the dynamic ecology of the city.

12   The landscape architecture historian Georges Farhat has made the observation that the customary view of human infrastructures set within natural environments has been inverted within the contemporary setting. So-called natural environments are now set within infrastructural systems as parts of this larger man-made system. It is a perception that is somewhat different from the more general observation that no natural or perhaps wilderness environments are left, but only a world remade by human activity. The difference lies in the persistent distinction between natural and human worlds and following from this that what is taken to be nature, which means some sort of landscape setting, is almost always set within and attached to infrastructural projects. Farhat made the observation in a lecture given at the John H. Daniels Faculty of Architecture, Landscape, and Design, University of Toronto, Fall 2010.

13   While I can imagine here someone calling upon affect theory to raise an objection to my insistence that no perceptions exist but through symbolic codes, the claim I am making is less sweeping. It is only that the discrimination between camouflaged and uncamouflaged things occurs at the center of a symbolic logic, not that logic which is an eminently symbolic cognition. In addition, whether there really are affective responses of the precognitive sort free from symbolic registers is debated by Ruth Leys, "The Turn to Affect: A Critique," *Critical Inquiry* 37/3 (Spring 2011): 434–472. I would like to thank Andy Payne for leading me to this article.

14   See www.vanalen.org/gateway/exhibition.php

15   See Michael van Valkenburgh's foreword in James Corner and Alex S. MacLean, eds., *Taking Measures Across the American Landscape* (New Haven, CT: Yale, 2000), ix–xi, which makes explicit the relationship of vernacular landscapes to an aesthetic project through the comparison he makes to Le Corbusier's famous use of silos (among other objects of a utilitarian vernacular) in the establishment of his aesthetic program for architecture.

16   Consider here the relationship between, one the one hand, Scott Brown and Venturi's observations about the vernacular logics of the Las Vegas strip and, on the other, how these were made to migrate into their design practices. Venturi Scott Brown's adoption and adaptation of the mandates of the automobile city, in which signage and image overwhelmed the physique of buildings, did not change the fact that their own work had to be taken as a form of reflection on the infrastructures of communication. Sometimes Venturi Scott Brown built in settings similar to the strip of their study, but they often transposed, to great polemical effect, the phenomenon of the strip to sites traditionally protected from its effects (such as the university campus).

17   Christopher C. M. Lee, Sam Jacoby, eds., *Typological Formations: Renewable Building Types and the City* (London: AA Publications, 2007), 116–125.

18   See Richard Weller, "An Art of Instrumentality: Thinking Through Landscape Urbanism" in Waldheim, *op. cit.*, 69–85. Weller's contribution summarizes, as the title suggests, the role of instrumental logics in a number of contemporary sustainability-oriented design practices. His own view ends with a measure of skepticism directed at logics

that claim for themselves technical neutrality, since technique fails to offer criteria for judgment about what the goals of technique might be when they exceed mere survival (as they always do). Bart Lootsma, who figures in Weller's account of instrumentality, sheds light on a genealogy of instrumental thought within the recent Dutch context in "Synthetic Regionalism: The Dutch Landscape Toward a Second Modernity" in James Corner, ed., *Recovering Landscape: Essays in Contemporary Landscape Architecture* (New York: Princeton Architectural Press, 1999), 251–274. Given the influence of Dutch design culture his account is important, but it reveals the peculiarity of concrete local practices transposed beyond the site of their origins. Unlike Weller's account, his is the untroubled account of an advocate.

19   See Michael Hays, *Modernism and the Posthumanist Subject: The Architecture of Hannes Meyer and Ludwig Hilberseimer* (Cambridge, MA: The MIT Press, 1995) or the discussions on *neue sachlichkeit* in Frederic J. Schwartz, *The Werkbund: Design Theory and Mass Culture before the First World War* (New Haven, CT: Yale University Press, 1996).

20   Ulrich Beck, *World at Risk* (Cambridge: Polity Press, 2009).

21   Adam Phillips, *Terrors and Experts* (Cambridge, MA: Harvard University Press, 1997).

2

Faculty of Omnipotence

Catherine Ingraham

[M]en wish to be serious but they do not understand how to be so.
Between their acts and their ceremonies lies the world and in this
world the storms blow and the trees twist in the wind and all the
animals . . . go to and fro yet this world men do not see. They see the
acts of their own hands or they see that which they name and call out
to one another but the world between is invisible to them.

—Cormac McCarthy, *The Border Trilogy: The Crossing* (1995), 46

There is something in the question of nature that is relentlessly lunatic. Timothy
Morton, in his book *Ecology without Nature*, wants to throw nature out of the
picture yet it abides in his very words: "eco" in bed with "logos."[1] He means
technologized Nature, reified Nature, Kant's Nature, Romanticism's Nature,
Modernism's Nature—definitions of Nature that are capable of a certain kind of
gratification. He does not mean nature, which cannot be gratified because it is
essentially incalculable.

It is a huge philosophical ungainliness to keep calling out nature in Nature,
Nature in not nature, and so forth. The problem is that nothing is not nature, and it is
therefore impossible to throw nature out. Morton gets embroiled in this right away,
in spite of his ambitious suggestion that we jettison the whole philosophical mess
of nature/culture with its endless conceits and start over with speculative realism's
philosophy of coexistence. As Morton writes:

What is required is a view that recognizes nonhumans as partners on
"this" side of social space, no longer conceived as exclusively human.
What is also required is a view that refuses to reduce one entity to

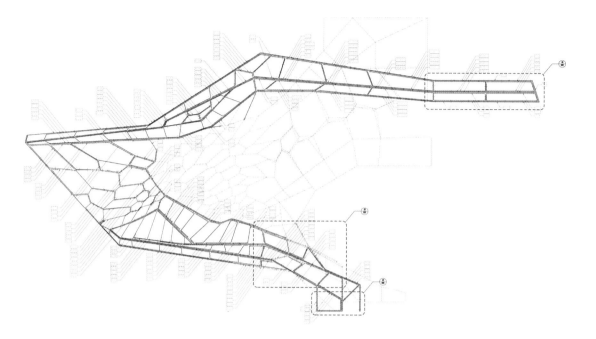

another—both reductionism and holism are problematic. In sum, we need to transition from the *time of nature* to the *time of coexistence*. For this, it is necessary to turn to the emerging object-oriented ontology movement, spearheaded by Graham Harman.[2]

The failure of current conceptions of sustainability in architecture, in Morton's view, has to do with how we "are not living in a *world*." And yet how to reconcile that world—McCarthy's between world—with this one? I will return to object-oriented ontology later.

Architects have clearly found fertile ground in the alliance between computation, theories of complexity, and neo-biological forms. Some have brought forth peculiar worlds. I am interested, for example, in the deep ornamentalism integral to work done by Hernan Diaz Alonso and Ruy Klein; and in Tom Wiscombe's modeling of various wing structures that perform at many more levels, and scales, than most surfaces of their kind (Figure 2.1). I am also interested in experimentation with structural systems that can carry the heavy differentiated skins so intricately composed in computer space, such as those designed by UNStudio for the Mercedes-Benz Museum in Stuttgart. Ben van Berkel seemed to be down on his knees at the construction site, the architect-engineer-tailor, measuring and bolting each unique building piece into its proper place. Diaz-Alonso and Wiscombe, in particular, are theorizing precedents for architecture that are not strictly architectural: Baroque art, existential narratives, insectoid organizations with inner workings that mimic adaptive developments, and floral complexity (Figure 2.2). This architecture is not biomimetic in any dedicated way, which is a good thing. Architects interested

in biomimicry tend not to grasp how dangerous it is to imitate another animal, plant, or geological system.[3] What are these built and unbuilt, sometimes balloon-like, sometimes wiry, labyrinthine, aggregated and ornate constructions, often afloat in inchoate post-apocalyptic hyper-industrialized space, trying to say about nature?

The immediate relevance of Giorgio Agamben's work to this question, in my view, has been the extremely serious attention he has given to the meaning of biological life now—not as a throwback or reduction but as a contemporary re-evaluation of the logics of political/cultural/biological life. In such writings as *The Open: Man and Animal*, Agamben's fleshing out of the philosophical implications of biomodernity in a direction Foucault implied but did not follow—more toward the animal one might say—has the potential to shift architecture's formal, aesthetic, and functional attention away from its still-obsessed relation to the modernist program and towards the complex living systems to which it is connected.[4] How the architectural program, with its tidy typologies of living, has kept life out of its thoughts sounds like, and is, yet another instance of lunacy. Biomodernity drastically unseats modernity in political and aesthetic terms. It argues that modernity's nature—the cartoon of nature that lies outside the autonomous architectural structure seated on its plinth—is now being recast as nature's modernity. In Agamben's discussion, biological life is precisely what is at stake in modern existence. Such a reversal is not a simple substitution of ecology or biology for culture; nor is it a sudden revelation about natural systems. Instead, it is a polemic that studies the complex entwinement of *bios* (natural life) and *zoe* (political life) in our own time. Architecture's claim for autonomy—which meant, in modernism, the freeing of architecture from history and historical precedents in order to establish a contemporary architectural language—may now have to face off against the *biological* definition of autonomy, which does not mean freedom. Biological autonomy is the formation and reformation of a system that must remain open to a large and complex outside. Is architecture a living system? Not exactly,

Catherine Ingraham

but living systems weave through it. Is architecture a social system? Yes, but in contemporary social theory, social organizations are intimately related to biological systems. These organizations substitute, if Niklas Luhmann is correct, an influx of meaning for an influx of energy in living systems.[5] The discipline and practice of architecture requires, inevitably, both meaning and energy. The better description might be to say that architecture is biotechnologically imbricated: biosphere and mechanosphere are united into a dynamic whole.[6]

Slavoj Žižek remarks, in one of his inevitable, and almost always persuasive, YouTube commentaries, that the problem for humans is not nature but our omnipotence over nature. Human beings in the *anthropocene*—the geologic age of humans—are, for the first time, making their own earthquakes. Žižek suggests that we stop being sad and nostalgic about nature and begin to exercise a certain discipline around the question of the scope and meaning of our omnipotence over it.[7] From such an inquiry, Žižek suggests, it would become clear that there is no nature for humans that is separate from our need and desire for omnipotence over it. This is similar—although coming from a different angle—to what Ilya Prigogine meant when he implied, at the beginning of *Order out of Chaos*, that there is such a thing as a successful dialog with nature that is not tragic.[8] A successful dialog with nature would mean, in Žižek's terms, a successful dialog with ourselves about omnipotence. That is part of what I want to attempt here: to capture just the barest hint of what such a dialog might mean for the war of the worlds that we are fighting. As always, my interests initially emanate from the discipline and practice of architecture, expand into different domains, then return to architecture with an argument (good or bad) in hand like a brace of pheasants shot on somebody else's property.

Omnipotence can mean many things. Ideas of omnipotence over nature, for example, have changed throughout history as human culture has fought its way out of divine, and into human, governance. Eighteenth-century developments, in particular, granted human omnipotence over nature the status of a Faculty. Faculty suggests that humans have not only a preference but, also, an aptitude for omnipotence. Aptitudes can be, ambiguously, learned or inherited traits, acquired or given. I am loosely borrowing the word "Faculty" from Kant because it is in Kant's theory of the sublime that we encounter a specific bridge between sensations of omnipotence, aesthetic experience, and claims for modern rationality. Aesthetic experience is something we routinely hope to harness to rational principles in architectural work. Kant's theory of aesthetic perception attempts this unification of experience with reason. His assumption is that experience is subjective and it therefore must be processed, universalized, by reason. Perception is one means by which reason processes experience. In the case of the sublime, nature overwhelms our senses, but reason helps us regain our sense of superiority over it. A necessary distance is reestablished; we need to keep pushing nature back into some proper, calculable, relation to ourselves. Our aptitude for omnipotence, in Kant's terms, depends on the varied meanings of this distance, and its periodic collapse and recovery. This faculty of omnipotence arises more purposefully, as an aesthetic/experiential theory, in Kant's age—the Enlightenment, the age of humanism—because humanism itself creates a separate nature for humans that sets it at a distance from some other nature, the nature of everything else. The modern concept of omnipotence over nature arising in the eighteenth century transforms earlier beliefs that nature is given by divine authority to humans—to use as needed—into a *right* that humans give to themselves. We have subsequently naturalized this right and rendered it irrefutable, not open to question.

This is a fairly blunt way of engaging with the very complex emergence of modern concepts of nature, reason, sensation, perception, power, divine and human rights, and historical process about which so much has been written and thought. But I am struck here by the self-evident fact that our so-called modern faculty of omnipotence, if such a thing exists, is rooted in utilitarianism. Once we became human, we no longer had any ground for sympathetic identifications with the non-human. Even our supposed sadness about nature is utilitarian. We lament the loss of our personal delight and pleasure in nature. When we became human we became, by definition, extremely different from every other living creature. The poet-scientist father of taxonomy Carl Linnaeus never actually defines the characteristics of the species *Homo sapiens*. He says something to the effect that if you want to know what kind of being a human is, you should look in a mirror.[9] Every other animal and plant is known by descriptions of physical structure and behavior. We know ourselves as a species, and as individuals, through self-reflection. We invented our modern human selves relatively recently, as Foucault reminded us in *The Order of Things*.

Architects routinely view architecture as a humanist discipline interested in the betterment of human life, as if we had taken the Hippocratic oath. But it is precisely the humanist position that now poses the dilemma. Use may still resonate with its nineteenth-century technological meanings of industrial consumption, extraction, and exploitation of nature, but now added to those meanings are new, potentially more virulent, uses such as medical and genetic research, visual exploitation (Planet Earth film series, Animal Planet television series, ecotourism), and political movements that use nature as a moral laboratory. On May 25, 2012, for example, two hundred climbers lined up to attempt to summit Mount Everest. On the way up they climbed over climbers who had failed in this same task several days earlier and now lay frozen in their path, still attached to the fixed ropes. Climbing Everest is pursued precisely as a pursuit of the sublime in Kant's terms. Oxygen bottles provide the necessary, if tentative, restoral of reason in the extremely dangerous death zone. Our non-industrial forms of utility, in particular, reinforce the confused presence, inherent in every manifestation of omnipotence, of lingering spiritual entitlements. These entitlements are now deeply lodged in rationalist scientific enterprises. Nature is simultaneously our natural enemy, hysterical, unstable, unpredictable, a place from which mayhem arises, and our dearest friend, our solace, refuge, our National Park, our mountain. In spite of evidence to the contrary—the dead climbers in our path—we feel a remarkable certitude about our right to control its moods and systems and we believe that nothing, not the climate, the icecaps, the oceans, the forests, the solar system and beyond, lies outside our future grasp. But just as you cannot completely throw out nature, you cannot throw out humanism either. Both are still morally persuasive.

I want to return to Kant's theory of the sublime briefly, in order to indicate a few other aspects of its operations. As Daniel Smith writes in the introduction to Gilles Deleuze's book on Francis Bacon, Kant "argues that perception requires a *synthesis* of what appears in space and time."[10] Three operations make up this synthesis: apprehension, reproduction, and recognition. The world is an incalculable multiplicity. To retrace again the sublime moment: when we encounter the world in a raw form—unmediated by the synthetic membrane of perception—we risk exposure to the chaos of its multiplicity. The sight of an overpowering and sublime nature throws our perceptual–organizational system and our powers of imagination into disarray, producing amazement, horror, and fear: "The sublime takes place when the edifice of synthesis collapses."[11] This is a transcendental moment in which omnipotence acts as the Idea that rescues the emotions from succumbing to a contest between nature and aesthetic (subjective) perception. The Idea of human omnipotence is incited, oddly, by the possibility of *nature's* omnipotence—*its* threat to overrun our system of aesthetic perception and appreciation. If human omnipotence is an idea, what idea is it? How does it curb our enthusiasm, so to speak? One thing at stake, in this scene of natural phenomena overwhelming our senses, is what Jacques Lacan calls the establishment of an orthopedic totality, a calculable figuration of the body that engages the world in setting the scale and size and completeness of the human body as a *gestalt* that forms identity.[12] This is a theoretical leap but it seems warranted by those images of the sublime that are routinely presented to us. Caspar David Friedrich's *Wanderer Above a Sea of Fog* (1818) is the usual example with its sturdy figure of a man with a staff, back turned to us, contemplating a vast, beautiful, and terrifying wilderness of rocks and mountains. The posture of the body shows an avid visual interest in, and a fitness to, the scene, but it also telegraphs complete dominance of the foreground from which the wildness is observed. This is a fantastical image of how humanness holds itself together against the world's turmoil by means of a cogent, and aggressive, figuration.[13] It is instructive that the wanderer has turned his back to us and that we cannot see his face. We see him contemplating what perforce we don't see and yet know we cannot understand, which is a way of representing the unrepresentable through a doubling of perception. The figure in Friedrich's painting is an analogue for Kant's observer, who stands outside the scene—of science, of nature—but whose posture of observation inevitably influences any account of the scene. We see from within a cage of humanness.

Omnipotence over a multitudinous and scaleless nature might belong, accordingly, to the same "psychic mechanism" that presents our bodies as illusory totalities to ourselves. Within Kant's eighteenth-century scene, omnipotence requires that we take a common measure of nature. What is synthesized in perception for Kant is subjective and has no measure: "[i]n the nature of objects there is no common measure."[14] Therefore, the unit of measure we use when we look at nature, Kant suggests, is the human body, which provides a "lived evaluation" of the unit of measure we use to form the object of our gaze. Daniel Smith thus remarks that aesthetic contemplation presupposed in Kant the "situatedness" of our bodies in the world, our "being-in-the-world."[15] In presupposing the body-as-measure in this way, merely *looking at* nature prepares the ground for both our omnipotence over it and our introspection into ourselves. The wholeness of nature in this context is not the late twentieth-century Gaia concept of a holistic interconnected nature, but the fostering of an illusion of nature as a whole entity that can be divided into parts and ultimately translated into property by the same mechanism we know of as self-possession. The modernist plinth, which established a precise geometric layer over vast ecological systems, perfected this translation in architectural terms. We take possession of ourselves as whole bodies in Lacan's mirror stage by looking at an image of ourselves in a mirror; Linnaeus's mirror reappears here.[16] It is important that Lacan's remarks about the illusory quality of our wholeness—illusory because it does not define the body from inside, as a living entity, but from outside, as an image—are not sinister. They describe, on the contrary, a crucial psycho-physiological adjustment we make in order to advance in our development as individuals. It is neurologically true, also, that the brain harmonizes the split picture delivered by the bifocal eyes into a continuous panorama or scene in order to simulate continuity. An additional step might be required, then, to move from the composition of an orthopedic whole, or a completed neurological scene, to projections of wholeness onto nature that demonstrate our aptitude for the faculty of omnipotence. How does individuality and self-recognition transpose itself into a theory of landscape and nature? Perhaps this extra step involves the enigmatic concept of the spiritual that Kant uses when he suggests that we seek to recover "spiritual" omnipotence over nature. Spiritual omnipotence implies a transcendental geographic shift in which a situated, all-too-human, body is elevated above the scene of nature and transformed into the eye of an overseer, remixing the secularity of scientific measure with some simulacra of the divine position of an "above." For Kant, this is the exercise of the faculty of Reason "by which humanity is revealed to be superior to Nature, pointing beyond Nature toward our spiritual destiny as moral beings."[17]

Deleuze's philosophy, as Smith argues, departs from Kant at just this point, and I want to use Deleuze to make a transition from Kant's idea of nature conceived through a situated body to what many have characterized as the dissipated body of posthumanism. The body, in Deleuze, is neither a whole nor a holistic entity. Ideas are still suprasensible in Deleuze, but they are associated with sensibility rather than reason. Ideas reveal the *forces* or intensities that lie behind sensations, which, in Deleuze's analysis, "draw us into nonhuman or inhuman *becomings*."[18] Nature's power thus lies, for Deleuze, in an immanence of the non-organic life of

Catherine Ingraham

things. He believes that art, in particular, can make these forces visible, such as Van Gogh's paintings of sunflowers that render visible the germinating force of sunflower seeds and Cézanne's mountains which render visible "the folding force of mountains."[19] And, as mentioned earlier, Francis Bacon: Francis Bacon, rather than Caspar David Friedrich, in whose paintings the myth of fitness or omnipotent contemplation is exploded, presenting us with profound moral dilemmas as to the status of our claims for superiority. Bacon wrestles with the figure. What emerges from that battle is, in effect, a color palette that paints both landscape and figure in colors drawn from the inside of the body: pinks and reds of flesh, various hues of blood-color, the white and grey-white of bone. If there is an arc in the passage from Friedrich to Bacon—early nineteenth century to late modernity—that encapsulates some of the themes I am discussing here, perhaps it can be extended now to the early twenty-first century. Tom Wiscombe's "dimensionalized painting," *Artic Mass*, could be described, for example, as an instance of a posthumanist dynamical sublime, in which both architecture and body have been dissolved as object-forms.[20] Thus, Friedrich's figure-in-the-landscape passes into Bacon's tortured body that, in turn, passes into Wiscombe's glowing neuro-scape (Figure 2.3).

For Deleuze, bodies cannot act as stable units of measurement because of the forces that convulse and contort the body at every moment: breath, energy, organs, language and communication, emotions, involuntary muscular movements, psychological disturbances; and also because of the biological operation of the body in its constant micro and macro adjustments to and within every aspect of nature. Bodies and nature are, thus, never distinguishable nor is the illusory whole of individual identity ever stable enough to capture nature as a calculable entity. The faculty of omnipotence fails to operate under such a theory. Events fail to be governed by executive orders.

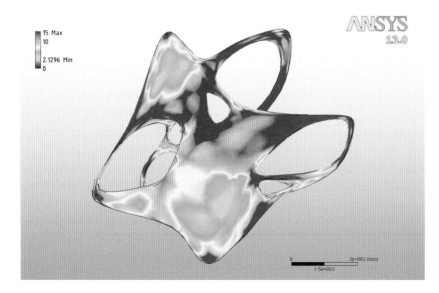

2.3
Tom Wiscombe, *Artic Mass-Painting*, 2011 (Courtesy of Tom Wiscombe).

Contemporary theories of biological identity—which begin with immunology—have created a field called neurophenomenology, which attempts to rethink life in terms of unconscious—rather than in conscious, reason-based, and intentional—processes, without reducing life to "mere" instinct or automatic processing. Our Spinozist concern to exist, "to carry on being," can only "operate as a movement that goes constantly *beyond* the given state of things." As the cognitive philosopher Evan Thompson writes, "this self-transcending movement of life is none other than metabolism."[21] Understood in this fashion, metabolism is that which organizes the organism in a particular way. There is no evidence—to link cognitive science with Deleuze—that we have any kind of intentional access to the sensibility of experience. This might pose a number of fairly tricky problems for architecture's usual agenda.

* * *

I was watching recently Robert Frank's film of the *Life-Raft Earth* project made in 1969 and was struck with a terrible boredom and irritation with the event (or perhaps it was with the film of the event).[22] *Life-Raft Earth* was that quintessential project filled with what now sounds like an inarticulate politics of a distracted group of campers (ourselves, in fact, in our youth) who surrounded themselves with an inflatable plastic wall in a parking lot in Hayward, California, in order to simulate a raft. We can now hear ourselves the way our parents heard us, and it sounds as if we had lost our minds, which is surely precisely what our parents thought at the time. In the interest of a didactic demonstration of the isolation of the earth—that we have only *one* earth, as the organizers put it—and to argue, rightly, that if we forget this fact we will all find ourselves starving, these campers proposed to starve for a week, at the end of which, for good reasons, they could hardly move much less argue. The event was later called "The Hunger Show." It does not need saying that most of the individuals inside the "raft" were from socioeconomic backgrounds that were, among other things, the most well fed in the world. Other vicissitudes—rain, legal constraints, the failure of the raft-space to hold itself together—conspired to destroy the symbolic momentum of the project and bring it down to what it was: a bunch of hungry people in an enclosed structure no longer able to sustain a discussion about politics. This was not unlike what happened in the Superdome in New Orleans after Hurricane Katrina, which went from an improvised shelter in a maelstrom to a place to lie down in your own detritus and forget about living (Figure 2.4). In both cases, one intentional and the other unintentional, some fundamental failure of resiliency was demonstrated. The enclosures, both of which were architectural in a broad sense and meant either symbolically and structurally to sustain life, became liabilities.

Why should life—the process of living—have any implicating power over architecture? We have a tidy conception of life in the architectural program and it would seem strange to ask the hardened material framework of an architectural building to be accountable to life's vicissitudes. But it takes only a very slight shift—

2.4
New Orleans Faces One-Year Anniversary of Hurricane Katrina (Photo: Mario Tama, Getty Images News, 71715040).

which, in fact, has been underway already for a long time—to suggest a profound organizational reciprocity between architecture and inhabitant that is brokered through both material and symbolic architectural acts. We sometimes say that buildings act as agents, but that concept deliberately does not express the degree of vitality or cognition involved. And we make constant historical and theoretical claims for architecture's power over personal and cultural life—the structuring of space, health, experience, perception, aesthetic effects, cultural developments, regime changes, and property relations. There is a system that develops, good or bad, between architecture and life that is intertwined with the metabolic relationship mentioned earlier: among other things, it is a combustible, energy-based relationship.[23]

The event of *Life-Raft Earth*, and perhaps the Superdome as well, showed political life (language, communication, law) fading through whatever means— hunger, fatigue, stress, fear—into nothing but biological life. And this condition, in turn, began to test the organizational logic of the structures themselves. Without resources or little capacity to revitalize resources, life and its orders begin to disintegrate. What is important in this disintegration is the loss of multiple membranes of identity that are simultaneously psychological, immunological and neurological, political, symbolic, and material. This may seem far too lyrical and general an account of the precipitating events—Hurricane Katrina's devastation of New Orleans, in particular. Like the implosion of the public housing project Pruitt-Igoe, Katrina revealed a series of shockingly mistaken assumptions that we hold about urbanism and architecture: the belief that American cities are stolid in their durability and supported in this stolidity by massive infrastructures that can stave off whatever nature might conjure; the belief that citizenry can survive an endless burden of cynical structures in the form of substandard housing and the abuse of systems upon which every city depends. But something in the sequence of events that transpired in both New Orleans and *Life-Raft Earth* partially confirm the physicist Erwin Schrödinger's remark that life "sucks its orderliness from its environment."[24] From the environment, Edgar Morin also theorizes, comes not only organization, but also energy and information.[25] The environment, in other words, is much much greater and far more complex than any given life system, and such systems, cities no less than organisms, depend on this multiplicity for their operation. They do so by making themselves less complex, or, to use the word that has, somewhat belatedly, recently appeared in architecture, they become *autopoietic*: self-organizing systems that are energetically open but operationally closed. For architectural work, it seems to me, the open yet closed aspect of life's organization is the most problematic. How to sustain, in any material sense, non-sequential organizations that are capable of sustaining paradoxical logics?

Life-Raft Earth, and the Superdome-as-refuge, demonstrated quintessential environmental and system failures of energy, information, and organization. The ensuing disintegration was not primarily socioeconomic, as has been sometimes claimed; the social classes of the people involved in each case were polar opposites. Nor was it primarily a mechanical or structural failure. The *Life-Raft* was built of inflatable plastic and the Superdome built with millions of tons of concrete. Neither failed completely and the structures, too, were polar opposites. What created the shared destitution of both worlds was that each architectural structure—one under-built, the other overbuilt, one filled with voluntary fasters, the other with those who were abandoned in the great exodus from New Orleans—remained somewhat intact but lost its organizational relevance to those compelled to stay within it. People, buildings, symbols, and systems were laid open to chaos.

It would come as no surprise that a temporary plastic inflatable barrier might falter beneath its symbolic and real loads. But the Superdome was, and is still, a concrete monolith fed by large urban infrastructures and supply routes, and its stadium typology, by definition, was intended to house thousands of people. It is the largest structure of its kind in the United States and it is not incidental that it was designed to look like a ship, specifically a spaceship.[26] Rafts (*Huckleberry Finn*) and spaceships (*2001: A Space Odyssey*) are legendary symbols of transport away from civilization and earthly orders. They are also tropes for dystopian and utopian voyages. When people were herded into the Superdome during the hurricane, it was certainly because that was the only place in New Orleans that seemed strong enough, and big enough, to protect them from the storm. But it was also regarded as an act of desperation, a last resort, the last ship for the last people who couldn't get out of the city.

It would make no sense to expect architects to fully anticipate how an

Catherine Ingraham

architectural work will ultimately be used, and no building has within itself the capacity to manage all and every kind of surprise—massive weather events or the sudden need to serve as a long-term camping spot for the residents of the flooded Ninth Ward in New Orleans. An over-concern with securing buildings against any and all eventualities would inevitably overstate the need for material protection. It would, in fact, eventually result in the removal of architecture from the building discussion. Securitization makes it extremely difficult to do architectural work, as we have seen in the long delayed, and massively over-secured, reconstruction of the World Trade Center in Manhattan. Hurricane Katrina temporarily blew the Superdome into a new place, so to speak. It became a coastal structure. Like other coastal structures that had failed to apprehend the infrastructural coherence of a coastal wetland system in relation to an urban system, the Superdome had to newly evaluate itself in relation to the very thing, nature, the wetlands, it had sought to displace and render irrelevant. This was quite radical, and short-lived, but deeply suggestive of one form of détente and hybridization with dynamic forces that architectural work now requires.

It would be tempting to cast the Superdome as an architecture of omnipotence and *Life-Raft Earth* as an adaptive hybrid, but it would be hard to say more. A number of architects might also say that, with our smart composite architectural skins, we have moved beyond both the Superdome and inflatable barrier structures. These structures were representative of their time. As structural types, they both span an architectural period after high modernism (1960s–1970s) that was deeply influenced by cybernetics, systems theory, and political resistance to modernism that began to temporalize architecture. Both of these types were also precursors to our contemporary computation of complex skins that seek smartness. But how smart are these new skins and what manner of smartness do they make possible?

* * *

By way of conclusion, I want to return to the beginning of this chapter and to the remarks that I made concerning speculative realism (a philosophical movement about which I am admittedly skeptical). Speculative realism introduces another aspect of a very diverse posthumanist movement referred to briefly above.[27] It concerns objects—and no less than the totality of nature—and seeks to regain some measure of the agency that rationalism and, later, deconstruction, ostensibly removed from them. Both computational architecture and its backlash—real buildings in real space—subscribe to the essentialist desires for the recovery of objects-in-themselves. This is where object-oriented ontology comes in. This theory argues that relations should be seen as ontologically secondary to things. Network relations, for example, "float 'in front of things'." I cannot vouch at this moment for all that Graham Harman, or Timothy Morton, point towards in a "thing," but the gist of their position is to suggest that networks are emergent properties of life forms and the world is a "non-totalizable plenitude of unique beings." Further, as Morton elaborates, "[g]enomic expression does not stop at the end of, say, a beaver's whiskers, but extends all the way to the end of the Beaver's Dam. . . . [t]he mountains we climb, let alone the air we breathe, are simply distributed expressions of DNA. A chalky cliff is the tale of millions of years of shells deposited by mollusks." An ecological view of reality, then, "must be irreductionist . . . it must cleave to unique beings."[28]

Much of this theory, which Žižek argues is really four theories, has enough provocation in it to persuade us of something.[29] "The two axes," Žižek writes, "along which these four positions are placed are divine/secular and scientific/metaphysical."[30] Graham Harman's work has at least two contemporary progenitors: Bruno Latour who is enthusiastically acknowledged; and Deleuze who is for some reason refused. The difficult part, however, is not the (questionable) irreduction of unique beings but the (unavoidable) irreduction of the double-think that accompanies any serious utterance about nature. In considering objects, relations do not seem dispensable. It is true that relations are not equivalent with objects and thus might be said to float, but the object inevitably also floats. There is more than a hint, in both Morton's and Harman's work, that they are specifically in flight from Jacques Derrida's theorization of double-think itself. Another part of the lunacy is the vast scale at which environments operate. No discipline can model the entire environment, but, were one to attempt it, the central assumption would be that scaling itself, as a concept and apparatus, would hold true no matter how large the system. Architects are perhaps particularly liable to make this assumption because in spite of being entrepreneurs of scale and space, even our largest buildings and infrastructures are minuscule in relation to nature. We have no use, in other words, for complex systems and theories of emergent properties in architectural design because our sampling of space and time is so small and tightly bound.

It is, in any case, not possible to get *behind* nature—it is, by definition, the "ungobehindable."[31] This may seem to argue for the irreducibility that Morton and Harman claim for "unique beings," but it is impossible to say. Francisco Varela, neuroscientist and Buddhist, believed that conscious experience was the irreducible process that constitutes the world. Molecular biologists view molecules as irreducible particles into which a substance can be divided and still remain a substance. Physicists regard fermions, the building blocks of all matter, as irreducible. Phenomenology required that we grant physical objects an irreducible reality as a matter of common sense, although the normative attitude we call common sense cannot act directly; for sense to be commonly held, it must pre-position reality.[32] The battle of irreduction is as old as science and philosophy. As a philosophical principle, irreduction typically requires a discourse of origins, faith, and all-encompassing orthodoxies, even in non-theological practices.[33] As a theoretical position, irreduction resurrects some version of a human omnipotence even as it might attempt to reorder the world away from humanness.

Žižek calls Harman's version of speculative realism a "panpsychism"—a "directly religious" or at least "spiritualist" view of nature.[34] Nothing about or in nature acts in a unified, homogeneous way, least of all its coalescence into "figures" or "unique beings" that can be taken forward as objects. In biological theories of nature formulated in the 1980s, for example, living beings begin to be understood through cybernetics and second-order systems theory, but it remains undecidable whether systems per se exist in nature. As mentioned earlier, we have understood animals for a long time in terms of taxonomic species although it is obvious that only individuals exist in nature. Edgar Morin recently noted that species and individuals cannot conceptually coexist: "Either the species disappears and the individual occupies the whole of our conceptual field or, on the contrary, the individual disappears, becomes something contingent or ephemeral and it is the species which abides through time and possesses the true reality."[35] We moved from taxonomic theories of organization to statistical theories in the mid-twentieth century, and there are, as yet, perhaps only a few theories, all of them fraught, of what it would mean to, first, think of ourselves (once again) as individual animals or what it would mean to think of other animals as individuals.[36] Linnaeus and the statisticians, each in their own way, continue to protect us from that sticky inquiry. Panpsychism may imagine itself as a theory of universal ethics, but it doesn't seem interested in navigating the paradoxes.

One of the ways second-order systems theory (complexity theory) has managed incompatible logics is through the concept, already mentioned, of emergence. Thus, in evolutionary terms, the individual is seen as an emergent phenomenon that arises in populations. In Wolfram's computational universe, for example, emergent mathematical formulations deliver, he believes, entirely new solutions to old problems. Emergence is fascinating, but it is also troubling in its generic application. It is, very nearly, a neo-rationalist version of Intelligent Design—the creationist hypothesis that the world is too complex to have (merely) evolved. The concept of emergence gives hierarchy to incompatible logics such as those that might arise, for example, in the co-presence of individuals and species mentioned above. In the search for unique beings, further, immunology now defines one kind of uniqueness, sociability defines another, psychology another, and perhaps panpsychism yet another. This is all only to say that while the idea of an individual unique being is not entirely meaningless—we uphold its various meanings every day, often in neo-theistic terms—the standing concepts of individual, subject, and group have been put back in play. And, so it seems, mysticism, animism, and vitalism are also back on the table.

One last excursion into the lunatic seems pertinent here in order to understand a little more about how computation itself fits into this discussion. The five architects that I mentioned at the beginning of this essay—Hernan Diaz Alonso, David Ruy and Karel Klein (Ruy Klein), Tom Wiscombe, and Ben van Berkel—each privilege and explore computational work quite differently. None of these architects believe parametric architecture to be an end in itself. In their diverse investigations, these architects are engaged, I think, in playing out a contemporary drama between brain, mind, and machine. What we are seeing, in their work, is a reimaging and restructuring of that drama as it pertains to living and nonliving systems.

It is quite important, given the assumptions we make about computation in architecture, that most neuroscience research argues that the human brain works in a radically different way from the computer. There is nothing brain-like about computation. This wouldn't matter except for the fact that cybernetics initially modeled the computer after the central nervous system (of humans and animals), and its central project, since the 1940s, has been to model the way the brain knows, remembers, and stores information. The most salient differences between computer and brain are that computing is sequential and concerned with the elimination of noise, while the brain works through re-entry, which is far more complex than feedback, and it runs on noise. If part of our plan, in computational architecture, is to model nature with the computer, we will run into this discrepancy. Our current desire to know nature anew has already run into this discrepancy. The massive weather and infrastructural data sets we possessed of New Orleans prior to Hurricane Katrina led to a particular theory of urban order that had been written into the infrastructure of the city since the 1950s. That particular order was unable to withstand not only the failure of its central structures—the levee system—but also the unfolding of the catastrophe as it was organized, and contended with, by its victims. *Life-Raft Earth*, for its part, spoke to the question of resources with the univocal voice of death: no resources, no life. Another kind of experiment might have tested ways in which a portable barrier can suffocate, or galvanize, a living system. Managing the radical differences between machine/apparatus information and bio-neurological knowledge—each with its own system, each historically requiring the other in some form—conditions almost every aspect of our contemporary ecological crisis: energy, information, governance, urbanism, infrastructure, sustainability.

Gerald Edelman, the neuroscientist whom most architects were reading in the early part of this century—because of an avid interest in epigenetic phenomenon— argues that an organism is composed, neurologically, by neural activity as it acts upon stimulation from the world and upon itself. Minds operate according to the evolutionary structure of the brain. This is what he calls the "reentrant dynamic core,"[37] in which the "outside scene" of aesthetic contemplation is formed by "thoughts [that are] themselves . . . the thinker."[38] Re-entrant circuits evolve in animals and are coupled to physical space-time in the "remembered present" of primary consciousness. Mental states cannot be split and over-defined, Edelman says, as philosophy is prone to do, because they do not ever have one focal point. And the ability to generalize is more important for communication than conceptual precision. As Edelman writes:

> The pervasive presence of degeneracy in biological systems is particularly noticeable in neural systems, and it exists to a high degree in the reentrant selective circuits of the conscious brain. In certain circumstances, natural languages gain as much strength from ambiguity as they do under other circumstances through the power of logical definition.[39]

Catherine Ingraham

Thus, our body, brain, and consciousness, Edelman remarks, "did not evolve to yield a scientific picture of the world." He means that science and philosophy, in their historical desire to analytically develop descriptions of the world upon which our most significant technologies have been based, produce a kind of systemization that is at odds with how our brains works. Technology thus "works"—when it does work, when we want to go to the moon and we get there—through a very different process than we imagine. Technology might require more noise, more somatic awareness, than it can currently afford. It seems now fairly clear, in architecture, that what we are looking for in the so-called "intelligent skin" is not yet possible in any direct sense, no matter how many sensors we plug in or how much data we collect.

Because of this constant upset in the principles that have shaped our infrastructures, cities, superdomes, atom accelerators, dams and levees, streets and sewers, plinths and platforms, houses and skyscrapers, we are still facing, again, although with more urgency, the same question that almost every philosopher, scientist, and witch doctor in human history has asked: How can we face a chaotic and vast environment and not be blown away by its chaos? Modernity's continuing solution—that we keep marshaling forth new versions of human omnipotence over nature—now falls far short of the question.

Notes

1   Timothy Morton, *Ecology without Nature: Rethinking Environmental Aesthetics* (Cambridge, MA: Harvard University Press, 2009).

2   Timothy Morton, "Architecture without Nature," *Tarp* (Spring 2012), 20.

3   Roger Caillois, "Mimicry and Legendary Psychasthenia (1936)," trans. John Shepley, *October* 31 (Winter 1984): 16–32. If you imitate an animal you are subject to the dangers that animal encounters.

4   Giorgio Agamben, *The Open: Man and Animal*, trans. Kevin Attell (Palo Alto, CA: Stanford University Press, 2004; originally published in Italian, 2002).

5   Niklas Luhmann, *Social Systems*, trans. John Bednarz, Jr. with Dirk Baecker (Palo Alto, CA: Stanford University Press, 1995), xxiii. "[S]ystems that operate on the basis of consciousness (psychic systems) or communication (social systems) require meaning (*Sinn*) for their reproduction."

6   Sanford Kwinter described futurism in art as an attempt to "link the biosphere and mechanosphere within a single dynamical system." I think we are now in some version of the future that futurism imagined. See Sanford Kwinter and Umberto Boccioni, "Landscapes of Change: Boccioni's 'Stati d'animo' as a General Theory of Models," *Assemblage* 19 (December, 1992): 50–65, 53.

7   "Slavoj Žižek—Nature Does Not Exist," www.youtube.com/watch?v=DIGeDAZ6-q4

8   Ilya Prigogine, Isabelle Stengers, *Order out of Chaos: Man's Dialogue with Nature* (New York: Bantam Books, 1984), 1–23.

9   Agamben, *op. cit.*, 27. As Agamben writes (25, 30): "In truth, Linnaeus's genius consists not so much in the resoluteness with which he places man among the primates as in the irony with which he does not record—as he does with the other species—any specific identifying characteristic next to the generic name *Homo*, only the philosophical adage: *nosce te ipsum* {know yourself} . . . The humanist discovery of man is the

discovery that he lacks himself, the discovery of his irremediable lack of *dignitas.*" Also see Carl Linnaeus, *Systema naturae*, 1735 (original Latin text reprinted by the University of Michigan Library).

10   Daniel Smith, "Deleuze on Bacon: Three Conceptual Trajectories in The Logic of Sensation," in Gilles Deleuze, *Francis Bacon: The Logic of Sensation* (Minneapolis: University of Minnesota Press, 2003), vii–xxvii, xv.

11   *Ibid.*, xix.

12   Jacques Lacan, "The Mirror Stage," in *Ecrits* (New York: W. W. Norton, 1977), trans. Alan Sheridan, 2–4. "[T]he total form of the body by which the subject anticipates in a mirage the maturation of his power is given to him only as a *Gestalt*, that is to say, in an exteriority in which this form is certainly more constituent than constituted, but in which it appears to him above all in a contrasting size . . . that fixes it and in a symmetry that inverts it, in contrast with the turbulent movements that the subject feels are animating him. Thus, this *Gestalt*—whose pregnancy should be regarded as bound up with the species, though its motor style remains scarcely recognizable—by these two aspects of its appearance, symbolizes the mental permanence of the *I*, at the same time as it prefigures its alienating destination; it is still pregnant with the correspondences that unite the *I* with the statue in which man projects himself, with the phantoms that dominate him, or with the automaton in which, in an ambiguous relation, the world of his own making tends to find completion. . . . I am led therefore, to regard the function of the mirror-stage as a particular case of the function of the *imago*, which is to establish a relation between the organism and its reality—or, as they say, between the *Innenwelt* and the *Umwelt*. . . . The *mirror stage* is a drama whose internal thrust is precipitated from insufficiency to anticipation—and which manufactures for the subject, caught up in the lure of spatial identification, the succession of phantasies that extends from a fragmented body-image to a form of its totality that I shall call orthopaedic."

13   Friedrich's painting is part of a powerful nineteenth-century history of figurative painting that Deleuze explores negatively through Francis Bacon's rejection of the figure as a whole entity. In Deleuze's analysis, Bacon uses diagrams and sketching to wrestle with this history; he scrubs the figure in order to interrupt its tendency to frame a linear narrative.

14   Deleuze, *op. cit.*, xvii.

15   *Ibid.*, xviii.

16   See the introduction to Carl Linnaeus, *Systema naturae*, 1735 (original Latin edition reprinted by the University of Michigan Library). Agamben remarks in *The Open* that "[a]n analysis of the *Introitus* that opens the *Systema* leaves no doubts about the sense Linnaeus attributed to his maxim: man has no specific identity other than the ability to recognize himself" (*op. cit.*, 26).

17   Deleuze, *op. cit.*, xxii.

18   *Ibid.*, xxii.

19   *Ibid.*, 49.

20   Tom Wiscombe Design, *Artic Mass-Painting*, Anaheim, 2011. Wiscombe describes this project as "somewhere between the disciplines of sculpture and painting," registering as both mass and graphic. The project is an "attempt to force the brain to hedge and guess in its 'modelling' of physical reality."

21   Evan Thompson, "Life and Mind," in *Emergence and Embodiment* (Durham, NC: Duke

Catherine Ingraham

University Press, 2009), 85. This and previous quotes, including references to Spinoza and the philosopher Hans Jonas, are taken from this essay.

22   Robert Frank, *Life-Raft Earth*, 1969.

23   Sanford Kwinter, lecture delivered at the Part-Animal Conference, Columbia University, February 29, 2008. Kwinter recounted his visit to the Kalahari Desert in Botswana and described the vivid impression that the animals were "combusted" out of the landscape.

24   Erwin Schrödinger, *What is Life?* (Cambridge: Cambridge University Press, 1992), 73.

25   Edgar Morin, "On the Subject of the Self," in *On Complexity* (New York: Hampton Press, 2008), 67–81.

26   The Superdome (Louisiana Dome) was designed by the architectural firm Curtis and Davis in 1967. After Hurricane Katrina it was repaired and renamed, in 2011, the Mercedes-Benz Dome.

27   See Cary Wolfe, *What is Posthumanism?* (Minneapolis: University of Minnesota Press, 2009). Posthumanist studies include work by Donna Haraway, N. Katherine Hayles, and many others who have identified different thresholds for the end of humanism. The movement breaks roughly into two parts: posthumanism as emancipatory and posthumanism as pathological.

28   Morton, *op. cit.* (n. 2), 21. Previous and following citations are also from this source.

29   Slavoj Žižek, *Less than Nothing: Hegel and the Shadow of Dialectical Materialism* (Durham, NC: Duke University Press, 2012), 640. The "four orientations" are: "[Quentin] Meillassoux's 'speculative materialism,' [Graham] Harman's 'object-oriented philosophy,' [Ian Hamilton] Grant's neovitalism, and [Ray] Brassier's radical nihilism."

30   *Ibid.*, 640.

31   Thompson, *op. cit.*, 90. The term "ungobehindable" was used by Francisco Varela to refer to cognitive experience. For Varela, lived (cognitive) experience is "where we start from and where we all must link back to." Also see Francisco Varela, "Neurophenomenology: A methodological remedy for the hard problem," *Journal of Consciousness Studies* 3/4 (June 1996), 334. The concept of the irreduction of conscious experience refers to the transcendental principle that the mind is embodied in a living body.

32   Varela defines common sense as "our bodily and social history" in Francisco Varela, Evan Thompson, and Eleanor Rosch, *The Embodied Mind: Cognitive Science and Human Experience* (Cambridge, MA: The MIT Press, 1991), 150. Such a history also requires a pre-positioning of notions of reality.

33   Phillip E. Johnson, "Is Genetic Information Reducible?," *Biology and Philosophy* 11/4 (October 1996): 535–538. As Johnson, 535, emphasizes, George C. Williams, for example, has pointed out that genes contain both information and material, and "the information encoded in DNA is fundamentally distinct from the chemical medium in which the information is recorded." This incompatibility makes any kind of reductionism of the process to a single entity impossible, yet evolutionary biology remains committed to a reductionist theory of the gene.

34   Žižek, *op. cit.*, 640.

35   Morin, *op. cit.*, 67–81.

36   The bioethicist Peter Singer analyses in *Practical Ethics* (Cambridge: Cambridge University Press, 2011), why and how the interests of living beings should be weighed.

Unlike Kant, who only considers the interests of rational beings, Singer includes the interests of animals in his bioethical argument. The argument is utilitarian, but the weighing of interests across the spectrum of living beings does not privilege humans over animals, so omnipotence, as a specifically human faculty, is mitigated.

37 Gerald Edelman, *Wider than the Sky: The Phenomenal Gift of Consciousness* (New Haven, CT: Yale University Press, 2004), 72.

38 *Ibid.*, 134.

39 *Ibid.*, 135.

3

The Raw and the Cooked

Sylvia Lavin

Despite computer-animated appearances and the cries of impending ecological doom to the contrary, architecture is in the midst of a widespread turn to what eighteenth-century theorists would have simply called first principles. Geometric primitives, the laws of nature, ecology and the will to shape experience directly and forcefully make contemporary architectural discourse uncannily reminiscent of the discourses of Quatremère de Quincy, Cuvier and Condillac. While the list of issues that preoccupy architects today, when seen in the context of the contemporary world, seems to be made of items that belong to radically different categories of thought and action, their historical analogues reveal instead that the list shares a fundamental attachment to an almost Rousseauian world view; his state of nature may now be today's tribal chic, but both look to the possibility of the unmediated as model, to the thing outside the vagaries of culture and to the notion that such a state of rawness will make possible for architecture a new form of synthetic agency.

It took a couple of hundred years to develop, but Lévi-Strauss's opposition between the raw and the cooked is the ultimate expression of the effects sought by Enlightenment thinking. His structuralist anthropology, rooted in the notion that culture obeys universal laws that can be scientifically explained, was fully articulated in what is considered by many to be his most important work, *Mythologiques*, of which *The Raw and the Cooked* is the first volume.[1] One aspect of his prodigious achievement was the virtually minimalist elegance with which he turned the morass of ideas distinguishing the natural from the cultural that had been developing since the end of the Middle Ages into a simple and straight line not only between but opposing the natural and the cultural. Both the economies and the confidences that lay beneath this diagram have long since given way to an emphasis on the continuities between these states. However, the traces of this opposition remain at work today, sometimes in the thinking of those who seem most devoted to its undoing. As a result, and even if as a rhetorical straw man, the vicissitudes of the raw and cooked are a surprisingly useful barometer of contemporary architectural commitments.[2]

A quick survey of the field reveals that an initially gentle and tentative introduction of natural themes in architecture—which had been expunged by the linguistic turn of the 1970s—has picked up speed and changed its character. (A proper account of the frank prohibition of matters of nature and of experience in architecture in the wake of the linguistic turn of the 1970s is beyond the scope of this short chapter. Let it suffice to say that what ultimately became architectural theory of the 1990s was predicated on the total eradication from the discourse of questions of material, phenomenology and other naturalisms as then understood). At first, "nature" paradoxically re-entered the architectural scene through the mechanisms of the theory that had at first exiled it; poststructuralism in literary circles became aligned with chaos theory from mathematical circles and their conjunction led to an interest in, amongst many things, calculus, topology and, step by step, to fractal geometry. Indeed, it was only with this final step that an intellected proposition became a pictorial platitude kept safe from criticism because the pictures were of nice natural scenes (who can confess to not liking nature). It perhaps does not arise to the occasion of irony that one of the most radical schools of thought in the postwar period could result in design studios filled with buildings shaped like trees and bigger trees and even bigger trees. But, despite the dead-end path taken by fractals in particular, what started as a small shift from complex language and cultural knots into complex weather systems and butterfly effects turns out to have been the beginning of a still unfolding drama of architecture "going native."[3]

There are too many steps to recount between the first signs of love for fractals and slime molds and the current marriage of the National Architectural Accrediting Board (NAAB) and the American Institute of Architects (AIA) to sustainability, but the trail from "nature" as element of cultural analysis to "nature" as signifying system and at times moral code mandating standards of building behavior is nevertheless evident. The craze for Mandelbrot's groovy scaling shapes was quickly tempered by the natural histories of Herzog & de Meuron, presented in the most coyly artificial manner as possible. There could have been nothing more unnatural than the cloud of the Blur building except perhaps Frank Gehry and Greg Lynn's zoo for exotic sea animals filled with giant robotic creatures making a show located between the display of Paleolithic specimens and the Archigram-like spectacle of moving buildings. Jason Payne recently conducted a studio in which the material used for design was cow rawhides bought via the Internet. The Museum of Modern Art (MoMA) filled PS 1 with farm animals, and François Roche tried to power a building with elephant shit. And all the while that such disciplinary struggles have been taking place, laboring to transform architecture from its status in the 1990s

Sylvia Lavin

as text, representation and panopticon into an articulate and forceful agent in the material world, professional practice has been expanding its market share with corporate buildings that breathe fresh air, are covered with plants and encourage the reduction of carbon footprints, conducting its own struggle for agency in the world of capital and power. At no time in the recent past has the conflict between the discipline and the profession been more acute; their two realities, the way the profession claims it's time to "solve real problems" (now ecological more than social) and the way the discipline claims to question what is real, what is a problem and what is a solution, are stretched across a seemingly enormous divide.

"Going native" covers a lot of ideological ground being trod upon by everything from celebrity philanthropy to the Environmental Protection Agency (EPA) to the flows of global capital. But the one thing that crosses this divide is the desire for rawness and the conviction that the raw is no longer to be merely opposed to the cooked, but should be helped to assert itself as the dominant term in the binary. This inversion of modernity's traditional temperament is nowhere more evident than in the contemporary cultures of both food and architecture. They have a long history of entanglement, from corn on the capitals to theories of taste and *le bon goût*, through which the notion of a special sixth sense governing the appreciation of all things aesthetic from the culinary to the architectural took root. But beyond these historic associations, in the modern period food and architecture share with fashion a unique proclivity to operate as purveyors of contemporary culture. Their embeddedness in matters of survival, pleasure, meaning and above all cycles of production allow them to serve as particularly useful nodes for understanding the values attached to these various forces. For example, it was not so long ago that elBulli, the Catalan restaurant run by chef Ferran Adrià and famous for its molecular gastronomy and the most scientifically concocted of cuisines, rose to the top of the food chain to become classified as one of the great cultural achievements of the late twentieth century. At elBulli, the use of food and its preparation to stage the intercourse between the cultural and the natural became instead a means to use carbon dioxide, nitrogen and centrifuges to spin every last natural molecule out of consumption. Tomatoes were transformed into the essence of tomato, a rosy piece of air with neither food value nor taste value but rather a pure exercise in culinary abstraction. ElBulli is now closed, perhaps as a result of slow food, which so slowed food down that it could not make it to elBulli's laboratory in time, slow enough that giant agro business farms could become "organic" fields of green, so slow that food finally found its way back to Rousseau's state of nature. ElBulli has been left in the wake of the raw food movement (which does not really preclude cooking as such, just heating above a temperature of 40°C), and architecture is working hard, since it would seem to be more difficult to identify a raw building than it is to distinguish a raw potato from a McDonald's French fry, to discover what its state of nature might be.

There are many different flavors of raw architecture operating today. Indeed, one of the most interesting features of this range is that none of them recognize each other as kin: how less related could Leadership in Energy and Environmental Design (LEED) certification and rawhide be? Yet the refusal to acknowledge fraternity is a necessary condition of the commitment to the raw; recognition of the fact that there might be two ways not to cook a building would betray the constructed features of all "raw" architecture as a category. Rawness in architecture can only be staged since never under any circumstances could any kind of architecture be produced outside the operations of culture. Architecture is by definition cooked, even if only lightly simmered or steamed to below 40°C.

So let me rephrase: today there are two principal ways of cooking up raw architecture, two rubrics into which many of the myriad efforts to cook architecture less can be divided, whether less cooking be understood in relation to carbon footprints, building refuse, naturalizing forms or the solicitation of unmediated forms of perception. The first category is the neo-primitivist, which includes such diverse things as rawhide, the interest in base affect and the decidedly not anthropological interest in substandard housing from Mumbai to Brazil.[4] The second category is the ecological, which also ranges widely from interest in environmental control systems, toxic land reclamation and the impact of architecture on the nervous system or how to have architecture engage human subjects through the apparatus of animal perception.[5] As different from each other as they are expected to be and as rooted in extremely current conditions, both rubrics are best understood as a contemporary unfolding of the long tradition of imitation in the visual arts. Mimesis is back.

The single most persistent theme in the history of the visual arts in the West since antiquity, the tenet that made art artful and cooked as opposed to a raw material, a tool and a labor, was its imitation of nature.[6] Mimesis management was the one skill shared by every artist and architect from Phidias to Frank Lloyd Wright. What sustained this almost eternal attachment to mimesis was the often-vituperative disagreement about how to effect the imitation. Although stemming from an antique philosophical dispute about the nature of Divine creation, Alberti codified the conflict as a core element of art and architectural theory through the distinction between *natura naturata* and *natura naturans*. The principle of *natura naturata* defined art in terms of its capacity to interpret nature and to produce works that most closely represented nature and its forces. This notion gave the visual arts autonomy from the dictates of ideality, permitting Leonardo, for example, to draw grotesques and everyone from Caravaggio to Van Gogh and to Warhol to depict dirty or poorly shod feet as appropriate subject matter for works of art. *Natura naturans*, on the other hand, was a more active principle that argued art could operate in the manner rather than the image of nature, could harness its forces and could even improve on natural phenomena. *Natura naturans* thus freed artists from the "as found," making it possible to understand things not existing in nature as natural; the most famous example of this type was the technique of selecting a nose from this figure, a toe from that one, a torso from the other, and putting them together to create an even better subject than nature could make itself.

Sylvia Lavin

The fundamental distinction between *natura naturata* and *natura naturans* remains in force in the dissention between today's neo-primitivist and ecological paradigms. The neo-primitives share with Leonardo a quest for points of departure within what they deem nature but outside the conventions of traditional ideas of beauty and ideal states of matter. The continuity between the primitive hut and the geometric primitives that abound in computer-aided design and parametric discourse is not generally recognized, but both have been constituted by architecture as "as found" and "original" objects from whence variations can then be derived. Log cabins and deformed squares are used as a means to produce unprecedented interpretations of nature, to discover subnatures, to provoke novel responses to nature and to expand the range of natures considered to be worthy of imitation. The ecologists, on the other hand, are both more idealizing and more driven by abstraction than the neo-primitivists. They produce landform buildings, epigenetic landscapes and use multiple species as models for and subjects of architecture to intellect natures that do not and could never exist. They seek to produce extra large buildings that function as ecologies through their scale and programmatic complexity.

Both strategies have their strengths and their pitfalls. The risk for the neo-primitivists lies in how they define objects as within nature but outside convention; shifting from platonic forms to Mobius strips has evidently expanded architecture's geometric and hence organizational range, but the shift becomes more problematic when the outside is defined not in formal or diagrammatic terms but in social and political ones. For example, the transformation of the everyday urbanism of Lagos into the natural basis of the special urbanism of OMA turns neo-primitivism back into old school primitivism and into an Africanist version of Said's *Orientalism.*[7] While the lines of colonial power are no longer those simply between the East and the West, defining anything within a state of this kind of nature remains the first step towards its colonization and subjugation. The more absolute primitivism becomes, the more it corrupts absolutely. The ecologists, on the other hand, risk reproducing essentializing arguments in artificial terms. Suggesting that architects should model environmental experience on the visceral response to being in a tree on the savannah surrounded by predatory animals inadequately accounts for the many different ways there are to find yourself in such a tree: because you are a bird, because you are on a first class safari or because you are out hunting up dinner. While ecology helps us understand ourselves as within the animal kingdom, our perceptions inevitably pass through culture on their way to consciousness, and that culture is neither color- nor class-blind.

The raw and the cooked, cooking techniques to replicate rawness and using previously uncooked materials to cook up new architecture, are not novelties but serious engagements with the history of architectural thinking. Recognizing this engagement makes it possible to recognize in turn that while the ecologists criticize the neo-primitivists for being principally concerned with representational issues and with the appearances of nature rather than its procedures, the ecologists have their own system for replicating natural systems. While producers of code claim innocence, it is not by a process of natural selection that the forms generated by their scripts look, well, organic. Shifting the object of mimesis from a natural object to a natural force is a shift in degree rather than in kind. And while the ecologists claim for themselves a more active role in environmental management with immediate and "real" sustainability enhancements, the neo-primitivists may be better at causing the ideological realignments necessary for any substantive transformation in ecological policy.

Picking sides is not a question of nature or even of architecture, but is rather an ethical matter arising from one aspect of what used to be called human nature. Historically speaking, many an evil thing justified its will to power by recourse to the authority of natural law. Most of today's architectural naturalists were trained by yesterday's historian/theorists, so one can be quite confident that the current inattention to the historical record is not a demonstration of ignorance but rather a repression, or worse, a deliberate erasure of a troublesome lineage. The attractions of matters pertaining to sustainability, both financial and personal, are luring architects closer and closer to using rhetoric that relies on what is now—or again—assumed to be the absolute value and authority of nature. Nature, which knows no such allegiance, is invoked as a means—beyond question—of privileging one form of practice over another. Gilles Deleuze was suspicious of arguments that began with the word "I" because he believed that the invocation of personal experience was the first step towards an inevitable privileging of this experience.[8] The logic of the I was for him intrinsically reactionary. Some architects are getting close to using nature the way Deleuze feared the I, to foreclosing other options, to privileging an often unintellected position and to smuggling reactionary thinking into the discipline in the guise of the uncontrollable forces of nature.

Many of these issues become clear when considering contemporary attitudes towards materials. No one believes anymore in the "nature of materials." Or do they? No one would ask a brick what it wants to be, but everyone would agree that using it again would be a good thing. Recycling is the new material nature, lending matter a protean capacity for endless transformation and regeneration. Recycling is as a means of transport—like Charon's ferry across the river Styx—that returns something from the state of having been cooked to a state of nature, allowing it to reenter the cycle of production and consumption in the guise of something raw. This almost mythical transformation has become a fundamental ethical preoccupation for citizens of industrialized nations, yet the question in this context is if and how such a preoccupation—which follows others of the same category: how to improve housing for the poor, how to improve conditions in the workplace, etc.—can be generative for the architectural discipline. The very fact that large corporate offices are getting larger and fatter by "going green" in one way or another indicates that there is a significant divide between the ways in which the professional and business aspects of architecture engage matters such as recycling and the way the discipline understands such questions. In an ideal world these two dimensions of architecture would of course converge—and that is certainly

Sylvia Lavin

the purported goal of New Practice—but in this less than ideal world, recycling in architecture risks becoming just another capitalist gambit to make money out of waste and to put a green spin on globalization. So before mounting a full-scale effort to calibrate the architectural contribution to environmental management by counting up piles of building waste or number of recycled materials used in an office tower, it would be interesting to examine the accounting ledgers of architectural firms and their principals to see how much money they donate to the Sierra Club, Greenpeace or other organizations who have it as their disciplinary mandate to solve environmental issues. Chances are good that such an exercise would demonstrate that architecture as an economic venture has no less but certainly no more purchase on environmental improvement than law, dentistry, rocket science or any other profession.

Instead of this sort of pseudo amelioration through which architecture has demonstrated time and again that it is a weak player in the world of global capital where urgent problems are both produced and solved, architecture should spend its resources elsewhere. Indeed, architecture is best equipped for playing a role in catalyzing the remediation (rather than return) that will be necessary to achieve a contemporary version of Rousseau's state of nature by doing what it does best: thinking about questions such as what is an environment, how do we determine which aspects of any environment are worth preserving or reusing, what kinds of reuse are tolerable and which are not and, finally, what kinds of materials can cycle through the states of nature, production, overproduction, abjection, until they become available again as raw agents. Recycling will never work as an ecological diagram if the goal is to take the cooked and make it raw; it is the quest for rawness itself, for a state of nature even if artificially manufactured, with all the elements of purity, control and virtue such a state implies, which is intrinsically futile and contra-ecological. Instead, by looking at the vicissitudes of the raw and the cooked, by recalibrating the values attached to materials as such, by reconsidering how much is enough and if waste is just a good thing in the wrong place, architecture can be a strong ally to substantive environmental thinking and potent opponent of ideologies determined to continue opposing the raw and the cooked. The new mimesis need not signal the end of architecture as a cultural practice as long as we understand that it reveals no natural laws and carries no absolute weight. Instead, it is the arguments about mimesis that sharpen architecture's understanding of the multiple natures it generates, and it is in turn these debates that will sustain our field.

Notes

1   Claude Lévi-Strauss, *The Raw and the Cooked*, trans. by John and Doreen Weightman (New York: Harper & Row, 1969).
2   These thematics were taken up in the exhibition *The Raw and the Cooked* curated by Dan Cameron held at the Reina Sofia Center, Madrid, 1994.
3   See the discussion of going native in Bill Ashcroft, ed., *Key Concepts in Post-colonial Studies* (London: Routledge, 1998).

4   I use the prefix "neo" because there is a long history of primitivisms in modern. There is a wide literature on this subject much spurred by the exhibition held at the Museum of Modern Art in 1984. See William Rubin, ed., *"Primitivism" in 20th Century Art: Affinity of the Tribal and the Modern* (New York: Museum of Modern Art, 1984).

5   There is a growing literature on ecology and architecture. Some recent examples include Stan Allen, Marc McQuade, eds., *Landform Building: Architecture's New Terrain* (Baden: Lars Müller, 2011), David Gissen, *Subnature: Architecture's Other Environments* (New York: Princeton Architectural Press, 2009) and Charles Waldheim, ed., *The Landscape Urbanism Reader* (New York: Princeton Architectural Press, 2006).

6   Befitting its subject, there is a massive literature on mimesis. Two good points of departure for this discussion include Rensselaer W. Lee, *Ut Pictura Poesis: The Humanistic Theory of Painting* (New York: W. W. Norton, 1967) and Anthony Blunt, *Artistic Theory in Italy, 1450–1600* (London: Oxford University Press, 1978).

7   Edward W. Said, *Orientalism* (London: Routledge & Kegan Paul, 1978).

8   See his statement in Gilles Deleuze, *Negotiations*, trans. by Martin Joughin (New York: Columbia University Press, 1997), 12: "Arguments from one's own privileged experience are bad and reactionary arguments."

Case Study I

MOS Architects, afterparty, PS 1 YAP Pavilion (2009)

An afterparty always follows the main event. Once the real party is over, the afterparty appears as a kind of lower level byproduct—a shadow, echo, aftershock or some other form tethered to what preceded it. Even if it is popular to say that the afterparty is often better than the party, this can only be true in comparison; you can't go straight to the afterparty no matter how hard you try. This is especially apparent when the discipline of Architecture feels like it's over (always, again). During these times, it's tempting to look for meaning in our origins—something primitive and genetic and reassuring—an escape from the Vagueness of Art towards the Realism of Life.

In this sense, we believe that today architecture is in productive disarray; afterparty is an attempt to collapse the primitive with the parametric in order to enfranchise another kind of space. Before we designed anything, we produced software for catenary and cellular aggregation to help define the form and organization. Catenary software produced structural arch shapes, cellular aggregation software produced agglomerations of hyperbolic conical domes. But we never wanted the architectural effect to be about geometry or tectonics. Instead, the effects of the afterparty occur through simultaneous registers: a functional system of "stack-effect" cooling towers, a formal means of form-finding and aggregation, and a haptic-visual apparatus of ugly-thatched-furry "wooly mammoth" or "Snuffleupagus" material. The superimposition of these effects produces something else. The project's defining character is the act of getting it wrong—a second-order performance figured as much by attitude or affect as by technique.

The party, for us, was a Positivist circus both at war and in love with itself. Its main genres were technique driven: the mannerist iconic, the tautological parametric and the scientific performative. The afterparty uses and abuses each of these genres on and with the others. The result is not a collage or high-end act of bricolage. The afterparty pavilion is perhaps more "natural" and sincere in its awkwardness and artifice. When we talk about a "return to nature" in the context of our work, this is the process in which the vast arsenal of contemporary techniques becomes naturalized in the service of design. The complexity of technique has shifted; 1990s-era traces of process or dynamic movement are nowhere to be found, nor does one see the feigned effortlessness of the algorithmic automaton.

We have argued that afterparty "is what it is," but that depends upon how one defines what the meaning of the word 'is' is—a take, perhaps, on the literalism of Judd or Morris. In the office, afterparty became a sort of monument of ambivalence and ambiguity for a generation that absorbs, processes and digests both the new and the natural at an exponentially accelerating pace. To evoke this asymptotic condition through architectural form would be the most banal form of autopoietic mimesis. Surprisingly, perhaps, for something so matter-of-fact, afterparty captures the noisy and consensual spirit of simultaneously projecting and shedding the burden of didactic self-awareness that has by now become second nature . . .

1
Looking at afterparty's series of furry chimneys from Jackson Avenue (Photo © Courtesy of MOS).

Case Study I: MOS Architects

2
View from the third floor of PS 1 during an event (Photo © Courtesy of MOS).

3
One of 16 *oculi*. Here the structure rests on the concrete wall and continues over to the other side (Photo © Courtesy of MOS).

4
Sitting inside one of the large domes. Scales are continually shifting depending on the size and grouping of arches, generating different spatial and thermal effects (Photo © Courtesy of MOS).

5
A singular conic section crosses over the wall (Photo © Courtesy of MOS).

6
The raw metallic interior is aluminum mesh combined with a radial scaffolding system of arches and domes (Photo © Courtesy of MOS).

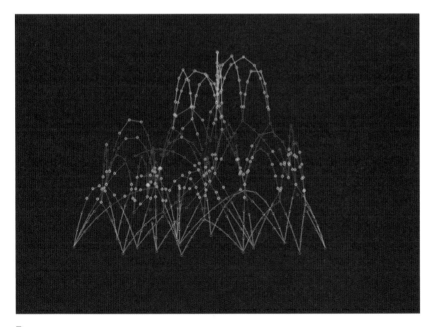

7
Output from the form finding software developed for the afterparty is a serialized system of catenary arches that grow into a variety of extruded paraboloids (Photo © Courtesy of MOS).

8
A top view image produced as an experiment in growth/aggregation formation (Photo © Courtesy of MOS).

9
Another top view image produced as an experiment in growth/aggregation formation (Photo © Courtesy of MOS).

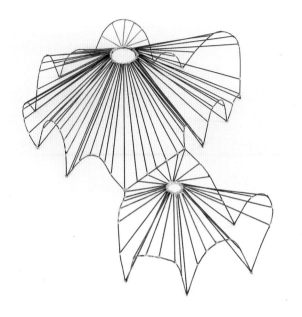

10
Wire frame structural study model. A series of physical models were used to test the formal idea of serial things and potential serial structure (Photo © Courtesy of MOS).

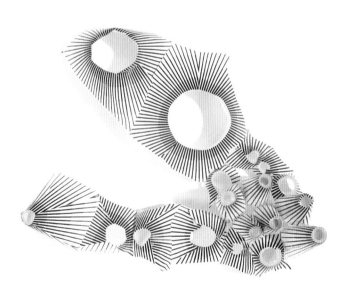

11
Final configuration of domes, cones and chimneys set with thatching patterns and future material densities (Photo © Courtesy of MOS).

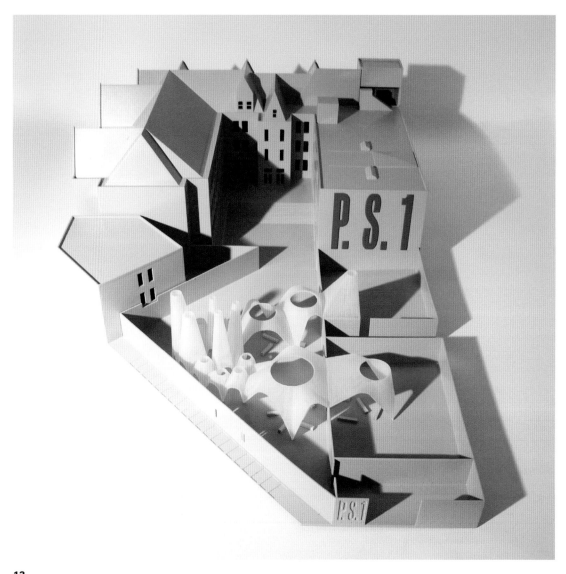

12
3-D-printed prototype showing design organization without any material effects (Photo © Courtesy of MOS).

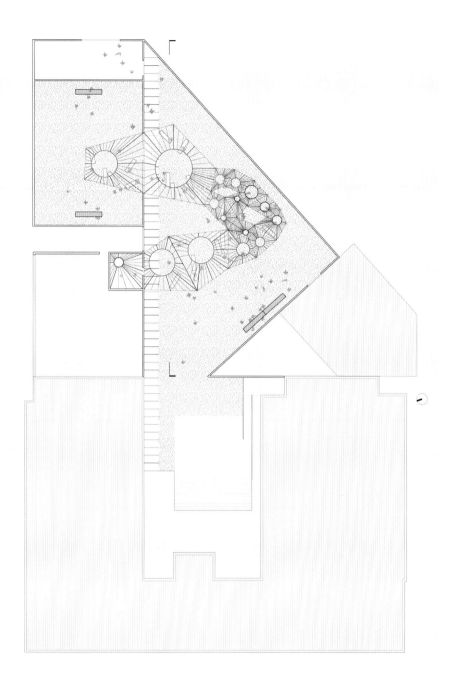

13
Plan: afterparty (Photo © Courtesy of MOS).

afterparty, PS 1 YAP Pavilion (2009)

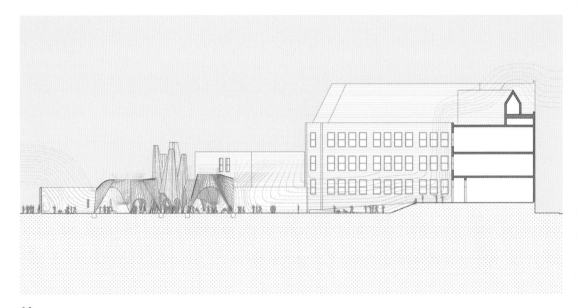

14
Section: afterparty (Photo © Courtesy of MOS).

Part II

The Sublime Past

4

The Nature Parallel

Barry Bergdoll

What I present in the pages that follow operates quite differently from K. Michael Hays's following analysis of Mies van der Rohe and the sublime, although I think that what I have to say will intersect and provide us with many more concrete examples to test his hypothesis. Mine are a series of impressions, and being trained as an art historian I can't help but put together images in the hopes of staging or proposing comparisons, contrasts, points of collision as well as of coalescence. That said, my first example is singular for I don't want to suggest a dualism either between historical and contemporary approaches or, for that matter, between human nature and the natural realm. However something of that complex dualism reminds us of the issues with which we are dealing as part of modern experience; those issues go back to the earliest philosophy preoccupied with the relationship of man *and* nature, man *as part of* nature and all of the tensions incumbent there. This relationship is taken up in different moments in relation to retreat, to self-consciousness (which will be my line of reading Mies), to stewardship and ultimately to the sublime—an attitude that suggests in its evocation both an enormous respect of nature but also a fear of an impassable chasm between inner experience and outer nature.

I find it interesting in view of all the discussion of Kant (whose philosophical concepts will not be glossed here) simply to reflect briefly upon an art historical artifact—a provocative form—that is contemporary with that definition. This is, of course, Goethe's famous and still perplexing monument in his garden-house at Weimar: the so-called *Altar of Agathe Tyche* (1777)—sometimes called the Altar of Good Fortune—which appears on the scene sometime between Burke's and Kant's aesthetic definitions of the sublime and the beautiful.[1] The point isn't really that this is a monument to the sublime but, rather, that it seems to function as a reference to an interest in the notion of aesthetic autonomy—this, in a garden that Goethe

4.1
WORKac, P.F.1 (public
farm 1) (Photo: Peter
Stegner, Courtesy of MoMA
PS 1).

carefully cultivated and in which he undertook his own natural history research. So his search for the primordial plant—his fascination with, simultaneously, the diversity and the elementarism of natural form—is complemented here by what would seem to be an absolute autonomous distinction from its natural surroundings. I would like to suggest that there are a number of discourses and practices currently out there in the architecture (the architecture not only that we look at but that I curate), which emphatically *don't* seek out such absolute autonomous distinction.

There are examples like this one by WORKac, P.F.1 (public farm 1) from the Young Architects Program at PS 1, which one might think of as a fragment of some notion of sustainability (Figure 4.1).[2] Or one could turn to projects by Aranda/Lasch to represent the current, and I think quite self-perpetuating, fascination with form-making that is meant to have its basis in some kind of biomimicry. Whether it be Aranda/Lasch or in the art world at the Venice Biennale or currently downtown in New York (Matthew Ritchie working with those same architects), generally all this has led to a remarkable proliferation of form-making without any, to my mind, evidence of the architectural project to which it might be connected and in ways that are actually hardly recognizable as a reflection on nature or on a relationship of architecture to architecture. Yet such form-making seems to be proliferating in rather extraordinary ways in studios and in galleries. There is also a more literal expression of biomimicry to be found in the sort of Neo-Art Nouveau forms of Greg Lynn's silverware for Alessi for example. In both contemporary practice and, as we shall see, in the larger history of modern architecture since the Enlightenment, there are conflicts between different attitudes about architecture's relationship to nature. Just to end this contemporary prelude, we read on the website of the prominent New York practice Hanrahan Meyers Architects not only that "Design is a frame for nature," but that biomimicry, following Janine Benyus, is "an emerging discipline that seeks sustainable solutions by emulating nature's design and processes."[3] As a historian, this makes me extremely nervous when I think back as recently as the Rococo and the Art Nouveau. I am indeed hard-put to find anything extremely novel in this notion that biomimicry is an "emerging discipline" rather than an established trope in architectural practice, which in all likelihood goes back to the gardens of the ancients. Such assumptions need to be questioned, particularly when we go on to read on the same website about the roof profiles of the new Battery Park Community Center where "naturally occurring wave forms determine the shape of the building's roof." The result, in fact, is beautiful and elegant, but the willful and bizarre confusion between the arbitrary and the necessary leads one to wonder to what extent natural metaphors are necessarily enriching architectural investigations today. After all, the determination of the sustainability of the roof in energy terms, rather than in terms of rising sea levels with climate change, seems not to find its most natural inspiration in the qualities of hydraulics.

Let's go back to where I'm on safer ground: in the eighteenth, nineteenth and earlier twentieth centuries. This will ultimately lead us to Mies. There are two paradigmatic examples we need to have in mind here. The first is Charles Eisen's frontispiece for the second edition of Marc-Antoine Laugier's *An Essay on Architecture* (1755), which is almost always used instead of Laugier's actual words to herald the famous appeal for a return to a natural model. What did he mean by a natural model? He never actually refers to the biomimicry inherent in the frontispiece; his forms do not actually grow out of the ground. Yes, Laugier describes something that is quite parallel to nature—something along the lines of what we might call "natural reason"—but in no way does he seek to advocate an imitation of nature itself. Rather, his is an argument about the fact that architecture finds its model within itself, and this emerges quite clearly when one refers to the text rather than to the many misreadings that have subsequently been fueled by image, which, lest we forget, doesn't seem to have been authorized by Laugier.

But there is a whole other strain, which is represented by Joseph Michael Gandy's famous watercolor, *Architecture: Its Natural Model* (c. 1838) (Figure 4.2). Here, architecture is seen to grow quite distinctly from the geological formations that had been detailed in Charles Lyell's *Principles of Geology* just a few years earlier. There is, throughout the nineteenth century, a fascinating counterpoint between discoveries in the natural sciences (geology and mineralogy especially) and architectural explorations.[4] The interesting thing, however, is that throughout that century one finds very little biomimicry, which comes back into architecture only very late in the century. In the eighteenth century, studies of natural origins and early architectures often sustained results that were elementalist without

4.2
Joseph Michael Gandy,
*Architecture: Its Natural
Model*, c. 1838 (Photo:
Courtesy of the Trustees of
Sir John Soane's Museum,
London).

mimicry. To compare Gandy with, say, an image of the Doric Greek Temples at
Paestum engraved by Thomas Major or a drawing of the same by Jacques-Germain
Soufflot is to realize this same primitive Doric order could give rise to very diverse
architectural primitivisms. Gandy here too is inspired by the structural order of the
basalt columns in the geological forms of Finnegan's Cave in the north of Scotland,
a favorite inspiration for the practice of the sublime. The point here is the fascination
of architecture and nature as two parallel but quite distinct worlds.

Enter into my most familiar territory, and there we would be led to the
interactions in German Romanticism between a major figure like Karl Friedrich
Schinkel and the German naturalist Alexander von Humboldt, which took place
quite literally on the grounds of the royal gardens at Potsdam. Consider Schinkel's
own representations of his Court Gardener's House, one of a series of buildings he
erected in that great landscape garden as he both revised and extended it with the
landscape designer Peter-Joseph Lenné (Figure 4.3).[5] Such images have typically
been misread as translations of the English picturesque in German contexts, when
it's clear that what Schinkel is showing us is an absolute distinction between the
realm of nature and that of architecture. Architecture is here conjugated from
primitive pillar forms through a whole series of an emerging order—a kind of natural
architecture that parallels nature itself (and, indeed, one can trace the origins of the
arch as well in another of these images). But there is no attempt whatsoever to look
for the literal appearance of nature in architecture. Instead, what is sought is a kind
of parallel logic to the way nature structures itself. This occurs over and over again

Barry Bergdoll

in Schinkel's work and, as a result, one needs to insist not only on the important role played by the forms Schinkel's architecture took but, also, on some understanding of his profound notion of architecture as a matrix: in this case, a kind of framework from which one might contemplate nature as something adjacent to—yet resolutely outside of—the architectural frame.

Schinkel's fascination, in many aspects of his work, with the ability of architecture to create the possibility for a practice of Romantic self-consciousness is something else that returns in the years after 1900 with the reappraisal of Schinkel's oeuvre, in other words, the historical crucible out of which Mies's architectural project would be born. This, too, is a truly fascinating moment: the return of nature almost exactly a century ago at the very turn of the nineteenth to the twentieth century, which we associate with Art Nouveau. There are obvious examples, but one that remains particularly fascinating is connected yet again to natural history. I'm speaking of the extraordinary impact on architecture of underwater oceanography and biology in the late nineteenth century, which teetered on the edge of a kind of biomimicry all the while revealing a distinct architectural project held in relation to the undertaking, in natural history, of the exploration of the invisible. With the appearance of the microscope and the telescope came depictions such as this one of miniature sea-life forms here seen in one of the least lurid plates from the so-called *Kunstformen der Natur* (c. 1899–1904) or *Art Forms from Nature* by the German neo-Romantic "Darwinian" Ernst Haeckel (Figure 4.4). This was taken over by the French architect René Binet in his great gateway to the Paris Universal Exposition of 1900, a rewriting of the Eiffel Tower now in concrete and metal but also a rewriting in terms of his interest in the self-generating forms in nature (Figure 4.5).[6] This exchange between the detail of formwork and the microscopic view of deep-sea organisms exposes what the rapport of architecture to new discoveries

4.4
Ernst Heinrich Philipp
August Haeckel,
"Cyrtoidea," *Kunstformen
der Natur* (Leipzig and
Vienna: Verlag des
Bibliographischen Institut,
1899–1904), plate 31
(Photo: Courtesy of author).

about nature might be, and the most interesting thing is that the designer has an a priori project that drives his applied vision of nano discoveries about nature's underlying architecture. There is, in other words, a project in Binet's architecture; it includes creating a span even greater than the Eiffel Tower that can stand on three feet instead of four and that can be self-sustaining in a different tectonic way. To take account of that scale might seem to bring us into the world of Aranda/Lasch and Matthew Ritchie, yet the idea of scalability is completely related to architectural issues of the quest for a civic form that might reframe for a season the experience of Paris. Binet, in sum, set out to fulfill an architectural problem rather than a purely

Barry Bergdoll

formal one. Interestingly Haeckel's correspondence is filled with a kind of fan mail from architects and artists (likely with no one more sycophantic than Binet).[7]

To contextualize Hays's brilliant discussion of Mies van der Rohe's American years, I would like to glance back to the issue of nature in his formative years, those years in the early 1920s when he comes into his own and adopts his new name, rechristening himself "van der Rohe." Again, this is a moment marked by dualisms. In my role as a curator I'm obsessed with objects, and we acquired two a couple of years ago just as I was arriving at the Museum of Modern Art that highlight vastly different attitudes toward nature in the Berlin avant-garde. The first is the work of Hugo Häring, an unfinished, unrealized part of his famous so-called organic farm at Gut Garkau in the north of Germany. And the second is a long lost drawing by Mies van der Rohe for the Eliat House outside of Potsdam, this classic territory of Schinkel. Now the interesting thing about these drawings, besides some stylistic similarities in their rendering, is that they were in all likelihood actually made in adjacent rooms in Mies van der Rohe's studio in the years when Mies and Häring shared space at Am Karlsbad 24. The two architects did not share a complete point of view but they must have had some kind of exchange (and one would really love to have the transcripts of the conversations if there were any desk crits between

4.5
René Binet, Monumental Gateway, Paris Universal Exposition of 1900 (Photo: Collections of the Library of Congress Prints and Photographs Division).

these two projects). This is still the Mies of villas rendered in brick and brought to visibility by sunlight; any nature in which he might have been interested involved the interaction of light with architecture rather than a biomimicry. Discernible is the absolute distinction in both cases between what we call the staffage of nature and the radically different explorations of form.

Now these are two figures who have often been put in opposition by, say, Nikolaus Pevsner, Sigfried Giedion or even Kenneth Frampton or Alan Colquhoun in more recent accounts. Häring is seen over and over again as a key figure in the development of modern organicism, with his theory of organic architecture often in my view misinterpreted as the equivalent of learning from nature. Whereas the notion of the organic in Häring and, later, in Hans Scharoun (a disciple of sorts), comes from the notion that architecture should not be imposed as a preconceived idea but, rather, should be discovered as an exploration of the place and conditions that the building is intended to serve. In other words, there is an organicism of the unfolding of the project through both program and form, and therefore of the interrelationship of those forms one to another as the project develops. In that sense, the opposition with Mies is not nearly as radical as the outer forms of the buildings might suggest at first glance. One of the reasons that I have been invited to be part of the discussion in this volume, I suspect, is that I am the person in our generation to have attempted to put nature back into Mies—but not in order to create a biomimetic or picturesque Mies at all. The title of the essay I wrote that reflected on Mies's early villa designs and the role of domestic space in particular as his laboratory in the German period was called "The Nature of Mies's Space."[8] The title was meant to be a play simultaneously on his fascination with nature and his evolving ideas of nature. I want to focus on this in closing not only in order to leave some open-endedness about images with which we might play further, but also in order to address what really preoccupied him, which was the nature of space rather than Nature with a capital "N."

Much of my thinking on the matter actually came out of a course that I was teaching simultaneously at Columbia University and at the Harvard Graduate School of Design before the Mies project began. I'm thinking back to the moment when I went to grab a slide of the plan of the Barcelona Pavilion and thought, "Oh that's no good, the back steps aren't there." I then began to realize not only that the back steps weren't there but that the whole relationship to the site wasn't there—and it began to dawn on me that the drawing had been redrawn for publication in *The International Style* (1932) as had the plan of the contemporaneous Tugendhat House (both were commissions of 1928).[9] What had been removed were all of the pictorial references by which Mies indicates the wiggly lines of nature absolutely adjacent to the ruled lines of the architectural creation. It's curious that whoever redrew this (I still don't know, but let's say it was Philip Johnson or someone else under his instigation) kept Mies's obsession with drawing all of the furniture even in the free plan. Yet all of the plants are removed, even from the conservatory and then from the adjacent site. The plantation there was clearly related and part of the

Barry Bergdoll

composition, but I would not go so far as to say that therefore Mies was attempting to make any kind of natural architecture. Rather what he was contemplating, primarily, was the idea of architecture as a frame for experience. This experience involved a deep reflection on *the nature* of nature inasmuch as it can be known as well as the nature of human consciousness.

In my 2001 catalogue essay, I spent a great deal of time talking about Mies's relationship to Schinkel. I think the comparison is compelling, and there are many formal gestures to which we can turn to substantiate it: the insistence on the great pedestal, the building that is set apart, the building that incorporates nature without ever attempting itself to bend in any mimetic way to nature. Tugendhat and Barcelona, both, are projects that have enjoyed canonical status as demonstrations of architectural autonomy. Both, indeed, are seen as seminal examples of the International Style. But, more importantly, both stem from a moment when Mies was actively thinking about the triangulation between architecture, nature and technology, so this is a third element. This was a period when, as Fritz Neumeyer has noted, Mies was actively engaged in a self-critique of an earlier enthrallment with technology.[10] And here the key text for us is Mies's own: the publication of some of his philosophical jottings, quite aphoristic, sometimes emerging in rare moments into actual paragraphs. We find him writing as early as 1924, "We agree . . .," so this is right after the concrete house, the glass skyscrapers and all of that: "We agree with the direction [Henry] Ford has taken but we reject the plane on which he moves. Mechanization can never be a goal; it must remain a means. A means toward a spiritual purpose."[11] It might be tempting to re-read that phrase with "nature" appearing at the key juncture instead (but I don't like to transpose words). The point is that this triangulation of architecture, technology and nature must remain just that, a triangulation, rather than a collapse—and this notion of a means towards a spiritual purpose is, I think, the key phrase in 1924.

By 1927–1928, the most important commissions of the German period all came into the office: the Barcelona Pavilion, the Tugendhat House, the Lange and Esters Houses in Krefeld and quite a few others. Mies writes at that time, "there are people who would like to make a Ford factory out of nature."[12] In an important lecture, "The Preconditions of Architectural Work" (1928), Mies concluded:

> We have to become master of the unleashed forces and build them into a new order, an order that permits free play for the unfolding of life. Yes, but an order also that is related to mankind. . . . We do not need less science, but a science that is more spiritual. . . . All that will only become possible when man asserts himself in objective nature and relates it to himself.[13]

Consider this call to assert oneself in objective nature and relate it to oneself with one of the more beautiful renderings for the Tugendhat House (for which there are countless sketches by Mies's hand unlike the Seagram Building for which there are but two, analyzed by Hays). One sees this object in delicate balance in relation to its site but, by the same token, as distinct in its forms from the site; the latter is taken up in the small scale, in the incorporation of this little wire trellis for planting, which, like the ordering cruciform column, becomes conjugated throughout the building. Mies invents a whole new order for architecture, keeping these things in a dialogue with nature but never, as I have been saying, merging them into it. Mies was preoccupied with these issues in the months before receiving the Barcelona and Brno commissions and the Tugendhat commission. "We want to give meaning to things again," he noted from the Roman Catholic philosopher Romano Guardini's *Von heiligen Zeichen* (1922).[14] "There is a totally untouched nature," he also wrote, "and the longing for it is itself a cultural phenomenon. Nature is truly affecting only when it begins to be dwelled in; when culture begins in it. Piece by piece nature is formed. Man creates in his own world, not only of a natural need but with deliberate purpose, serving spiritual ideas."[15]

Let me suggest that we could go through the entire career in Berlin from the first building to the last, and see how something like the brilliant plan of the Tugendhat House sets up a dialectic. We could go back to it, to its exterior, and to the parts that had been planned by Mies as an extension of interior space as well as a play between the blurring of inside and out (epitomized by the juxtaposition of window panes that disappear) and those instances where nature is caught between panes of sheet glass (in the interior conservatory). The house, as I concluded in my reading of it some years ago, is a frame for a specific type of experience of both family life and individual contemplation—of the relationship between the self and the external world. Grete Tugendhat had been a student, in the months before the commission, of Heidegger, and she spoke very specifically about this.[16] Tugendhat might almost therefore in her own work represent a strategy for achieving what Mies, now her architect, had called for in his 1928 lecture. "It must be possible," he said, "to solve the task of controlling nature and yet create simultaneously a new freedom."[17] The client soon weighed in as well in response to a now famous debate on whether one might live in this vast undifferentiated space with its lack of protection from the great outdoors. The critics saw in the house the luxurious play of an architect's notion of pathos and the grandeur of nature being reduced to amazingly beautiful materials: perhaps here a suggestion of the sublime, onyx and mahogany.

"What has the architect given us?" Greta Tugendhat memorably responded to the critics. "An important feeling of existence [*Daseinsgefühl*]," she stated in a direct evocation of Heidegger. "I had never experienced the rooms as possessing pathos. I find them large and austerely simple—however not in a dwarfing but in a liberating sense. . . . For just as one sees in this room every flower in a different light, and as every work of art gives a stronger impression, individuals too stand out more clearly against such a background."[18] In short, Grete had found for her house a vehicle for contemplating the self in the realm of nature: in other words, the type of practice we admire today perhaps in the work of Olafur Eliasson, which mediates

Barry Bergdoll

between the fallacies of biomimicry and an invitation to contemplate ourselves in a realm of nature; the type of practice which is now often merged with technologies in ways that essentially mean nature is never a static category. Put another way: mimicry can only be maintained in relationship to an image we have at the moment of nature. What we need is a profound engagement with nature, both for our own project of self-critical definition and for the confrontation of the real challenges we have with a nature that is as threatening to us as we are to it.

Notes

1   In his poem "Urworte. Orphisch" (1817), Goethe describes "Tyche, das Zufällige" as chance: "Die strenge Grenze doch umgeht gefällig / Eine Wandelndes, das mit und um uns wandelt . . ." See Theo Buck, *Goethes "Urworte. Orphisch": Interpretiert und mit einer Dokumentation versehe* (Frankfurt am Main: P. Lang, 1996); and Karen Lang, "The Dialectics of Decay: Rereading the Kantian Subject," *Art Bulletin* 79/3 (Sept. 1997), 422.

2   Amale Andraos, Dan Woods, eds., *Above the Pavement–the Farm! Architecture and Agriculture at P.F.1* (New York: Princeton Architectural Press, 2010).

3   <http://blog.hanrahanmeyers.com/2009/10/hma-research-biomimicry-and-designfont. html>. The statement summarizes the views presented by Janine Benyus, *Biomimicry: Innovation Inspired by Nature* (New York: William Morrow, 1997).

4   See Barry Bergdoll, "Of Crystals, Cells and Strata: Natural History and Debates on the Form of a New Architecture in the Nineteenth Century," *Architectural History* 50 (2007): 1–29.

5   See expecially Barry Bergdoll, *Karl Friedrich Schinkel: An Architecture for Prussia* (New York: Rizzoli, 1994), 153–167. See also Iain Boyd Whyte, "Charlottenhof: The Prince, the Gardener, the Architect and the Writer," *Architectural History* 43 (2000): 1–23.

6   This exchange was the focus of the exhibition, "René Binet and Ernst Haeckel's Collaboration: Magical Naturalism and Architectural Ornament," at the Charles Deering McCormick Library of Special Collections, Northwestern University, March 31 to October 31, 2011. Writings on the subject include Erika Krause, "L'influence de Ernst Haeckel sur l'art nouveau," in Jean Clair, ed., *L'Ame au corps: Arts et Sciences (1793–1993)* (Paris: Gallimard, 1993), 342–350.

7   See Barry Bergdoll, "Les esquisses décoratives de René Binet" in *René Binet (1866–1911), un architecte de la Belle Epoque* (Sens: Musée de Sens, 2005), 101–109. See also Robert Proctor, "Architecture from the Cell-Soul: René Binet and Ernst Haeckel," *Journal of Architecture* 11/4 (2006): 407–424.

8   Barry Bergdoll, "The Nature of Mies's Space," in Barry Bergdoll, Terence Riley, *Mies in Berlin* (New York: Museum of Modern Art, 2001), 65–105.

9   Henry Russell Hitchcock, Jr., Philip Johnson, *The International Style: Architecture Since 1922* (New York: W. W. Norton, 1932).

10   See Fritz Neumeyer, "A World in Itself: Architecture and Technology," in Detlef Mertins, ed., *The Presence of Mies* (New York: Princeton Architectural Press, 1994), 71–83.

11   Ludwig Mies van der Rohe, "Lecture (1924)," in Fritz Neumeyer, *The Artless Word: Mies van der Rohe on the Building Art*, trans. Mark Jarzombek (Cambridge, MA: The MIT Press, 1991), 250.

12   Ludwig Mies van der Rohe, "Notebook (1927–1928)," 60, in *ibid.*, 288.

13   Ludwig Mies van der Rohe, "The Preconditions of Architectural Work (1928)," in *ibid.*, 301.

14   Ludwig Mies van der Rohe, "Notebook (1927–1928)," 62, in *ibid.*, 289.

15   Ludwig Mies van der Rohe, "Notebook (1927–1928)," 40, in *ibid.*, 281.

16   As daughter Daniela recalled: "My parents, especially my mother, were concerned with the philosophy of Heidegger. The closest friends of my mother were students of Heidegger; through them she was introduced to his lectures even before the publication of *Sein und Zeit* (*Being and Time*) in 1927"; Daniela Hammer-Tugendhat, Wolf Tegethoff, eds., *Ludwig Mies van der Rohe: The Tugendhat House* (New York: Springer, 2000), 27. Greta and Fritz Tugendhat's son, Ernst, later became a philosopher whose writings include *Der Wahrheitsbegriff bei Husserl und Heidegger* (Berlin: Walter de Gruyter, 1967), which he dedicated to his mother.

17   Ludwig Mies van der Rohe, "The Preconditions of Architectural Work (1928)," in Neumeyer, *op. cit.*, 301.

18   Cited in Bergdoll (2001), *op. cit.*, 99.

5

Next to Nothing

K. Michael Hays

I wish to rewrite the oldest maxim of art theory, that art imitates nature. I shall rewrite it like this: Art (or in this case architecture) is mimetic of a Nature that does not exist; or, architecture emerges next to nothing. The point I'll be making is the Kantian one that there are conditions we can conceive, yet neither see nor show. The architecture of interest, then, is an architecture that presents the unrepresentable. And, finally, what I want to emphasize in this rewriting of the maxim is the dialectic of a radical negativity that is bound up with a utopian vocation.

In the Kantian system, works of art are phenomenal expressions of the noumenal realm (a realm independent of the senses, the realm of Mind), and the perceived beauty availed to us in the aesthetic appreciation of such works also enables us to regard Nature itself as a phenomenal manifestation of that matrix in which things are truly what they are—which Kant calls a "supersensible substrate." The supersensible designates that which transcends experience.

The judgment of taste is purely subjective, but the subjectivity is mediated by Nature insofar as the judgment of beauty depends on our ability to experience an appropriateness of the object for cognition that is also the promise of the unity and harmony of Nature. In the beautiful, we experience our own subjectivity through the "naturalness" and the rightness of Nature, through Nature's ability to form the coherent whole, the total system we assume in our search for knowledge. Which means we find and found ourselves in the mirror of Nature. According to Kant, while we should be conscious that art is art, with an external, intentional cause, and not Nature, which has no such cause, nevertheless the purposiveness (*Zweckmässigkeit*) of art—the "merely formal purposiveness" freed from the constraints of use or arbitrary rules—makes it seem as though the presence of beauty in an object of art just *is* the presence of Nature itself.

5.1
Ludwig Mies van der
Rohe, Illinois Institute of
Technology, Chicago, IL,
1939–1941. Composite
photograph of site plan
(Photo: Hedrich Blessing.
Courtesy of the Chicago
History Museum).

This, then, is Kant's version of the maxim, Art imitates Nature. Kant's sublime, on the other hand, goes beyond Nature; it works its disruption in relation to our place in Nature; it is an aesthetics of "de-naturing." The sublime throws the subject into an out-of-time, a beyond-time, where the time of sense experience and the system of Nature are no longer limiting.

The work of Mies van der Rohe reaches for a spatialized version of the Kantian sublime.

Take the Illinois Institute of Technology (IIT) campus plan (Figure 5.1). A first gloss confirms the received view of Miesian planning as a kind of idealist decoupage: first, a cutting away of the existing fabric of Chicago's South Side in an effort to reveal the more essential underlying matrix that ideally should order all of space; and then, into that ideal matrix, a demiurgic reinsertion of a swath of sensible, material, public space that symbolizes the *polis* itself and sets itself in a negative dialogue with the surrounding fabric. Enough has been made of the Miesian universal space and infinite grid—the utopia of the unmixed—to allow this preliminary reading. But it is as if, in the confrontation of the actual material of the degraded American city and the supersensible substrate to which it is here compared, the architectural imagination finds it impossible to adequate the one to the other. What results is what we might think of as a spatial trauma.

In Mies's plan, Crown Hall faced outward from the campus; it was the hinge between the campus and the city, the fold of ideality and reality. In it, we might hope to find the reconciliation of the immediate and sensible and the transcendent supersensible. But the space produced by Crown Hall is not really as resolved

K. Michael Hays

as the received Miesian paradigm is supposed to be. Colin Rowe long ago noted that because Crown Hall has no effective center from which the observer might contemplate the whole, there is no "spatial climax" but rather a constant, unstable "rotary, peripheric" swirl effecting an outward pull that forever defers the formal fix Mies's North American work has been famously supposed to offer.[1] What is more, the spatial continuum of the clear-span pavilion is utterly contradicted by the treatment of the glazing, frosted on the bottom panel to a line just above eye level so that any visual calibration of the space outside the pavilion becomes impossible, while scenes from the far away are effectively collapsed onto the glass along with the close to (Figure 5.2). This to-and-fro movement is then caught up in the sideways movement of space against the glass surface resulting in an unstable, traumatic space—figure of the metaphysical panic that is the first stage of the Sublime.

5.2
Ludwig Mies van der Rohe standing in S. R. Crown Hall on Illinois Institute of Technology Campus, Chicago, IL, ca. 1955–1956 (Photo: Hedrich Blessing. Courtesy of the Chicago History Museum).

Mies's attempt can best be described, I think, as the *transubstantiation* of the reality of its site into an appearance as such, *eine Erscheinung*—a shining forth. That is, the IIT campus plan and its architecture articulate the virtual possibilities of South Side, tracing (in the grid and the frame, primarily) what is most "promising" about the context, what is latent in its structure. But that promise is precisely what, in the present social order, the context of the campus can never actually become. Reality thus bleeds through, but only in the forms and fragments ideality allows. This is not to deny that Mies's architecture is also a positive proposal beyond the virtual, but rather to point to the power of its negativity in itself, which emerges as the concept of another dimension that disrupts the normal order of phenomena—a fleeting, anticipatory glimpse of a possible world (in this case a transcendent world) made out of the very substance of what exists but which momentarily appears or shines through the Miesian matter that has replaced it and which, in the next instant, is already lost.

To express this critical predicament of irresistible utopian forces expending themselves on immovable ideological objects, Mies has taken recourse to the sublime. At this point, however, it is incomplete. Let us take the next step.

Look at the sketch of the Seagram project, one of two nearly identical sketches, the only development sketches by Mies in the archives (Figure 5.3). Traces of Schinkel's landscape narratives, which Mies explored in his villas, are there in the asymmetry of the large proscenium-tree on the right and the foreground edges, but movement has been stilled. Crown Hall is there with its five bays and human figures drawn in and its "universal" space of the clear-span pavilion, but the horizontal spatial plenum meets a vertical plane. The New National Gallery is prefigured in the wisps of trabeation, not in the same plane as Crown Hall but perhaps just in front of it. But mostly there is just the space of what will be the plaza and the few props—edges, planes, and frames—needed for its definition. What will become the building itself is indicated by a series of hasty zigzags, as if in an afterthought, or perhaps the reverse: as if Mies already knows the solution to that part of the project and needs to put his energies elsewhere.

One is tempted to read the Seagram Plaza as a staking out of a space for contemplation or a "space of appearance" in Hannah Arendt's sense, with all the promise for profundity of subjective experience that notion holds out. Either of these views is consistent with the Kantian system. But it's hard for me to understand Mies's ethos of repetition and renunciation as promising anything like subjective experience in this sense. Rather, his effort joins Arendt's space of appearance with what Mies called *beinahe nichts*, next to nothing, in order to deny that the one is any longer possible without the other; if the space of appearance is to be found it will not be a positive, substantial space, but rather a space adjacent to a nothing. Thus are both emptiness and fullness, discontinuity and difference, introduced into the previously continuous plenum of the real. To say it another way: architecture, of course, cannot eradicate appearance altogether, cannot become literally nothing without destroying itself, turning into a reductive materialism and leaving behind

K. Michael Hays

5.3
Ludwig Mies van der
Rohe, Conceptual sketch
for the Seagram Building
Plaza, New York City,
ca.1954–1955. Graphite on
tracing paper 7.0 × 21.4
cm (Photo: Courtesy of
Collection Centre Canadien
d'Architecture/Canadian
Centre for Architecture,
Montréal).

the unmediated symptoms of the unsatisfactory reality it hopes to change. But Mies now regards with distrust any positive expression since with that concept comes the nagging worry that what's driving the architectural expression, what's behind the appearance, are just those social forces—instrumental technology, the market, the chattering masses, the superficiality and inauthenticity of the public sphere—into whose service architecture is constantly being pressed. Nature, in whose mirror the subject hopes to find itself, has been too effectively dominated and fetishized to play such a role in the architectural imagination; it is rather the world system of technology and finance that now exceeds our power to grasp and represent to ourselves. So architecture must become virtual. If architecture could do away with expression, if one could come forth next to nothing, making virtual conjunctions from the myriad bits and pieces of architectural possibilities, then perhaps some other kind of experience could make an appearance.

Recall that Kant's account of the work of art considers the object only through the (contemplating or producing) subject. Mies insists that the desubjectified affects and percepts that enter into virtual conjunction construct cognitive content in the object itself, a content that is not exhausted either by the subjective intentions of its

5.4
Ludwig Mies van der Rohe,
Exterior detail, Seagram
Building, New York, NY,
1954–1958 (Photo: Courtesy
of David Turturo).

producers or by the subjective responses of its consumers. The abstraction of Mies's architecture arises out of the central tension between the desire to desubjectify the aesthetic phenomena—to displace the subject-centered categories of experience, consciousness, interiority, and the like with the elementary bits and pieces of the object world—and the commitment to produce a new aesthetic experience which maintains some last dimension of fully achieved engagement with form, which the desubjectifying desire cannot wish to deny.

This is the first divergence of Mies from Kant: the priority of the object over the subject. The second divergence is that, for Mies, there can be no radical separation between the transcendental and the empirical. He pursues a single substance, immanent to itself, *immanence without the opposition of transcendent.*

Let us look at Seagram's wall (Figure 5.4). The Seagram's famous I-section steel mullion is crucial; it is the nexus of meaning of the entire building surface: functional, factural, symbolic; utterly commonplace yet raised to representational status in the matrix that is the Seagram's surface; the primary mark out of which the surface's tissue of effects is produced. A close view emphasizes the facture, materiality, and immediacy of Mies's sublime. But as we move back to view the curtain wall at a distance, the facture of the primal elements is taken over by their visual effect, which is to say by a logic of surface perception. The series of bronzed steel mullions now casts shadows on the bronze glass, erasing themselves as figures and the glass curtain wall as ground into a continuous spread of surface. The modulations of the surface—the reticulated grid of welded mullions and panels—as tectonically thick as they are, cannot be read "deeply." Rather, they can only be scanned for textural effect. There is only an immanent evenness of surface persisting from start to finish as if unencumbered by subjective intent. The sublime

K. Michael Hays

object keeps the scanning movement of apprehension continuously in motion as a way of denying that our comprehension ever settles.

There are two moments in the surface of the Seagram, then, one that stresses the quiddity of materials and tectonics and the other that takes us toward the Beyond of the supersensible. Mies pursues a single substance in the sense that immanence and transcendence are pressed together; the surface *is* substance, that is, immanent to itself, but produces the supersensible. To think such a surface adequately is to think next to nothing—the transcendent within immanence. This is where Mies parts with Kant.

At IIT there is a hidden matrix or structure necessary to produce the architectural effects. There is a transcendent organizational principle to which the formation, development, and consequent effects of the campus plan and its buildings relate. At Seagram there is a different matrix, which does not seek to represent an ideal but rather brings to immanence the experience of sheer abstraction. The supersensible remains but as an abstract intensity, an alongside of nothingness, which joins with a bodily intensity of materials and facture. Mind is no longer to be conceived as a self-contained field, substantially differentiated from body, nor as the primary condition of unilateral subjective mediation of external objects or events. Rather all real distinctions (mind and body, idea and matter, interiority and exteriority, natural and artificial) emerge together in a single substance. The sublime of the Seagram could therefore be said to be still mediated by Nature in a Kantian sense, but it is a Nature that does not exist.

There are two different planes of construction which architecture can activate in its work of representation. The first plane is the plane of Idea; it contains instructions and templates for organizing forms and functions to which it stands in a transcendental relation. This plane is deeply imbricated in Nature, which serves as its ground and guarantees its processes. But neither the plane nor Nature is given; they can only be inferred from their effects, such as, say the campus plan of IIT.

The second plane is a plane where immanent materials and events circulate. It is the plane of Desire. This plane hovers just above or just below the parts (like an electromagnetic plate organizing metal filings according to patterned flows of energy). Nature no longer exists as stable ground or source of models in this plane. Indeed, it no longer really "exists" at all; it "is" nothing but the constant flux of immanent molecules and particles, including architectural percepts and affects, and their organization and enfolding into architectural elements—such as metrically controlled glass and metal panels of the Seagram, the series of I-sections, the bronze coating, as well as certain qualities like reflectivity, dullness, or brightness. This second plane brings together such heterogeneous elements and makes them function together, creating non-preexistent and continually shifting relations without unifying them. The nature of this plane is not to produce a whole but to constantly search for the new. Its nature is virtual and abstract.[2] Paul Klee already commented on the plane of Desire: "Kunst gibt nicht das Sichtbare wieder, sondern Kunst macht sichtbar."[3] Art does not reproduce what is already there, but rather organizes forces and presents individuations that are not in themselves visible. Which is to say, art appears next to nothing.

Notes

1   Colin Rowe, "Neo-'Classicism' and Modern Architecture II" (1957), *The Mathematics of the Ideal Villa and Other Essays* (Cambridge, MA: The MIT Press, 1976), 148.

2   I have borrowed here, with some abuse, from what Deleuze and Guattari call the Memories of a Plan(e) Maker: "There are no longer any forms or developments of forms; nor are there subjects or the formation of subjects. There is no structure, any more than there is genesis. There are only relations of movement and rest, speed and slowness between unformed elements. . . . There are only haecceities, affects, and subjectless individuations that constitute collective assemblages. . . . It is necessarily a plane of immanence and univocality. We therefore call it the plane of Nature, although the natural has nothing to do with it." Gilles Deleuze and Felix Guattari, *A Thousand Plateaus: Capitalism and Schizophrenia* (Minneapolis: University of Minnesota Press, 1987), 266.

3   Paul Klee, *Kunst-Lehre* (Leipzig: Reelam, 1987), 60.

K. Michael Hays

6

Nature after Mies

Diane Lewis

I

By tracing a sequence of plans that directly address the issue of nature and the sublime, the definitive contributions made by Ludwig Mies van der Rohe are clearly illuminated. Pivotal among the architects who were directed toward radical innovations in plan syntax from which new orders and spatial forms broke with conventional ideas of style in architecture, he was simultaneously able to sustain the presence of architectural memory against the onslaught of technocracy. The work on these objectives resulted in a dramatic vision of nature transformed in and by his time.

A succession of plans demonstrates the engagement of a select set of architects who embedded their thought on the manner in which Nature speaks to architecture as one component in the derivation and advancement of the new plan form of the twentieth century, that is, the free plan. Nature was addressed within the language of the free plan by imbuing decisions on form with the dialectics that are intrinsic to the subject of nature as it pertains to architecture.

Mies's address of these issues in plan was pivotal among architects concerned with innovation in plan syntax as it impacted structure and space, and rescaled the relation between the orders, technology and the natural world. By emphasizing the search for a continuity of architectural memory in a new definition of the orders, Mies's work resulted in a dramatic vision of nature transformed by the threat of the erasure of memory presented by the destruction of civilization as it unfolded in his time.

His redefinition of the relationship between interiority and exteriority, nature and artifice, manifest his poetic and structural derivation of the "orders" executed in completely new terms. These delineations of order employed a dramatic expression of gravity in shear connections, double cantilevers, long spans, and negative corners. This new order sustained the evolution of the structural expression established by Wright's determination to "destroy the box." The elements Mies derived and the new typologies of structure and space he invented confronted the academicism of precedents that prescribed an adherence to solely formal and stylistic rules of the Classical orders. The visceral power of the ancient and the archaic temples was re-embodied.

II

This commitment to the reinvention of the orders is manifest in the application of the free plan to the expression of the single order temple. A temple cropped from the structural "field" condition provided in a free plan can be recognized as the accomplishment of one of the new typologies: from Mies's Barcelona Pavilion to his Neue Nationalgalerie, in Le Corbusier's Heidi Weber Pavilion and onto the Wall House of John Hedjuk. Reading the memorable or definitive free plans, and selecting this itinerary for the "Sublime" is a process defined by T. S. Eliot in his essay "Tradition and the Individual Talent" (1919):

> what happens when a new work of art is created is something that happens simultaneously to all the works of art which preceded it. The existing monuments form an ideal order among themselves, which is modified by the introduction of the new (the really new) work of art among them. The existing order is complete before the new work arrives; for order to persist after the supervention of novelty, the *whole* existing order must be, if ever so slightly, altered; and so the relations, proportions, values of each work of art toward the whole are readjusted.

III

The following sequence is one that I have detected and developed over years:

- *The Barcelona Pavilion (the anti-pictorial plan)*: There is no greater example of an existentially determined, anti-pictorial plan than that of the Barcelona Pavilion. Mies's signature photographic representation of the pavilion is focused on the figure suspended in space and time; he attained a new dimensionality and a range of unpredicted architectural phenomena that were most pronounced in the photographic image. The photograph of the Barcelona Pavilion is clearly a definitive response to Edmund Burke's 1757 literary formulation of the "Sublime": "The passion caused by the great and sublime in *nature*, when those causes operate most powerfully, is astonishment; and astonishment is that state of the soul in which all its motions are suspended with some degree of horror. In this case the mind is so entirely filled with its object, that it cannot entertain any other. . . . Terror is in all cases whatsoever the ruling principle of the sublime." The resultant plan stood as the definitive statement of a "new sublime," which was anchored to Mies's ability to observe terror with remove, and to witness its source with humility by shielding the gaze.

This new detachment was a radical act that penetrated his ability to "*temper*" form. As he stated in his "Letter on Form in Architecture" (1924): "My attack is not against form, but against form as *an end in itself*." The recognition of this in his plan initiates a detachment—a theatre of the sublime existing independently from an interaction with the natural world— and deconstructs the conventional dualities supported by earlier definitions of natural paradise. The figure at Barcelona hovers in metamorphic fields of surface, space and elements. The figure floats—reflected and reversed without an explicit condition of enclosure—and is thereby suspended in an exterior vertical continuum with sky above and reflection below.

- *Laugier's rustic hut (the root of the free plan)*: The encyclopedic definition of the word "nature" is focused on distinguishing the world of human creations from that which exists outside of it. This opposition is expressed in architectural terms as a natural outside and an artificial inside by means of the bearing wall structure, that is, by means of the pre-exposed structural frame, which precedes the free plan and conventionalizes architecture primarily as enclosure or shelter. It can be argued that the free plan was born with Laugier's ideas about the purity of the free-standing column and the entablature of which his "little rustic hut" is comprised; these allow the distinction between the essential and the superfluous, and in this way Laugier's tenet of reduction to the essential sets into place the fundamental principle of the free plan. The hut paralleled concerns for democracies and the rights of man, for structures similar in their objectives for freedom, transparency and paring down: thus the name "plan libre," which forged new gradients between the natural and the man-made.

- *Semper's plan of the Caribbean hut (a magnet for gathering)*: Semper's Caribbean hut, with its emphasis on a central hearth, set forth the limits of architectural content and the significance of reduced structural expression as a basis for form that has no precedent in Neoclassicism or the imagery of empire. Laugier and Semper broke open the pre-existing structural conditions that encompassed only simple oppositions: the natural opposed to the artificial, the outside opposed to the inside. But the derivation of the frame— as an imperative based in a strictness of values—and the requirement of objectivity have motivated attempts to overthrow the roots of these principles. Thus contemporary formal arguments for structure to exist as skin only are formed in accordance with causalities or processes analogous to that which is not man-made or conceptualized through notational memory.

- *From Wright's Robie House to Mies's Brick Country House (new temples of planar elements)*: If Semper's hearth was posited as the primary element of civilization and central mass, Frank Lloyd Wright's hearth was positioned as the idealized element of support for the spanning element of shelter: the roof-bearing hearth. Cantilever is implicit as is the expansive infinite surround. The domicile is considered the model for the temple, and with this civic dimension, the impact of the individual on the collective is considered. Wright employs the pier and the wall in lieu of columns to replace the frame (which can still be linked to the architecture of empire), and a new temple form of planar elements emerges as an alternative to the pure frame.

  Mies's Brick Country House plan can be seen as a re-reading and re-writing of Robie, for the autonomous tectonic masses register an attempt to draw the plan from the characteristics of the Wright elevation.

- *Le Corbusier's Maison Domino (variable syntax within a structured continuum)*: Maison Domino, a virtuosic demonstration of the impact of free plan on sectional innovation, can be seen as a direct syntactical reading of the implications of Semper's hut as well as an experiment with three diverse conditions of the interior/exterior boundary and continuum. This led to the fact that the Villa Savoye is a stack of three diverse free plan typologies, which offer the most varied syntax ever seen within a structural continuum and the most unrecognizably different plans ever consolidated into a singular structure.

- *Le Corbusier's Heidi Weber Pavilion (infinity in the diamond diagram)*: The diamond, instantiated by Piet Mondrian, not only asserts the frame as aperture—a window on the beyond—but rotates that frame all the while ensuring that the Cartesian condition of horizon remains constant. Mies would rotate the structural grid to a four-point diamond; he arrived at the double cantilever, a manifestation of Neoplatonism in spatial projection. This structural prototype is the basis for both a domestic and civic typology as projected in the Fifty by Fifty House and the Neue Nationalgalerie. Meanwhile, Le Corbusier proposed his infinity diagram in his last letters as the text for future exploration and revelation. Infinity as he sliced it, adding the sun and the moon, became the diagram of day above and night below the horizon. With the courage of the individual creating a collective text through an exploration of notational language, he built his Parthenon explicitly as a hieroglyph. He worked to conceive an entry to it by deriving the condition of the horizon as its access; one enters through the place where dimension begins, the point where consciousness generates and inhabits the horizon. The Heidi Weber Pavilion renews the potential of the diamond.

Diane Lewis

- *Hejduk's Wall House diagram (the potential of the hieroglyph)*: In the 1960s, John Hejduk embarked on the labor of the Wall House diagram and spent the next 35 years on the permutations derived from it. The notation instigated by the Wall House brought the themes advanced and explored in the sequence I have just described to bear on a new temporal and spatial collapse or impaction. The infinite field of Mies's Brick Country House, the potential of the diamond, and the courage of the hieroglyphic are all present here and contribute to the continuation of an open text in the discipline of architecture.

This sequence brings together memorable formulations that set the stage for the necessary tension between the autonomy of architectural innovation and that of its circumstantial content. The sequence bears witness to a profound conversation of plans made in response to one another. Each is profoundly meaningful for the discipline as a whole, a benchmark within the language of plan. Taken together, they denote a progression of recognizable breakthroughs in a language that when "played" in the mind, in the manner of a musical score, will allow the architect to envision previously inconceivable spatial, structural, programmatic and material implications: a sublime phenomenon. When Frank Lloyd Wright stated that a good ground plan is more valuable than any of its manifestations, he was describing this phenomenon.

IV

The sequence shows traces of a number of variables employed in the derivation of the free plan and indicates what principles the authors of the discourse on plan have shared and focused upon. The plans reveal the search for structural elements that no longer bear any resemblance to the picturesque aspects of the Neoclassical columnar order. The research on the significance of reciprocal autonomy between form and program, and the implicit and explicit memory of specific forms with respect to their site and cultural heritage, are areas of discourse that are revealed and refined as the free plan leaves its founding typologies and confronts international and cross-cultural problematics. However, the series of works included here must exclusively serve the purpose of examining how the philosophical address of nature was employed in the derivation of the free plan.

V

The very first step of this development toward abstraction occurs between the rustic hut illustrating the second edition of Marc-Antoine Laugier's *Essay on Architecture* (1755) and the plan view of the Caribbean hut by Gottfried Semper, which he had seen at London's Crystal Palace in 1851 as part of the Great Exhibition. Here the transition away from any pictorial representation of nature is already evident. The new structural and spatial order was derived from nature then proceeded to confront it. From there, the order progressed onwards towards an abstract spatial model that rejected nature as exteriority, a condition whose promise was latent when the emptiness of the stripped frame first appeared in plan as a field of points.

VI

Strictly in tune with the methodologies of abstraction, these experiments were carried out without any a priori formal assumptions, just as the twelve-tone composers (such as Arnold Schoenberg) committed to a new anti-hierarchal structure of the scales in order to generate a temporal and spatial dynamic in music. These experiments with the free plan frame the examination of the earlier opposition of nature to artifice by means of a new spatial continuum predicated on a structural dialectic. The genetic line I trace begins with the significance of the word "nature" and the interest in defining the "sublime" in the period of revolutionary thinking on the rights of man, and the emergence of questions on the role of the individual vis-à-vis the collective in history as in art.

VII

The architectural parallel was the interest in Laugier's little rustic hut and its later relation, Semper's simple plan of the Caribbean hut; Semper employed this parallel in order to return to origins and thereby to the definitive conditions of an architecture liberated from any association with the orders within the moribund tradition of academic styles. The rejection of style as bourgeois affectation, necessary to the revolutionary acts of deposing monarchies and their constructed environments, was supported by Semper's search for an ethnographic origin for architecture as the deeper aspect in the founding of civilization as structure. It is also possible to recognize that a taste for the austerity of these pursuits set the tone for the sublime free plans, where there is a subtext signaling a restoration of the consecrating functions of architecture. The memory as well as the severe tone of dignity and silence that this architecture embodies emanate from a radical origin and have been sublimated by the formal readings of its raison d'être. It is impossible to understand the text if it is read through the formal conventions of any architecture based in aesthetics and in the idea of natural paradise.

VIII

At the inception of post-monarchial democracies, it was useful to see architecture as derived from the simple frame system embodied by the little rustic hut precisely because it connected with human origins. The Laugier reduction is the recognizable antecedent of the Maison Domino, which is, as is its inspiration, neither a formal nor a design-oriented model but, rather, a conceptual modus operandi. Wright's model is an alternative to the Domino, striving to be an order of and for the American continent. Wright rejected the column as linked to Classical empire and explored the element of the hearth as well as the pier-wall relation.

IX

As an integral aspect of the structural support, it is interesting that Mies adopted, explored and advanced an order of this type in the Brick Country House instead of a columnar one after the Domino concept. The radical innovation of articulating a primary vertical member in his vocabulary of plan appeared with the new integration of both systems in Barcelona. There, his invention of the intersection column was a contribution to the evolving formulation of this new set of elements. The intersection is, in my view, an entropic column that faces out. The mark of the I-beam in plan is more a Merzbau principled formulation. Both are his foray into this challenge. With the Domino concept, the palette of elements that ultimately stems from Laugier's principles as well as Semper's formulates a new order lodged in architecture's collective memory. In so formulating, it evacuates all formal accretions accumulated over centuries of monarchy and tyranny. That first purging of stylistic and academic uses of structure remains necessary to any building that resists an appearance of contemporaneity. This is, of course, a requisite for the sublime; the building must attain an un-datable, timeless, eternal material identity.

X

Mies's breakthrough and the definitive character of his thought came into view with the "explosante fixe" imagery of the project at Barcelona. Mies achieved a timeless character in the constructed facts of his architecture, and that particular condition of the sublime inspired such works as Paul Rudolph's Art and Architecture building, Louis I. Kahn's Kimbell Art Museum, Gordon Bunshaft's Beinecke Library and a host of other works in which one detects phantom aspects of the Barcelona Pavilion's comprehensive character of the archaic modern. Mies's assertion that the grid is related to the "earth having been measured" implies that his projects can be considered "crops" of a continuous field. Those projects assert an existential discomfort struggling against the desire for the pastoral and the pictorial. Even the

Resor House collage of the great mountain seen through the structural frame has as its focus not nature but, instead, a confrontation with the scale of the columns and the slabs by means of which it holds the memory of the ancient temples siting the geographical formation to which they orient their gaze.

These projects and others belong in the lineage I have formulated, but the genetic sequence has been closely edited in order to evidence the main armature of the sublime plans as they address nature. Nature appears in Mies's work as one of the variables he can orchestrate in plan notation. Nature is an omnipresent floating field in the larger field that his plan syntax implies. Nature is no longer outside of architecture but instead a component of its artifice. Here, the natural world functions as a "frottage" that amplifies the existential dimension of the architecture and applies technological and structural advances of its time to achieve the mythic presence and the autonomy between form and program, structure and use, which the ancient typologies attained. This is not the functionalism described in form follows function. The existential sense is the main programmatic objective. Mies reaches for the ancient Greek and Roman drama of architecture and its response to earthly features, reinstating a sense of the pagan severity informing plan orientation and presenting extreme confrontations of scale and span possible only from the twentieth century forward. Nature exists in his nuanced tectonic field—a field that exudes a spatial entropy and a decisive emptiness, a field that asserts the threatening challenge of reintroducing the consciousness provided by the ancient temple and inserting it into the domestic and civic realm of everyday life.

Case Study II
Michael Bell Architecture, Gefter-Press House, Hudson Valley, NY (2007)

The Gefter-Press House, sited on a 12-acre property in the Hudson Valley, is accessed by crossing a quarter mile expanse of farming fields before passing into a forested site. The slow approach to the prismatic glass house is the initial phase of movement that instigates the general organization of movement and time in the building. Four views plotted on the site plan—including the entry into the living area, the courtyard, and the two offices—emphasize crucial vantages along the house's exterior; as the sun fades, outside and inside become animated by light. Aspects such as the cutaway entry and the courtyard further contribute to rendering the house visible to itself both from the outside and the inside. Conceived as a series of planar organizations, the pictorial depth of the approach and of the view through the house serves to counter the shallow spaces and movements of the interior where the building is as narrow as ten feet.

The programming of the building is harmonized with the carefully orchestrated play of visual depths. Social relations are coordinated by floor heights, by relations to grade (above, at or below grade) and by diagonal vistas though the house and across the courtyard. The floor plan underscores the elegant restraint of the interior configuration. For example, the kitchen island is situated opposite the living room while a suspended fireplace above the basement stair orients itself both towards the courtyard and the living room. Offices marking the end of each of the two wings allow refuge in separate work areas, which are both equally enhanced by uninterrupted views of the surrounding forest. The master bedroom sinks slightly below the extended concrete corridor to become a singular space. So as to close off the guest bedroom from the rest of the house and ensure privacy, a bookcase is integrated into a sliding wall. Vents running along the base of the glass panels add radiant heating throughout.

The building's structural glazing system—9 by 14-foot wide insulated glazing units—allows the gaze to pass through the private as well as public spaces. The axonometric section of the plenum details demonstrates how the placement of the glass just below the floor conceals the edges; the sills are recessed two inches below floor level. The glass is at the same time cantilevered slightly outside the structural steel in order to produce subtle shifts in perception. In this way, the glazing is either flush with the building volume and projected inboard of the structural framing (on the east/west elevations) or six inches outboard of the structural framing (on the north/south elevations). The effect is to project the interior margins of the building volume outward and to asymptotically flatten the exterior view against the interior surfaces. Thus the background is elastically pulled to the foreground and the sense of a middle ground is diminished. The interior is precisely defined, but it also dissolves into the extended spaces and clearings in the forest. Vision, which is immediate, shimmers between proximity and distance. This simultaneity brings the space of the wilderness into the immediate circumstances of private life. The house can be opened to form a single volume: the two bedrooms open with interior sliding doors that match the glazing systems and form two oculi; when approaching the house, they form a binocular effect that bifurcates the singular vantage of the architecture. The minor dimensions of a relatively small building thereby cross a threshold opening to the wider field of the site.

Design Architect:	Michael Bell Architecture
Project Team:	Michael Bell, Thomas Long, Eunjeong Seong
Associate Architect:	Stephen O'Dell
Structural Engineer:	Nat Oppenheimer
Mechanical Engineer:	Alteiri Sebor Wieber LLC
Photographs:	Richard Barnes and Bilyana Dimitrova
Glazing:	Rochester Insulated Glass
Contractor:	Mitchell Rabideua, William Satter, Cav-Ark Construction
Owners:	Philip Gefter, Richard Press
Location:	Hudson Valley, New York

1
View from west. Approach by car circumnavigates west-facing façade. Main living spaces to left; bedroom spaces to right. House set 20 inches above grade (Photograph: Bilyana Dimitrova).

2
Cantilevered steel deck forms entry. North–South-facing glazing cantilevered six inches from structural steel tube frame of building. East–West glazing flush with outboard edge of structural steel channel. Courtyard is seen at entry and forms a simultaneous private and public zone in the house (Photograph: Bilyana Dimitrova).

3
View from northeast. North façade and entry set 20 inches above grade. East façade set four inches above grade. House and foundation terrace building site and incrementally create a domestic landscape of terraced interior plans (Photograph: Bilyana Dimitrova).

4
View from east. Structural framing painted black cuts horizontal line through forest of trees. The building program is layered in parallel planes organizing immediate daily life within deep volumes of exterior space (Photograph: Richard Barnes).

5
View from east. Two office/studies are completely private with different vantages into the forest: the east office/study is virtually at grade and within the forest; the west office (to the distant left in image) is set 20 inches above grade and has long controlled vistas across a lawn. Both studies turn away from the courtyard (Photograph: Richard Barnes).

6
View from south. A south-facing courtyard captures winter sun in a very cold climate. The two building volumes are shallow, forming a series of layers between the forest and the field. The library and gallery also serve as circulation and frame the courtyard creating a promenade along its full perimeter (Photograph: Bilyana Dimitrova).

7

View from living room into bedroom. Structural steel wide-flange and custom steel window framing form a complex corner. Insulated glazing units are set in structural silicone and set outboard of building structural framing. Glazing unit becomes an object and mass set within traced volumes of interior and exterior space (Photograph: Bilyana Dimitrova).

8
View to west from within living room. The living, dining and kitchen spaces share an 800-square-foot volume. Glazing units as large as 14 feet wide by 9 feet tall extend the horizon line and dilate the viewing field to bring nature to the line of enclosure. Glazing is set within, flush with and outboard of the interior volume (Photograph: Bilyana Dimitrova).

9
View from west. Living, sleeping, library, office, baths, courtyard and forest beyond are set into a syncopated layering of planes (Photograph: Richard Barnes).

10
View from study/office. A shallow office space offers a diagonal view to nature or a frontal view to a shallow but wide desk. Fixtures are not final. Sliding doors open office to the forest behind (Photograph: Bilyana Dimitrova).

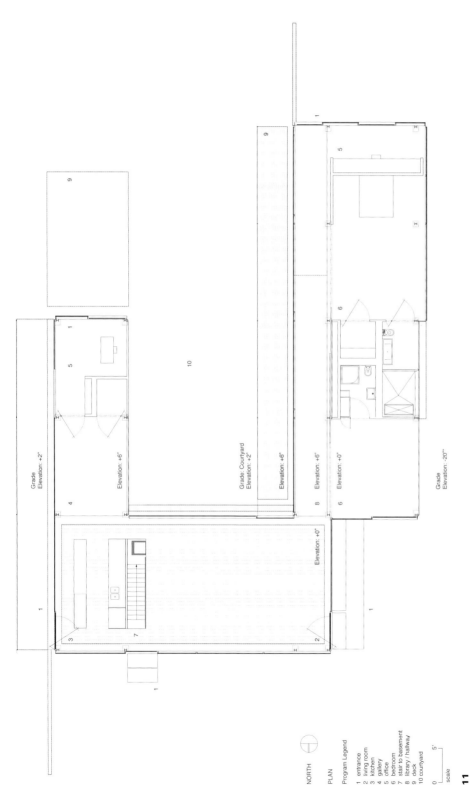

NORTH

PLAN

Program Legend

1 entrance
2 living room
3 kitchen
4 gallery
5 office
6 bedroom
7 stair to basement
8 library / hallway
9 deck
10 courtyard

0   5'

scale

11

Plan. The 2,280-square-foot one-story house is organized around a 25-foot wide courtyard. Three building wings organize program but sliding interior partitions will open the interior to a loft-like single-room house. The widest volume is twenty feet creating a shallow dimension that allows light to deeply penetrate the house. Combined with an interior terracing, the occupant encounters either a courtyard or forest that are virtually at the same grade level as the finished floor; or a distant view over a lawn/field set 20 inches below the floor level (Courtesy of Michael Bell).

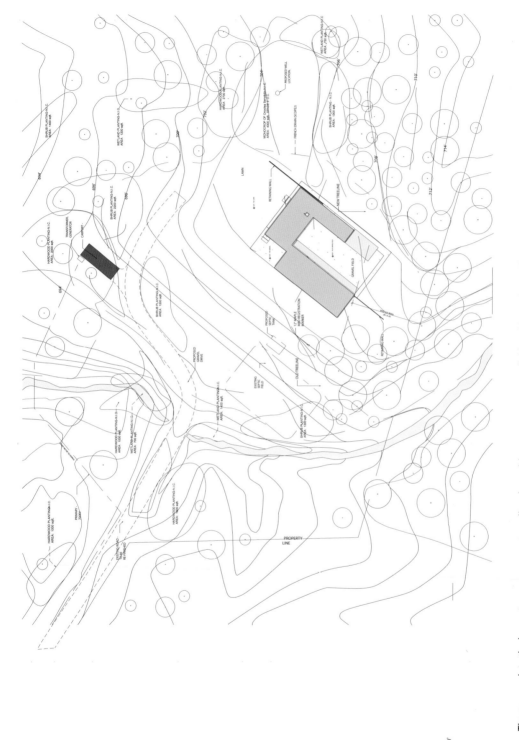

NORTH

SITE PLAN

0   20'
scale

12
Site plan. The approach to the house traverses a quarter mile private driveway over an open field and into a forest. The house is sited at the apex of this arrival; a car moves slowly to the north at the building entry and the occupant approaches the house from the diagonal. A seasonal stream segregates the house from the forest and fields (Courtesy of Michael Bell).

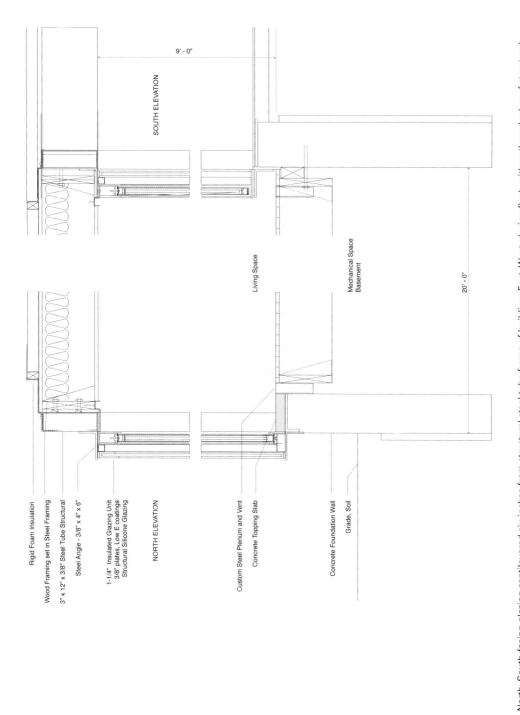

Rigid Foam Insulation

Wood Framing set in Steel Framing

3" x 12" x 3/8" Steel Tube Structural

Steel Angle - 3/8" x 4" x 6"

1-1/4" Insulated Glazing Unit
3/8" plates, Low E coatings
Structural Silicone Glazing

NORTH ELEVATION

SOUTH ELEVATION

9' - 0"

Living Space

Mechanical Space
Basement

Custom Steel Plenum and Vent

Concrete Topping Slab

Concrete Foundation Wall

Grade, Soil

20' - 0"

North - South Section

0   1'-0"
scale

13

Building section. North–South-facing glazing cantilevered six inches from structural steel tube frame of building. East–West glazing flush with outboard edge of structural steel channel. Wood floor with radiant heat is set within rather than on top of foundation walls. Other parts of the building have concrete floors. The building acts as a dam, terracing the sloping grade of the forest behind to the final interior finished floor level (Courtesy of Michael Bell).

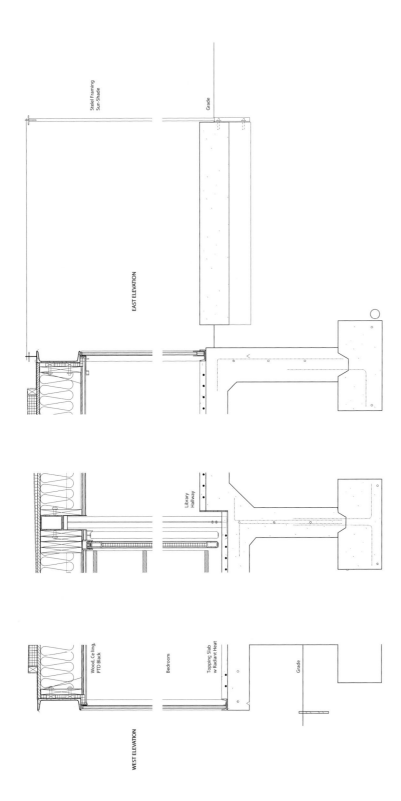

EAST ELEVATION

Steel Framing
Sun-Shade

Grade

Library
Hallway

WEST ELEVATION

Wood, Ceiling,
PTD Black

Bedroom

Topping Slab
w/ Radiant Heat

Grade

East - West: Site Section

0   1'-0"

scale

14

Site section. East–West section shows terracing of grade and orchestration of being "on-grade" to being cantilevered over grade. Roof level is consistent; floors decline and simultaneously slide forward over foundation walls forming cantilever (Courtesy of Michael Bell).

Part III

Sustaining Nature

7

On Limits

Andrew Payne

But where danger is, the saving power also grows.
—Friedrich Hölderlin, *Patmos* (1802)[1]

Limits on carbon emissions, limits on growth, limits on consumption: to speak of sustainability is invariably to speak of limits. But what are the limits of sustainability itself? Presumably this is first of all a question of semantic limits and of just what state of affairs the term "sustainability" may be thought to signify. However, this semantic question comes laden with ethical implication. For if, as Amir Djalali and Piet Vollard contend, "no one can take a stand against sustainability [when] there is no definition of it," it is equally true that no one can be "for" sustainability in the absence of such a definition.[2] The semantic question is also and immediately a question of what sorts of practice, what mobilizations of human energy and commitment, this word may be thought to recommend or command.

In light of such an ethical inflection, it is perhaps noteworthy that at least two twentieth-century thinkers, Jacques Lacan and Ludwig Wittgenstein, argue that ethics is nothing but a passage to the limit—a passage to the limit of the living in the case of Lacan, and to the limit of the sayable in the case of Wittgenstein.[3] With that in mind, let me put the question of sustainability's limit as follows: to what border or extremity does the term convey us, we whose species' destiny it is to live life in language, and so at that threshold where Lacan's order of the living touches Wittgenstein's order of the sayable? To what inhuman edge or precipice does this word compel us, we whose fate it is to live by words? And if we can detect, within the discourse of scarcity and limitation that this term so readily attracts, no sense of our being compelled to some such edge or precipice, what does this suggest about the term's status as a possible object of our ethical attention?

These questions seek to measure the quality and magnitude of the claim sustainability makes on our ethical and political attention. It is my hope that such measurement might go some distance in at once prying the term away from any narrowly technical construal of its implications and subjecting it to closer theoretical scrutiny. This seems to me a task of some urgency in a situation in which the perspectives of the natural sciences, guided by an essentially cybernetic orientation to the ecosystem, dominate our understanding of the nature and implications of the current environmental crisis. It is also my hope that these questions may serve to identify the term "sustainability" as an important contemporary locus for an issue of long-standing importance for historians and theorists of architecture: what sort of latitude for ethical and political engagement does the professional, intellectual, and disciplinary commitment of the architect permit or mandate? Is there, to borrow Karsten Harries's phrase, an ethics of architecture?[4] And if there is, how does the vocation for architecture inflect in particular ways our status as citizens of secular modernity, assuming that this is to what our ethics still commit us? Or is it the case that rationality consists in building a firewall between ethics and technical expertise, in not confusing the game of citizenship with the game of professional conduct?

If sustainability represents a special locus for such questions, it must immediately be added that current usage of the term tends to obscure the tension between the ethical and technical dimensions of architecture in its relationship to the project of modern rationality. Sustainability also serves to obscure a host of political problems and considerations that rise up in the gap between ethical and technical expertise. It does this, first, through its often implicit appeal to an ethical imperative—save the planet—that serves as a species imperative, a question of survival, and as such trumps the conflicting political interests that have a stake in the eco-technological disposition of planetary life. It does this, second, by welding the task of "saving the planet" to the task of saving humanity in such a way that the former appears, contrary to all available evidence, as essentially contingent on the latter. It does this, third, by creating the assumption that, having effectively bracketed the political, it is now at liberty to translate an ethic of animal humanism into a complex of techniques whose universal application will insure the planetary implementation of that same ethic. Most importantly, perhaps, it authorizes itself to perform these three mystifying operations only after having initially excluded from consideration the possibility that the ethical and political vocations of humanity might stand in a complex, even contradictory, relationship to its biological disposition. For all these reasons, the term "sustainability" does not seem to me very promising for theorizing the practical and ethical dilemmas posed by the now very advanced deterioration of our biosphere as well as the role that architecture and urban design may have in addressing those dilemmas. Still less does it seem to offer an adequate framework for theorizing architecture's relationship to the confluence of technological, economic, and political modalities of governance that today determine our relationship to our surroundings. At the

Andrew Payne

conclusion of this chapter, I will suggest that the inadequacy of the concept of sustainability to any description of our contemporary condition concerns not merely the political, but also the aesthetic and psychological dimensions of that condition.

From Biopolitics to Ecogovernmentality: Foucault and After

I have suggested elsewhere that the semantic limits of the term "sustainability" and the forms of ethical and political commitment implicit in these limits must be established with reference to the broader conceptual terrain it occupies: a terrain I designated with the term "biopolitics."[5] I would like here to clarify and develop this connection between sustainability and our larger biopolitical destiny by suggesting that the emergence and growing currency of this term cannot be thought apart from what some consider to be a new episode in the evolution of modern biopower—an episode in which the technological, political, and economic regimens of governmentality described by Michel Foucault converge on the environment as the shared destination of their respective operational logics. The environmental dimension of biopower was not lost on Foucault, as is apparent in his gloss on a remark made by the eighteenth-century demographer Jean-Baptiste Moheau to the effect that "it is up to the government to change the air temperature and to improve the climate . . . to create a new soil and a new climate."[6] Says Foucault:

> The Sovereign deals with a nature, or rather with the perpetual conjunction, the perpetual intrication of a geographic, climatic, and physical milieu with the human species insofar as it has a body and a soul, a physical and a moral existence; and the sovereign is someone who will have to exercise power at that point of connection where nature, in the sense of the physical elements, interferes with nature in the sense of the nature of the human species, at the point where the milieu becomes the determining fact of nature.[7]

According to Foucault, biopower emerges at the moment when the practical issues and related exigencies of government associated with sustaining this "perpetual conjunction" begin to outstrip the conceptual resources of sovereignty as a political fiction and operational framework.[8]

I will return presently to the new primacy given to the term "environment" in contemporary discussions of geopolitical governance. So as to set the stage for that discussion, I will recall the broad lineaments of Foucault's argument concerning biopolitics and briefly describe the elaborations to which that argument is subject in the environmental theories of more recent thinkers like the political scientist Timothy Luke and the sociologist Ulrich Beck.

Foucault's theoretical development of biopower emerged from within the context of a broader project interrogating the logic and historical genesis of the concept of man. According to Foucault, the concept of man only fully disengages itself from its mythopoeic prehistory with the emergence of man as both subject and object of positive knowledge, that is to say, in the second half of the eighteenth century proximately speaking. Foucault referred to this particular conception of man as the "empirico-transcendental doublet."[9] He then argued that knowledge of the concept's empirical aspect concerns three dimensions of human existence: man's biological being, man's productive being, and man's being in language. The primary issue in the first of these, the biological, is the relationship between the human organism and the environment, while the second dimension, the productive, concerns the transformation of our environment as a consequence of the industrial application of our productive powers. Hence one of the implications of the new primacy given to man's biological condition and productive capacities, in considerations of his social destiny, is a new focus on the environment as a complex comprised not only of ecological factors but also of technological, economic, and social–cultural ones. For Foucault, biopolitics is politics as practiced from within this new bio-anthropological framework. More importantly, it is a real politics that benefits from the application of knowledge gained from the new sciences corresponding to the empirico-transcendental doublet (biology, economy, linguistics) and to questions of political and sub-political governance.

In his lectures at the Collège de France between 1977 and 1979, Foucault, in an effort to explain the emergence of this novel conception of politics, described a situation in which the theories of sovereignty that had guided seventeenth- and eighteenth-century understandings of the political—theories that emphasized the territorial extension of the sovereign—gave way to a conception of politics in which the governance and administration of populations was central.[10] With the latter, we move from territory to milieu. At the end of the first of these lectures, Foucault drew on the work of his teacher Georges Canguilheim in order to delineate the migration of "milieu" from its origins in Newtonian mechanics to the life sciences at the end of the eighteenth century—a migration that, on his account, served as prelude to the entrance of the concept (if not the term) into the theories of governance that were emerging contemporaneously. That entrance marked, following Foucault, the transition from Sovereigntism to a security paradigm of power. Foucault also introduced a third modality of power between sovereignty and security: that is, the disciplinary.[11] He turned to examples taken from late seventeenth- and eighteenth-century French town planning: the ideal town plan proposed by Alexandre Le Maître in *La metropolitée* (1682); the modular plan based on the model of the Roman encampment employed at Richelieu; and the proto-ecological planning strategies employed in Nantes. He then argued that each of the modalities of power—sovereignty, security, disciplinarity—imply distinct approaches to the conceptualization and fabrication of social space. Summarizing the difference between these three styles of spatial occupation, Foucault remarked:

Andrew Payne

Sovereignty capitalizes a territory, raising the problem of the seat of government, whereas discipline structures a space and addresses the essential problem of a hierarchical and functional distribution of elements, and security will try to plan a milieu in terms of events or series of events or possible elements, of series that will have to be regulated within a multivalent and transformable framework.[12]

The disciplinary mode needn't concern us just yet, since it is in the description of the transition from sovereignty to security that the environmental dimensions of Foucault's arguments come most boldly into view. Having said that, we will confront disciplinary power again in the concluding discussion of the aesthetic implications of contemporary biopower.

In Foucault's sovereigntist paradigm, power finds its essential expression in the sovereign's right to put his subject to death. Under the biopolitical model that succeeds it, and in which security is dominant, power consists rather in the ability to positively promote life, or in Foucault's words: "to administer, optimize, and multiply it, subjecting it to precise controls and comprehensive regulations."[13] To this new model corresponds the plethora of new sciences and applied sciences—genetics, statistics, demographics—which lend themselves to measuring and reshaping the population. Also to this new model corresponds a conception of architecture that emerges contemporaneously. Architecture begins to relinquish its classical vocation, which consisted in the simultaneously mimetic and conventional representation of order thought to be operative throughout the natural universe. What surfaces in its stead is a new vocation for the reorganization and regulation of the human environment in conformity with strictly functional and operational criteria.

According to Foucault, the regulation of birth and death rates, the control of disease and the monitoring of hospital patients—along with more contemporary manifestations like the collection of consumer data, health insurance, and psychological and sexual profiling—become intelligible only within the context of the biopolitical paradigm. Biopolitics is a paradigm of governance rather than rule in which the fiat of monarchical or popular will is progressively replaced by the anonymous protocols guiding collective decision-making in complex bureaucracies increasingly driven by the specialized mandates of diverse professional and disciplinary communities. Foucault gave the following as early examples of the operative nature of this biopolitical orientation of governance: the English poor laws, the so-called "medical-police" of eighteenth-century Prussia, birth control programs in England and France, urban hygiene efforts in Paris, and hospital reforms in London and Paris. We could certainly add to this list the current forging of environmental policy and associated legislation at a global scale—policy and legislation that, on the one hand, reflect the enduring imbrication of technological, economic, and political regimens Foucault associated with biopolitical governance and, on the other, routinely deploy the same applied sciences Foucault associated with such governance (namely statistics, demographics, political economy).

As the political scientist Timothy Luke observes, the concept of sustainable development, and of sustainability in general, is a key symptom of the new prominence that the environment assumes in contemporary biopolitics. For Luke, the emergence of sustainability as a key term in international governance must be linked to two factors: the increased importance of macroeconomic competition appearing on the other side of the dissolution of Cold War politics; and a growing sensitivity to the risks associated with environmental degradation on the part of the actors participating in this generalized state of economic competition.[14]

Teasing out some of the environmental implications of Foucault's genealogy of modern power (albeit from a theoretical perspective that is, in some respects, radically distinct from the latter's), the sociologist Ulrich Beck follows Luke in his assertion that our current encounter with the environment, as both generative source of and limiting condition on our species' destiny, is what chiefly orients the technological, economic, and political regimens of biopolitical governance. On his account, the emergence of a "politics of risk" is the signal feature of this new phase of bio-governmentality. As he argues, the *bios* at stake in such governance does not primarily concern the fact that political inequality increasingly implies uneven access to the mechanisms of collective decision-making as well as uneven access to the means for expanding one's level of material franchise. Rather, political inequality means as often as not unequal exposure to the medical and ecological hazards which are the inevitable correlatives of the ever-expanding demands made by actors in the global economy. As Beck puts it: "the social production of wealth is systematically accompanied by the social production of risks [so that] the problems and conflicts relating to distribution in a society of scarcity overlap with the problems that arise from the production, definition, and distribution of techno-scientifically produced risks."[15]

Beck links the emergence of environmental risk (which is a central stake in recent discussions of the interconnection between technological, economic, and political sectors) to the transition from a pre-reflexive to a reflexive modernity— that is, a transition that involves a reflexive inclusion to assess environmental risk as part of the social and economic value attributed to industrial products. On the other side of this transition, the management of waste threatens to supplant the management of wealth as the chief stake of contemporary biopower. Furthermore, these theorists have observed that contemporaneous with this transition, a migration of the mechanisms of collective decision-making has taken place: out of the arena of politics *sensu stricto* and into the bureaucratic mechanisms associated with contemporary planning and policy. As part of this new post-political framework of governance, the right to protection from the risks related to hypertrophic production and consumption at a global scale is increasingly decided not via the traditional fora for political deliberation. Rather, it is decided by means of an anonymous, pseudo-scientific subjectivity whose claims to legitimacy are based on adherence to a set of disciplinary protocols in which scientific, technical, and economic motivations overlap. As the environmental toxicologist and ethicist Marc Lappé remarks:

Andrew Payne

The potential for structuring society migrates from the political system into the sub-political system of scientific, technological, and economic modernization. A precarious reversal occurs. The political becomes non-political and the non-political becomes political. . . . The promotion and protection of "scientific progress" and "the freedom of science" become the greasy pole on which primary responsibility for political arrangements slips from the democratic system into the context of economic and techno-scientific non-politics, which is not democratically legitimated. A revolution under the cloak of normality occurs, which escapes from possibilities of intervention, but must all the same be justified and enforced against a public that is becoming critical.[16]

The political limit I would associate with current uses of the term "sustainability" concerns the relative failure, by those who undertake simultaneously to theorize it and to advocate on its behalf, to address the implications of these new modalities of governance now constelling around the environment, along with the new spatial logics and attendant social stratifications they imply at every scale of human existence. The progressive migration of political will into the sub-political mechanisms of governance—the signal feature of these new modalities—and the vitiation of that will by technological and economic rationalities has profound repercussions for how we understand the relationship between architecture and politics (a relationship that not so long ago dominated the critical discourse around architecture). Recent advocates of a post-critical architecture seem to me to be right in at least one sense;[17] the rapprochement of vangardist politics and aesthetics that drove what they characterize as the "critical" phase in architecture dissolves in the face of the confluence of economic, technological, and political forces at the heart of contemporary biopower. The question of the environment, both as concept and as lived reality, will be central to any future articulation of the relationship between politics and architecture. Furthermore, the task of forging a critical theory of the built environment *as environment* remains a crucial, and to date largely uninitiated, task for architectural theory.

Today, the forms of post-political governance characteristic of contemporary biopower establish bureaucratic and juridical frameworks in which ecological initiatives in architecture are imagined and put into operation. This is perhaps never more the case than when those initiatives are thematized as sustainable. In *Hijacking Sustainablility*, the design theorist Adrian Parr observes how sustainability has come increasingly to imply a position in which compliance with the mechanisms of neo-liberal governmentality represents the real, if not the royal, road to urgently needed environmental change.[18] In addition, a growing number of political theorists such as Alain Badiou, Jacques Rancière, and Slavoj Žižek have identified environmental crisis as the central ideological trope of a post-political condition in which the mania for consensus and security has eclipsed any sense of the political as the site of an agon between competing social classes and interests. This understanding of the new prominence of ecological issues in the collective imagination informs Badiou's characterization of ecology as "the new opiate of the masses," a slogan around which Žižek and others have subsequently rallied.[19]

If ecology is the new opiate of the masses, then sustainability is their laudanum—the original delirium diluted and re-branded for broad consumption. For this reason, sustainability has become increasingly problematic for those who view meaningful environmental change as contingent on contestation of—and not capitulation to—the mechanisms of neo-liberal governance. Whatever its utility as a rhetorical tool for forging bipartisan consensus on environmental questions, it is far from clear how and to what extent the term "sustainability" may serve to enrich historical, theoretical, and critical perspectives on architecture's current condition. A good part of my own skepticism in this context concerns the inability of those who deploy it to integrate meaningfully ecological concerns into an expanded vision of architecture—one that would incorporate not only ethical and political considerations, but aesthetic and semiotic ones as well. It seems to me that any expanded conception of architecture's environmental mandate requires us to give some attention to how the notion of the environment has been deployed not merely in recent discussions of architecture but in discussions of adjacent arts as well. More precisely, attention needs to be paid to the shift from an aesthetics of the object to an environmental or atmospheric aesthetic, a shift whose influence has been significant. What might Foucault's insights into the environmental dimension of biopolitical governance bring to an analysis of this shift?

From Object to Environment: Biopower and Aesthetics

> Hence it would have to be admitted that after the end of History, men would construct their edifices and works of art as birds build nests and spiders spin their webs, would perform musical concerts after the fashion of frogs and cicadas, would play as young animals play, and would make love like adult beasts.
>
> —Alexandre Kojève (1980)[20]

Part of the answer lies in Foucault's observation that the aesthetic realm is primarily associated with the disciplinary mode of power, that "anatomo-politics," as he calls it, which finds its special locus in the human body to the extent that it represents a repository of productive force and affectability.[21] To this we must add that if the aesthetic realm is in Foucault's thought primarily aligned with the disciplinary mode of power, it is aligned with this mode as its subjectivating shadow—that zone of freedom in which the individual human organism experiences the power to contest or to comply with the social technologies in which it finds itself immersed,

Andrew Payne

and to discover in those technologies the image of its misery and desires. Now in our current biopolitical context, if Foucault is to be believed, the accent has decisively shifted from discipline to security, from docile subject to normalized population. What remains of the aesthetic on the other side of this shift? The broadest implications of that question come into view when we consider Foucault's remark, made at the beginning of *Security, Territory, Population*, that the security paradigm has its genesis in the moment when "modern Western societies took on board the fundamental biological fact that humans are a species."[22] In view of that remark, we can reframe our question as follows: what becomes of the aesthetic as we progressively apprehend the implications of this "biological fact"?

The answer arising from influential quarters in the worlds of art and architecture (albeit *sans* reference to Foucault) is that such an apprehension must involve an overturning of the ethical and intellectual claims made on behalf of the work of art by post-Kantian aesthetics (with its idealist and anthropocentric biases) in favor of a bio-aesthetic that would embrace the sensuous and appetitive dimensions of object experience (which post-Kantian aesthetics has so vigorously suppressed). Simply put, there is a growing consensus that good taste should taste good, should engage our physical senses, and most especially our non-optical senses. Frequently, if not invariably, this consensus is accompanied by a claim that sensualist aesthetics has the potential to transform the experience of art and architecture into a limit experience in which the difference between individual and collective identities all but dissolves and in which modernism's fixation on the object is overturned in favor of an ambient and synaesthetic receptiveness to the surrounding landscape.[23] Such an approach arguably leads away from the scopophilic subject and toward the multisensory herd, away from the object and toward the milieu. Gilles Deleuze and Felix Guattari offered its most philosophically sophisticated articulation, developing a territorial theory of the work of art based on Jakob von Uexküll's biosemiotic concept of the *Umwelt*.[24] A more accessible version is found in ecologist and anthropologist David Abram's best-selling *Becoming Animal*. Developing an argument already made in *The Spell of the Sensuous*, Abram describes sense experience as producing a state of "reciprocity," by which he means oceanic immediacy unfolding between individuals and their surroundings:

> As soon as we acknowledge that our hands are included within the tactile world, we are forced to notice this reciprocity; whenever we touch any entity, we are also ourselves being touched *by* that entity.
>
> And it's not just the tactile sense that exhibits this curious reciprocity. The eyes, for example, these luminous organs with which we hunt the shapes and colors of the visible world, are also *a part of* the visual field onto which they open. Our eyes have their glistening surface, like the gleaming skin of a pond, and they have their colors, like the auburn flank of a horse or a patch of pewter-gray sky. . . . Such reciprocity is the very structure of perception.[25]

What to make of such arguments? The anthropological bias of post-Kantian aesthetics is incontestable as is its hostility to sense experience. Notwithstanding differences over whether nature or art should serve as the privileged vehicle for aesthetic experience, both Kant and Hegel affirmed that the value of the aesthetic realm is tied to its status as a modality of experience capable of revealing the individual as a *subjectum*: a being of reason. For Kant and Hegel, the privileged type or model for such experience is that which is focused on an object.

This object-experience is distinguished from other forms of sensorial encounter by the act of contemplation that it implies and by means of which the object is notionally subtracted from its surroundings. The separation of the object from its milieu is accompanied, for both Kant and Hegel, by a corollary separation of our judgments concerning the object from any sensuous or appetitive desire related to it. Hegel does concede, in the context of a passing reference to the picturesque landscape, the possibility of an aesthetic experience arising from "a rich variety of objects both organic and inorganic . . . and proceeding therefrom a delightful or imposing harmony (*aüssere Zusammenstimmung*) which appeals to our senses and interests us."[26] However as Hegel's characterization makes clear, this represents an exception to the rule of philosophical aesthetics in which the singular object, isolated from all external circumstances and determinations, serves as the "sensuous semblance of the Idea."

The bias in favor of the object over its surroundings goes some distance in explaining the marginal status awarded by Kant and Hegel to environmental art, architecture, and landscape. In such an anthropocentric bias, the separated object is taken to be the correlative, in the external world, of the coordinated perceptual and cognitive powers that are distinctive of the human being. In this scheme of things, aesthetic experience becomes an imaginary nexus in which the environment slips into the background so as to produce an immediate correlation between the autonomous subject and the formally purposive object.[27] Hence the celebration of the supra-sensuous vocation implicit in the singular human capacity for aesthetic judgment and the fixing of aesthetic attention on an object isolated from its milieu are two sides of the same anthropocentric coin.

When seen against this background, the present erosion of our collective sense of species uniqueness, which has increasingly been placed under pressure as a result of explorations of the biological and cybernetic bases of human experience and cognition, has profound implications for how we imagine our current aesthetic condition. Depending on which of these bases one emphasizes, we are faced with reimagining the terms of contemporary aesthetic experience in one of two ways: either from the perspective offered by a neo-vitalist ontology of life (which stresses the continuities linking human life to other forms of animal life); or from the perspective offered by a neo-mechanist ontology of the letter (which stresses the continuities that link human life to the a-life of cybernetic machines). Regardless of which perspective is adopted—the work of art as *Umwelt* or as cybernetic network—we drift decisively away from the object and toward the environment,

Andrew Payne

that is, away from the contemplation of a discrete entity by a discrete subject and toward immersion in a milieu. This milieu is alternately sensuously manifold or artificially complex or, following the informational conception of life itself, offers some synthesis of the two.

Among those who have attempted to place the aesthetic commitments of contemporary architecture in context, Christopher Hight perhaps most explicitly links an interrogation of anthropocentrism to this shift of aesthetic attention away from the object and toward the sensorium (understood as a biotechnical milieu). Here is how he puts it:

> *Anthropos* (humanity) is stretched across the gap between subject and world, structured through a space of representation. In contrast, the relationship of the animal to the world is presented as consisting of intensive relations, including immediate visual sensation. Thus, for the architectural subject to be immersed in an environmentally affective volume suggests something closer to animal, or at least biological, intensity rather than the representational expanse of the human world.[28]

Echoing Abrams's arguments, Hight goes on to assure us that this animal aesthetic, and the imbrications of organism and milieu that it orchestrates, is sustainable or, at any rate, green:

> Many contemporary architects . . . seek to envelop within an atmosphere to produce an aesthetic response. But often this discourse continues the modern genealogy of aesthetics, which privileged visual and geometric orderings of the object, and objects distinct from subjects. Yet the idea of Green Pleasure, which necessarily implies an architecture whose design continually intertwines subject and object in both time and space, will be based on the production of effects that produce an intensive somatic affect in addition to, or even in displacement of, visually determined aesthetics of disinterest and distance.[29]

These words offer a convincing depiction of the remains of an aesthetic vocation at the moment when, to recall Foucault's phrasing, "modern Western societies took on board the fundamental biological fact that humans are a species."[30] Or at least that is what they offer if we take Foucault to mean that we are merely a species among others.

Against this view, Italian philosopher Paolo Virno argues that any adequate response to our current biopolitical condition and its attendant ecological crises must first consist in the following recognition: that the species *Homo sapiens* is anything but a species among others, and that the unprecedented quality of our current historical circumstances can only be assessed on the other side of a recognition of the singularity of our species' condition. Virno links this singularity to the development of the faculty of language, which he sees as exemplary of the "non-specialization" that distinguishes the adaptive potential or power (*dynamis*) of the human organism—a "non-specialization" he traces to man's "instinctual poverty":

> The language faculty confirms the instinctual poverty of the human animal, its incomplete character, the constant disorientation that sets it apart . . . Not everything that is innate has the prerogatives of a univocal and detailed instinct. Despite being congenital, the capacity to speak is only *dynamis*, power. . . . The animal that has language is a potential animal. But a potential animal is a non-specialized animal.[31]

According to Virno, this instinctual poverty and the peculiarly adaptive power to which it gives rise find their origin in the prematurity of human natality: "*Homo sapiens* has a 'constitutively premature birth,' and precisely because of this is an 'indefinite animal'."[32] Essential for our purposes here is the manner in which such indeterminacy transforms the human organism's interactions with the environment, rendering them uncertain and volatile:

> Biologically related to neotony [*the adult retention of juvenile characteristics*] the potentiality of the human has its objective correlate in the lack of a circumscribed and well-ordered environment. . . . It goes without saying that a non-specialized organism is an out-of-place organism. In such an organism perceptions are not harmoniously converted into univocal behaviors, but give rise to an overabundance of undifferentiated stimuli, which are not designed for a precise operational purpose. Lacking access to an ecological niche that would prolong its body like a prosthesis, the human animal exists in a state of insecurity even when there is no trace of specific dangers.[33]

In this "state of insecurity," which marks the human animal's comportment with its environment, we discover a paradoxical nature, because it is this animal's nature to have no nature (if by nature is meant an innate comportment with its surroundings). According to Virno, contemporary biopolitics involves first and foremost the sweeping away of all forms of cultural authority, which in traditional cultures had served to mediate the relationship between power and this biological invariant, thus paving the way for a direct appropriation of the productive potential deriving from it. As he puts it: "Human nature . . . constitutes both the arena of struggle and its stake. . . . The [new global] movement is rooted in the epoch in which the capitalist organization of work takes as its raw material the differential traits of the species (verbal thought, the transindividual character of the mind, neotony, the lack of specialized instincts, etc.)."[34]

Andrew Payne

Virno does not comment on the aesthetic implications of those "differential traits" he ascribes to humanity's indeterminate nature. However more than a half-century earlier, Lacan drew on a similar set of ethological findings. He linked a comparable set of traits—premature natality, instinctual maladaptation, and the compensatory hypertrophic development of the imaginary and symbolic faculties—to what he deemed a singular coordination of perceptual and cognitive powers defining the human animal's aesthetic encounter with its surroundings. In particular, Lacan's account of the imaginary and symbolic faculties provides the basis for a materialist aesthetic that evades the anthropocentric metaphysics in which the legacy of Kantian and Hegelian aesthetics remains steeped. At the same time, given its insistence on the enduring significance of the subject–object nexus, Lacan's account stands at a resolute distance from the ambient and the sensualist dimensions of Hight's environmental aesthetic.

Noting, like Virno, the state of permanent insecurity in which the human animal exists, Lacan stressed the significant role played by the image–object complex in structuring that precarious state. As he observed, the insecurity marking the human animal's relation to milieu correlates with the insecurity marking its relation to itself, to the extent that the sense of self as an integral whole possessing motor-coordination is not something with which one is born. Hence Lacan's sense of the singularity of the aesthetic rapport between the human animal and its milieu turns on a recognition of the consequences of bipedalism and the gradual nature of its acquisition. Chief among these consequences is a capacity and predilection for fixating on an optical object–image as a compensatory means: "The stability of the standing posture, the prestige of stature, the impressiveness of statues set the style for the identification in which the ego finds its starting point and leave their imprint in it forever."[35] Lacan gave the term "mirror stage" to the decisive moment—a developmental turnstile, as it were—in this process of acquisition, although he hastened to add that such a moment was structured by a temporal paradox, a chiasmus of past and future, memory and anticipation:

> This development is experienced as a temporal dialectic that decisively projects the individual's formation into history: the mirror stage is a drama whose internal pressure pushes precipitously from insufficiency to anticipation—and, for the subject caught up in the lure of spatial identifications, turns out fantasies that proceed from a fragmented image of the body to what I will call an "orthopedic" form of its totality—and to the finally donned armour of an alienating identity that will mark his entire mental development with its rigid structure. Thus, the shattering of the *Innenwelt* to *Umwelt* circle gives rise to an inexhaustible squaring of the ego's audits.[36]

In his argument concerning the "mirror stage" and the role it plays in coordinating the incoherent movements of the newborn, Lacan drew on the conclusions of Henri

Wallon who himself relied on the work of Charles Darwin, Charlotte Buhler, and others. According to Wallon, the human is forever condemned to apprehending its "proprioceptive ego" through the mediation of an "exteroceptive image."[37] Linking this process of apprehension to themes and preoccupations borrowed from Hegel and Freud, Lacan went on to assert that the ego, which he differentiated from the subject, is an image acquired only belatedly by the child (somewhere between 6 and 18 months after birth). This acquisition is realized through anticipatory identification with the Gestalt that is unified (because it is characterized by bipedal motor-coordination) and that the adult counterpart begins to present to the infant at this time.

Elaborating on these ideas in his seminar on the psychoses, Lacan observed that the precipitation of this ego image gives a decidedly paranoid character to subject–object relations. He linked the development of the human animal's will-to-know to this persecutory dimension of object identification, with all the aggressivity it implies as it is both masochistically and sadistically directed. He also stressed the discontinuity that separates the objects arising from these identifications from those that populate the *Umwelten* of other animal species:

> What did I try to get across with the mirror stage? That whatever in man is loosened up, fragmented, anarchic, establishes its relation to his perceptions on a plane with a completely original tension. The image of his body is the principle of every unity he perceives in objects. Now, he only perceives the unity of this specific image from the outside, and in an anticipated manner. Because of this double relation which he has with himself, all the objects of his world are always structured around the wandering shadow of his own ego. They will have a fundamentally anthropomorphic character, even egomorphic we could say. Man's ideal unity, which is never attained as such and which escapes him at every moment, is evoked at every moment in this perception. The object for him is never the final goal. . . . It thus appears in the guise of an object from which man is irremediably separated, and which shows him the very figure of his dehiscence within the world. . . . It is in the nature of desire to be radically torn. . . . If the object perceived from without has its own identity, the latter places the man who sees it in a state of tension, because he perceives himself as desire, and as unsatisfied desire. Inversely, when he grasps his unity . . . it is the world which for him becomes decomposed, loses its meaning, and takes on an alienated and discordant aspect. It is this imaginary oscillation which gives to all human perception the dramatic subjacency experienced by a subject, insofar as his interest is aroused.[38]

Approximately a decade after Lacan wrote about these matters, the paleontologist André Leroi-Gourhan made complementary arguments concerning the importance of bipedalism in establishing the human animal's rapport with its surroundings; in his case, the focus was the phylogenetic rather than the ontogenetic implications of this phenomenon. As with Lacan, the object has a central role to play in those arguments. However, Leroi-Gourhan's object is not an image but a tool. He linked bipedalism to a range of physiological phenomena: corticalization, the assumption of an anterior visual field, the shrinking and transformation of the hominid skull in a manner propitious for language development, and the freeing of the hand for the development of tools—all this to suggest that bipedalism, and not cerebralization, is the central event of human genesis. Referring to Louis and Mary Leakey's discovery, in Tanzania in 1959, of the first tool using hominid *Zinjanthropian boisei* (alias *Parenthropus boisei*), Leroi-Gourhan proposed that it "necessitates a revision of the concept of the human being" for whom the key event is not the expansion of the brain pan but the assumption of an upright stance. What follows from vertical orientation is a co-genesis of organ and organon, such that the human rapport with milieu must be understood as originally, not secondarily, prosthetic as well as mediated by the interposition of objects with which the individual identifies in complex and para-instinctual ways. Leroi-Gourhan echoed Wallon and Lacan in his assertion that the confusion of organ and organon implies the co-originality and codetermination of the interiority of consciousness and the exteriority of the material world.[39] The proximity between his arguments concerning the consequences of bipedalism and those of Lacan becomes apparent when we consider the link the latter drew, in his essay on "The Mirror Stage," between the Gestalt in which the human animal jubilantly assumes its ego image and that "automaton in which . . . the world of his own making tends to find completion."[40] From this perspective, humanity's aesthetic and technological vocations are understood as effects of the transformation of the hominid's rapport with its environment resulting from the adoption of an upright stance.

Lacan's description of the role played by bipedalism in reorienting the nervous–perceptual–cognitive hominid apparatus as well as his account of the significance that the objects of our perception (notionally isolated from their surroundings) assume on the other side of this reorientation are the antipode of Hight's championing of an environmental or atmospheric aesthetic. For Hight, the difference between animal and human dissolves. To this we may add that Lacan's account of the specificity of the "desire" that emerges from such reorientation— and by which man is "torn apart," radically estranged from his surroundings—puts in question the central conceit of Hight's account of "Green Pleasure," namely that what is desirable and what is sustainable are versions of the same thing.

There is a venerable tradition, extending from Augustine to Freud and beyond, that links the genesis of what we call desire to the emergence within the human organism of an instinct that tends in a direction contrary to the one driving the satisfaction of biological needs. The interest of Lacan's thought concerns his understanding that what we call "aesthetic experience" represents a privileged locus for this extra-necessitarian dimension of human existence. Any interpretation of our species destiny that excludes this all-too-human capacity for resisting or eluding the pressures of organic persistence, along with the forms of conduct they demand, is likely to prove unsustainable in the long term.

Perhaps what we most need today is not a sustainable aesthetic, but, to the contrary, an aesthetics against sustainability—against that animal humanism for which the term "sustainability" has come to serve as a post-political shibboleth. Perhaps what is most needed in our biopolitical circumstances is aesthetics as a practice that brings to the fore the scarcity that is also an excess and that lives upstream of bio-economic distinctions between scarcity and plenty, luxury and waste. Perhaps human survival—here understood not as a species concept but as the name of both a collective subject and its project—depends on the fact that what desire "desires" is neither the natural nor the sustainable, but that enigmatic Thing thanks to which "every cycle of being may be called into question, including life in its movement of loss and return."[41] Following Lacan, let us imagine the task of the artist and architect as one of finding objects negatively adequate to the thought of that Thing.

I have proposed that the limits of sustainability as a conceptual optic through which to view our contemporary environmental dilemmas concern, first and foremost, the naturalization of the political and aesthetic dimensions of our environmental condition promoted by the very term "sustainability." This naturalization expresses itself in a tendency to reduce complex and relatively autonomous social and institutional mechanisms to biological (or quasi-biological) and causal frameworks. In response to such a "return to nature," I have argued for the singular and highly plastic character of the human animal's encounter with the environment. Such singularity and plasticity finds their anatomical anchor in bipedalism, which established the physiognomic conditions for the development of speech, the assumption of an anterior visual field, and the freeing of the hand for the use of tools. What follows from this is the complex affective rapport that the human animal establishes with its surroundings (the translation of instinct and need into drive and desire) as well as the symbolic and technical mediations that are motivated by this rapport and that are interposed between our selves and our immediate biological condition. Given our current environmental circumstances, a fuller understanding of our singularity and its implications for thinking about the relationship between species life and polity remains an important task for those wishing to grapple with the contemporary implications of Foucault's theory of biopower. I would add that thinking through our singularity as part of the interpretation of humanly constructed environments represents the central task for any theory of architecture in our putatively "posthuman" present.

Notes

1   This, of course, is the verse parsed by Martin Heidegger in his essay "The Turning," *The Question Concerning Techonology, and Other Essays*, trans. William Lovitt (New York: Harper & Row, 1977), 42.

Andrew Payne

2   Amir Djalali and Piet Vollaard, "The Complex History of Sustainability," *Volume 18, After Zero* (Winter 2008); 33–41(33).

3   Jacques Lacan, *The Seminar of Jacques Lacan, Book VII: The Ethics of Psychoanalysis*, trans. Dennis Porter (New York: W. W. Norton, 1986), 262–263; Ludwig Wittgenstein, *Tractatus Logico-Philosophicus*, trans. C. K. Ogden (London: Routledge, 1922), 27 and *passim*.

4   Karsten Harries, *The Ethical Function of Architecture* (Cambridge, MA: The MIT Press, 1998).

5   Andrew Payne, "Sustainability and Pleasure: An Untimely Meditation," *Harvard Design Magazine* 30/1 (2009): 63–83.

6   Jean-Baptiste Moheau, *Recherches et considérations sur la population de la France* (Paris: Moutard, 1778), 154, cited in Michel Foucault, *Security, Territory, Population: Lectures at the Collège de France 1977–1978*, trans. Graham Burchell (New York: Palgrave Macmillan, 2007), 22.

7   *Ibid.*, 22.

8   This is perhaps the most controversial dimension of Foucault's argument, not to mention the one that has elicited the most consequential responses to it, namely those of Roberto Esposito and Giorgio Agamben. Agamben's project in *Homo Sacer: Sovereign Power and Bare Life*, trans. Daniel Heller-Roazen (Stanford, CA: Stanford University Press, 1998) and related texts is precisely to excavate the biopolitical underpinnings of the classical theory of sovereignty, and in so doing to challenge Foucault's claim that it is after 1750 with the withering of this classical model that man's biological condition entered into the realm of politics. For his part, Esposito argues in *Bios: Biopolitics and Philosophy*, trans. Timothy Campbell (Minneapolis: University of Minnesota Press, 2008) that Foucault's term "biopolitics" represents "an enigma" (15), which he then traces to a persistent "oscillation" in the latter's account of both the genetic and the structural links between sovereignty and biopolitics (31–35). For both Agamben and Esposito, it is not merely a question of how biopower was nascent in the sovereign paradigm, but also of how the sovereign paradigm survives within and alongside the new regime of globalized biopower.

9   Michel Foucault, T*he Order of Things: An Archaeology of the Human Sciences* (New York: Vintage Books, 1994), 318.

10   Foucault (2007), *op. cit.*, 1–28.

11   If, as I have observed above (note 8), there is a degree of ambivalence or oscillation in Foucault's account of the relationship between sovereign power and biopower, there is a similar ambivalence in his account of the relationship between the two modes of which biopower is comprised: disciplinarity and security. Typically, he describes that relationship as one of structural complementarity, so that discipline and security represent the distinct yet related registers of a biopower that succeed the classical paradigm of sovereignty. However in "Right of Death and Power Over Life," the final chapter of *History of Sexuality: Volume I: An Introduction*, trans. Robert Hurley (New York: Vintage Books, 1980), 139, the relationship is given a genetic dimension, with the disciplinary register of power "slightly" predating the security mode. That the sovereignty/disciplinarity/security series is here seen as having a genetic and not merely a structural–taxonomic sense begs a question: does the security of the population correspond to the *telos* of modern biopower, and, if so, what happens to

the "anatomo-politics of the human body" that Foucault associates with disciplinarity when such biopower achieves its most developed forms? Put otherwise: what happens to the individual as a somatic locus for the re-subjectivation of the processes of de-subjectification, which were put in play by the shift from docile individual to secure population? This is implicit in Giorgio Agamben's recent reflections of the Foucauldian concept of the *dispositif* in *What is an Apparatus and Other Essays*, trans. David Kishik and Stefan Pedatella (Stanford, CA: Stanford University Press, 2009), 1–24.

12   Foucault (2007), *op. cit.*, 20.

13   Foucault (1980), *op. cit.*, 137.

14   Timothy Luke, "Ecogovernmentality as Green Governmentality," *Discourses of the Environment* (Malden, MA: Blackwell Publishers, 1999), 121–151.

15   Ulrich Beck, *Risk Society*, trans. Mark Ritter (New Delhi: Sage Publications, 1992), 1. As Beck observes, the concept of "risk" is also central to Foucault's theory of biopower; see, for instance, Foucault (1980), *op. cit.*, 61.

16   Marc Lappé, *Chemical Deception: The Toxic Threat to Health and the Environment* (San Francisco, CA: Sierra Club Books, 1991), 186.

17   See especially R. E. Somol and Sarah Whiting, "Notes Around the Doppler Effect and Other Moods of Modernism," *Perspecta* 33 (2001): 72–77; and R. E. Somol, ed., *Observations on Architecture and the Contemporary City*, special issue of *Log* 5 (Spring/Summer 2005). See also Charles Rice, "Critical Post-Critical: Problems of Effect, Experience and Immersion," in Jane Rendall, Jonathan Hill, Murray Fraser and Mark Dorrian, eds., *Critical Architecture* (Abingdon: Routledge, 2007), 261.

18   Adrian Parr, *Hijacking Sustainability* (Cambridge, MA: The MIT Press, 2009).

19   See Alain Badiou, "Live Badiou—Interview with Alain Badiou, Paris, 2007," in O. Feltham, ed., *Alain Badiou—Live Theory* (London: Continuum, 2008), 136–139; and Slavoj Žižek, "Censorship Today: Violence, or Ecology for the Masses," available at <http://fordiletante.wordpress.com/2008/05/07/censorship-today-violence-or-ecology-as-a-new-opium-for-the-masses/>.

20   Alexandre Kojève, *Introduction to the Reading of Hegel*, trans. James H. Nichols, Jr. (Ithaca, NY: Cornell University Press, 1980), 159.

21   Foucault (2007), *op. cit.*, 377–378.

22   *Ibid.*, 1.

23   See Peter Weibel, ed., *Olafur Eliasson: Surroundings Surrounded, Essays on Space and Science* (Cambridge, MA: The MIT Press, 2002). The emerging preoccupation with both the physical—in particular, non-optical—senses and the environmental dimensions of aesthetic experience finds expression in two exhibitions which appeared in close succession and which prompted intense theoretical reflection in the accompanying catalogues. The first of these, Mirko Zardini *et al.*, eds., *The Sense of the City: An Alternate Approach to Urbanism* (Baden: Lars Müller, 2005), contains essays by an number of noted historians, anthropologists, and humanist scholars (including David Howes, Constance Classen, and Wolfgang Schivelbusch). The second, Caroline Jones, ed., *Sensorium: Embodied Experience, Technology, and Contemporary Art* (Cambridge, MA: The MIT Press, 2006), contains essays by Jonathon Crary, Peter Galison, Donna Haraway, and Bruno Latour. Jones's own essay is a historically informed and theoretically sophisticated defense of sensorialist tendencies in contemporary artistic practices. She emphasizes the opportunities for artistic invention arising from the

increased role technology—and, in particular, embedded technology—has in mediating the sensuous apprehension of our surroundings. This argument had already emerged in 1999 in connection with the theme of "hypersurface." See, for example, cultural theorist Greg Seigworth's "Protegulum," in Stephen Perella, ed., *Hypersurface Architecture II* (Chichester: Academy Editions, 1999), 40–47; here, the concept of the *viniculum* (join, bond, hinge) employed by Gilles Deleuze and Bernard Cache contributes to an argument that architecture must become "the activation of a supple partition turned reflecting wall" on and through which an ambiguous collusion of our optical, aural, and haptic capacities occurs. In this same volume, architect Mark Goulthorpe argues that hypersurface architecture appeals to "a negotiation between self and environment— an interactive uncertainty" (63). Philosopher Brian Massumi (also a contributor) has linked contemporary philosophical and scientific preoccupations with architecture, and his writing has fueled the attention given to sensation and affect in contemporary architecture. For a broader historical account offering a usefully nuanced critique of Massumi's borrowings from recent neuroscientific research, see Ruth Leys, "The Turn to Affect," *Critical Inquiry* 37 (Spring 2011): 434–472.

24 Gilles Deleuze and Felix Guattari, "Percept, Affect, Concept," *What is Philosophy?*, trans. Hugh Tomlinson and Graham Burchell (New York: Columbia University Press, 1994), 163–200.

25 David Abram, *Becoming Animal: An Earthly Cosmology* (New York: Pantheon, 2010), 58.

26 Georg Friedrich Wilhelm Hegel, *The Philosophy of Art*, trans. F. P. B. Osmatson (London: Thoemmes Continuum, 1920), 182.

27 In Kant's analytic of taste, the privileged device for producing this subtraction of the object from its surroundings is the *parergon* (or frame) by virtue of which the *ergon* (or work) is sequestered—cut off from its surrounding milieu—so as to become the object of an autonomous judgment; Immanuel Kant, *Critique of Judgment*, trans. J. H. Bernard (London: Collier Macmillan Publishers, 1951), 59–60. A relevant commentary on Kant's *parergon* is Jacques Derrida, *Truth in Painting*, trans. Geoff Bennington and Ian McLeod (Chicago, IL: University of Chicago Press, 1987), 37–82 and *passim*.

28 Christopher Hight, "The New Somatic Architecture," *Harvard Design Magazine* 30/1 (2009), 24–31(27).

29 *Ibid.*, 26.

30 Foucault (2007), *op. cit.*, 1.

31 Paolo Virno, "Natural-Historical Diagrams: The 'New Global' Movement and the Biological Invariant," in Lorenzo Cheisa and Alberto Toscano, eds., *The Italian Difference: Between Nihilism and Biopolitics* (Melbourne: re.press, 2009), 131–147(136).

32 *Ibid.*, 136.

33 *Ibid.*, 137.

34 *Ibid.*, 131.

35 Jacques Lacan, "Some Reflections on the Ego," *International Journal of Psychoanalysis* 34 (1953), 11–17(15).

36 Jacques Lacan, "The Mirror Stage as Formative of the *I* Function as Revealed in Psychoanalytic Experience," *Ecrits: The First Complete Edition in English* (New York: W. W. Norton, 1996), 78.

37 Henri Wallon, "Conscience et individualization du corps propre," *Journal de psychologie* (Nov.–Dec. 1931): 705–748.

38   Jacques Lacan, *The Seminar of Jacques Lacan: Book II the Ego in Freud's Theory and in the Technique of Psychoanalysis 1954–55* (New York/London: W. W. Norton, 1991), 165–166.

39   André Leroi-Gourhan, *Gesture and Speech*, trans. Anna Bosstock Berger (Cambridge, MA: The MIT Press, 1993), 10–20. Leroi-Gourhan's relevance for architectural theory has been explored by Catherine Ingraham, *Architecture, Animal, Human: The Asymmetrical Condition* (New York: Routledge, 2006). See also the account of bipedalism in Hans Blumenberg, *Work on Myth*, trans. Robert M. Wallace (Cambridge, MA: The MIT Press, 1990).

40   Lacan (1996), *op. cit.*, 77.

41   Lacan (1986), *op. cit.*, 211.

Andrew Payne

8

Eco-Pop
Mark Jarzombek

Part One: ARUPtocracy

In April 2010, Peter Head of ARUP came to MIT to give a lecture in which he showed this equation:

$$(CO_2 - 80\%) + 1.44 \text{ GHA/capita} + \text{HDI increase} = 2050: \text{The Ecological Age}$$

Head knows what he is talking about. He has had more than 40 years of experience in civil and structural engineering and planning, and has been involved in many leading projects in Asia, Europe, North America and the Middle East. The lecture in which this equation appears is now online and translated into Arabic, Chinese, Korean and Spanish.[1]

I am not sure I understand everything about this equation. After all I am not a scientist. But I do understand the equals sign, and it is at this point that I will aim my opening discussion. The equals sign intends to prove that the equation not only *will* work out, but that it has *already been* worked out. If science can accomplish anything, it has to be founded on the sanctity of the equals sign, and ARUP, one of the world's greatest engineering firms, has (so one can presume) now placed the weight of its considerable reputation on this mathematical symbol. 1.44 GHA cannot be 1.43 GHA. 80% is not 79%. 2050 cannot be January 1, 2051. My point is thus a simple one. This is a faux-equation built around a principle of elegance, as good equations, so some scientists argue, are meant to be. Thus the question is: Why in an age when science is often held in suspicion and when the science of global warming is so radically politicized, does ARUP play games with science? Why does ARUP produce an equation that discredits science even further?

Against the supposed science of this equation, I would like to propose another one that conforms better to the actual goals of ARUP: Technology + Control = Nature. It is a laudable ambition. But should we leave it at that?

I am not suggesting that ARUP engineers think that nature is something dialectically different from culture; they know that the nature they produce is just natural enough (for most people at least) that it cannot be mistaken for the artifice that it is. The result, of course, is that the natural has been evacuated of whatever naturalness it might have had. Everything, even nature, is not-nature. Architects will, of course, continue to ornament their drawings with green grass and trees while working with the Romantic image of a happy and contented nature. But we all know that this is all so much smoke and mirrors, for our globe is basically an enormous vivarium (Figure 8.1). Yet unlike the vivarium of old where we humans see—and construct—the difference between nature and its artifice (unlike the animals in the vivarium who presumably are unaware of this difference), we are not only living in the vivarium but also constructing its habitat at the same time. The controls and the dials are no longer "outside" the vivarium. They are inside and part of our daily human existence. Every breath we take, every machine we operate, and everything we purchase changes the dial. And yet, despite this, we seem to want to

Mark Jarzombek

be like the fish, snakes and birds that live an entire life—so we presume—without realizing they are in an artificial landscape. For this to happen, however, we need ARUP at the dials.

The nature around us is an illusion constructed in tight alliance with the world of pipes, ducts, and valves both real and metaphysical. But we should not just assume that this is a death of the natural world. ARUP's equation produces two natures. The first one is Nature-as-image and the second is Nature-as-Science. The equals sign gives us entrée into this latter form of nature, a nature that is rendered transparent through the elegance of the equation and at the same time comprehensible in the abstractions of science. The equals sign is an indication that in their eyes the new vivarium culture can actually work—that is to say, that we can live in the enclosure of the globe by manipulating its inputs and outputs (Figure 8.2). ARUP's equation is the governing principle of the new globe/vivarium.

The idea that Nature is not "out there," but that it is identical to science is an extension of Positivist techniques of observation, calculation and prediction. Positivism rendered matter as "dead" so that it could be enlivened by the equations of physics and chemistry that govern the world from their magisterial heights. Yet it is one thing to describe Nature through an equation and another to fiddle with the equation so that it "works out" to our (or perhaps their) convenience. $E = mc^2$. Now THAT is an equation. What ARUP proposes is not. For 2050 to be reached, heat has to be released and recaptured. Carbon dioxide will have to be measured and contained, bought and sold. Methane will have to be curbed and natural resources managed. But if 2050 comes around and we are not where ARUP wanted us to be, the mistake, according to them, was not theirs but ours! While this is astonishingly arrogant, we should follow their argument to its logical conclusion for what their equation tells us is that we cannot trust politicians to do the work of science. What we need, therefore, is a special brand of trained technicians and managers who supposedly have nothing to do with politics. If Aristotle wanted us to be ruled by an aristocracy, ARUP wants us to be ruled by an ARUPtocracy, which would reign supreme in the Ecological Age. ARUPtocracy would put an end to contested democratic inefficiency as well as to corrupt nation states. It would even enforce its will on the corporate world by arguing that it, too, is "a corporation" that understands the logic of big business.

In discussing ARUP in this way, I am trying to separate ARUP's ideology of management pragmatism from its philosophical position. We are often so infatuated by the promises of the former that we do not discuss the latter. ARUP claims the supra-legitimacy of a disinterested science over the distrusted and ineffective human institutions of governance and, as such, represents a form of disengagement from the more prosaic world of humans. This is modernism's (and modernization's) last great gasp.

ARUP's equation, furthermore, promises what it cannot deliver. The equals sign is a fiction, an expression of a utopian projection of a unified nature. This means that ARUP's approach to Sustainability is to architecture what Intelligent Design is

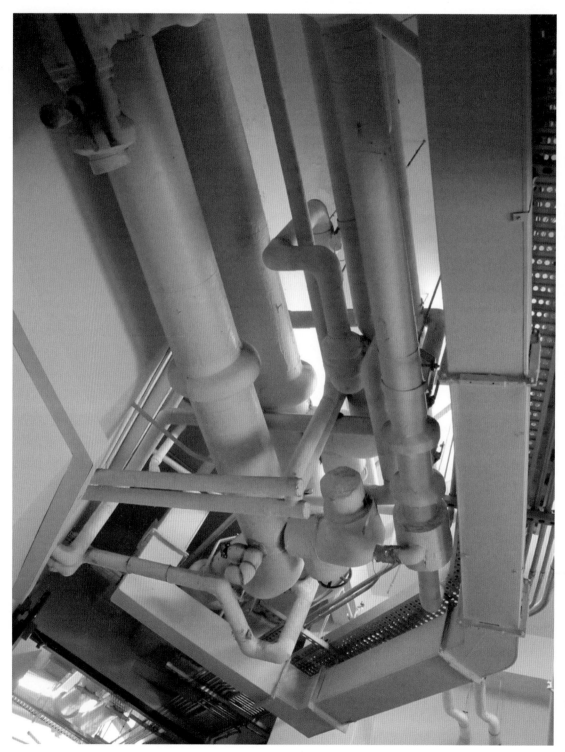

8.2
Producing the Natural (vivarium pipes) (Photo: Mark Jarzombek).

Mark Jarzombek

to the discussion of evolution: a joke or, worse yet, an extension of the false hope that there is a god in the system or, in this case, that there is a big equation in the sky. Why are we amazed that climate-change-deniers are so pervasive when our leading intellectuals and engineers play around with the equals sign?

The result is an architectural discourse about Sustainability that—from a cultural and theoretical point of view—is tottering on irrelevancy. And this is not because the globe is not warming. The reason we want the appearance of Nature and the illusions of Science to (co-)exist is that they hold out the promise of a fixed point on which to leverage design and policy. But that Archimedean point—and the utopian project of modernization on which it is founded—does not exist and to hold on to the illusion that it does is simply absurd. Just as religion is the opium of the masses, Sustainability is now the opium of architects, policymakers and technocrats.

So let me be clear. We live in an unsustainable world and we will *always* live in an unsustainable world. This means that we should build *and theorize* accordingly. The first theoretical act is to clear the air, get rid of the word "Sustainability" and learn to speak honestly about what it means to design in an unsustainable world. So I propose an equation that I know *will* work and that I know is *more* scientific than the one proposed by Peter Head:

$$(CO_2 - 80\%) + 1.44 \text{ GHA/capita} + \text{HDI increase} \neq 2050\text{: The Ecological Age}$$

Part Two: Eco-Pop

ARUP has magnified nonsense in the name of rationality and in so doing has proven that nature is nothing more than a shifting, if not actually empty, signifier. So using their beginning point, I want to carry the argument to the next level. If ARUP is producing fairy tales, why is architecture so serious about its mission to improve the efficiencies of our buildings and cities? Let us simply accept the truth that Nature = Shifting Signifier. That is where we should start. We must engage (or perhaps re-engage) architecture as a play of concepts, and what better concept to play with than Nature.

And this brings me to Pop Art, an art movement of the 1950s and 1960s that emphasized exaggeration and that took its imagery from advertisement, news, and generic cultural artifacts. It poked fun at postwar corporate seriousness. Though the movement is now long since forgotten, I propose to add Nature to the list of its targets. The fusion is Eco-Pop, a design strategy that embraces *all at once* the untenable cultural predicament of our current age, the vacuity of the idea of nature, and the fabulated ambition for a Sustainable future. Eco-Pop, just as it rejects the rhetoric of science and efficiency, does not ascribe to design-from-below either; it does not attempt to give some magically empowered voice to the non-architectural community. Unlike ARUP, which secretly points to a technocratic utopia from above,

Eco-Pop makes no claims about politics at all except that it needs an environment of free speech. Its goal is thus rather to think outside of the conventional design ethos of the professional architect and to make use of cultural productions, tropes, and critiques that may not require "design" themselves but that can be grafted *into* the processes of architecture.

Eco-Pop returns to the postmodern notion of pastiche.
> Eco-Pop shifts the focus from the technological to the philosophical. Nature, if it exists at all, is being filtered through the vortices of our cultural imaginaries, which means that architects need either to wake up to these cultural constructions or be left holding the empty promise of irrelevancy.

Eco-Pop seeks the truth of rupture over the myths of continuity.
> Eco-Pop accepts the truth that there is no single magic equation that explains all. There are hundreds and thousands of potential equations.

There is very little architectural history to Eco-Pop, since most design schools today would see an argument in its favor as preposterous, and this largely because designing an Eco-Pop building would mean something vastly different in pedagogical terms than going to a class on Sustainable Design. There are precedents, however. On the Pop side of the equation, one could list the Chiat/Day Building, Los Angeles (1985–1991) by Frank Gehry (Figure 8.3). Rarely do we talk about this building today, but one can hardly overlook its rather amazing binoculars. And if the Oldenburg tactics weren't enough, one is struck by the oddly aligned sticks holding up the roof. There was a time when tactical exaggerations and borrowings were considered

8.3
Frank Gehry, Chiat/
Day Building, Venice,
California, 1991 (Photo: 2007
Bobak Ha'Eri, GNU Free
Documentation License,
Version 1.2).

Mark Jarzombek

a legitimate part of an architectural way of thinking, but for various reasons this approach died. Even Gehry now has turned away from such cultural references.

The Urban Cactus of UCX with Ben Huygen and Jasper Jaegers seems to move toward the ideas of Eco-Pop. Unlike the other projects of UCX, which should be categorized as rather uninteresting examples of modernist reductionism, this building with its tree-laden curved balconies seems playful. But is it Eco-Pop? No. Unfortunately the UCX architects did not consult with Natalie Jeremijenko who not only heals "Polar Ice Cap Stress Disorder," but also plants trees upside down as part of her Tree Logic exhibition at the Massachusetts Museum of Contemporary Art (MASS MoCA). The trees survive quite nicely. Her project asks us to think about our manipulations of nature while at the same time showing us an extreme example of the non-natural.

As it is, the UCX project is little more than a tower with bourgeois balcony plantings. The architects, in other words, have caved in to the naive notion of nature as an ideal, though constructed, landscape for the wealthy. In accepting the status quo, they do not challenge us to rethink our attitudes toward nature. Jeremijenko's trees do. Had UCX really wanted to challenge the architectural cliché of photoshopped nature, they would have followed Jeremijenko's idea and hung the trees upside down from the ceilings of the apartment above.

Unlike the Urban Cactus, the Naha Harbor Diner in Naha City, Japan, is an excellent example of Eco-Pop (Figure 8.4). The project was designed by Takeshi Hazama and built by the engineering firm Kuniken Ltd.[2] There is some difficulty

8.4
Takeshi Hazama, Naha Harbor Diner, Naha City, Japan (Photo: Courtesy of Mark Jarzombek).

in knowing what to call it, but I will insist on calling it a building. Even so, the project would hardly earn a passing grade in a design studio, despite the relatively sophisticated engineering that went into its construction.[3] The tree's bark, for example, was made of painted fiberglass-reinforced panels supported by light-gage steel frames. Hazama created small cracks in the panels and inserted mats and plants so that moss could grow from the branches. Eighty thousand small lighting fixtures were also installed on the tree's skin and restaurant façade. At night, these lights illuminate and define the shape of the tree.

This unexpected pairing of nature and artifice is extraordinarily provocative, especially as an alternative to the seductive tree romance of the film *Avatar*, which I see as merely extending the heroic, animistic fantasy of a computational fusion of man and nature. The Naha Harbor Tree plays on the difference between the "natural" and the "man-made." It is not a conventional tree house either, but has a modern—and rather absurdly typical—concrete building montaged into the branches. The design does not hide the restaurant in the tree, but launches it implausibly into its upper reaches as if swept up there by a great tsunami. This multilayered, syntactical fracture, in which both the tree and the restaurant (and even the idea of Japan) are in quotes, is the key to this building's success. The disparate imaginaries out of which the diner is designed are ready-mades, but by

8.5
Takeshi Hazama, Naha Harbor Diner, construction drawing of the section (Photo: Courtesy of Mark Jarzombek).

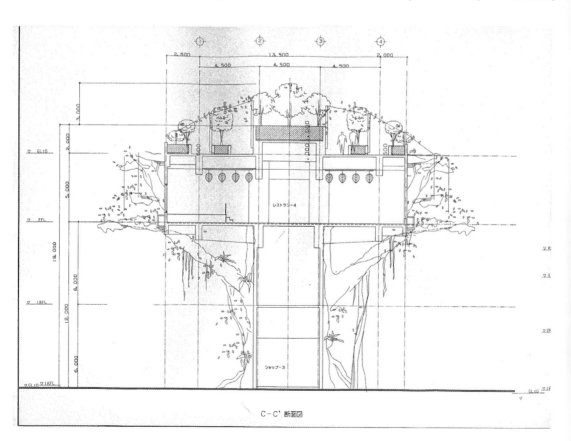

Mark Jarzombek

8.6
Stata Center Upgrade
(Photo: Mark Jarzombek).

putting them together in this way, the project undermines the presumption that aesthetic production has to be an extension of the super ego (Figure 8.5).

More can be done to expose the transitory state of the cultural product. We should, therefore, take the Naha Harbor Diner one step further. I propose to rebuild it next to Gehry's Stata Center designed for MIT along Vassar Street (Figure 8.6). The Stata Center, after all, is itself a replication of the Gehry brand. So if architects copy their own work, and corporations utilize the franchise model, why are we in the discipline of architecture so insistent on our principles of authenticity and autonomy? Such insistence has long since been obliterated as a cultural model and survives almost exclusively in schools of architecture. The new tree is, however, neither brand nor franchise, instead serving as an alien insertion—a photoshop that happily exposes the death of the *arkhitekton* and the related death of Nature, both of which are dialectically invisible in Gehry's building. The Vassar Street Diner, as I propose it, will remind us that the death of these concepts is the *only* theoretical platform on which architecture can legitimately operate. The new fiberglass tree is the future set against the backdrop of the old.

Notes

1   This equation and a lecture of his are now online at: http://www.arup.com/Publications/Entering_the_Ecological_Age.aspx [Accessed December 2011].

2   Takeshi Hazama is a registered architect in Japan although he has never been trained as an architect. He considers himself as a designer not an architect. Hazama lived for many years in Italy where he worked as an assistant art director for the Italian movie director Federico Fellini. He was hired by 20th Century Fox as an art director in Los Angeles for

several years. He then went on to produce TV commercials in Japan. Now, he bases his business in Japan as a designer–producer. He was part of the team that came up with some of the themes for the scenes of the opening and closing ceremonies of the Atlanta Olympics. Though he is a licensed architect, Hazama is what one might call a concept designer. The client of the restaurant was Kiyoharu Kakazu, the former head of Ryutou Inc., which used to be Ryukyu Seito, a local sugar manufacturing company. The site is between the city of Okinawa and the airport, and, according to the architect, lacks good "Ki" or "quality." The tree was meant to compensate for this. It represents the Gajumaru tree (*Ficus microcarpa*), which grows in the region. Hazama envisioned that the tree would form the basis of a commercial village around it, providing "Gokujo Kokage" (the Best Shade under the Tree). Feng shui was also taken into consideration. Four living Gajumaru trees were placed at the bottom of the tree.

3   I would like to thank Norihiko Tsuneishi, who interviewed Hazama for me and made the necessary translations.

Nature, Model of Complexity

Jean-François Chevrier

Nature as model in modern art and architecture remains fundamentally ambiguous. Is nature as model simply the legacy of the Beaux-Arts system or a new paradigm of creative and constructive activity? Is it both simultaneously? Is it a source of inspiration, a reservoir of formal types—that is to say, of "models" (in the strict sense of the term)—or a principle of regulation, which stands in contrast to an anarchic imaginary? Is it a sort of impersonal "archi-norm" to set against the multiplication of styles and idiosyncrasies or an antidote to the exuberance of virtual forms? Is it a moral criterion inherited from a Puritan past or a means of reattaching the living to a physical world (the *physis* of the ancient Greeks) in an age of information and biotechnologies? Is it an ensemble of preexisting givens to human actions, which is augmented by a selection of artifacts, or the past that has been bypassed by an ever-expanding artificial world?

These questions concern art and architecture rather directly. One could propose—and I rally towards this position—that nature, including life, is essentially a model of complexity, which, until proof to the contrary emerges, has not been obviated. By turning to the notable example of the work of Herzog & de Meuron, I would like here especially to emphasize the first of the ambiguities I have just described, for it touches upon the historical definition of architecture in relation to the visual arts (painting, sculpture, and other visual productions). In particular, I will analyze their recent project, the TEA (Tenerife Espacio de las Artes).

One of the distinctive traits of Herzog & de Meuron's projects has always been the attention to landscape as it appears in its material, multi-sensorial aspects as well as in its topographic preconditions. This can be seen in the conception of TEA in Santa Cruz de Tenerife, Spain. The project unfolded over the course of ten years between 1998 and 2008, instigating a sort of laboratory of architectural thought developed by the firm during a period in which the de Young Museum in San Francisco was being realized without delay. Despite vastly different urban contexts—the de Young Museum is sited in a park and includes a 144-foot tower overlooking the city—the two buildings present strong analogies both in the general parti and in the particular treatment of the envelope. Herzog & de Meuron are not currently in the process of rediscovering nature; their ideas about the project have always been guided by an acute attention to the site and its metaphorical potential. My own hypothesis is that the model of complexity that nature offers concerns simultaneously *the image of the body* (in the sense defined by Paul Ferdinand Schilder) as it forms itself in the built conception of the building and the metaphorical content of the site. The image of the body appears notably in the relations between the envelope, the skin, and the structure. The metaphors allow a transfiguration— the word is admittedly a little intense—of the functional appropriateness of the building for a local program. Any territory, as with any individual or any community, risks withering, a sclerosis, if it is assigned too rigorously to a strict geographical situation.

It seems evident that the return of the reference to nature in the practices of architects and urbanists corresponds to current ecological concerns and to the principle of sustainability, which is opposed to the ravages unleashed by the cycle of production and consumerism. The time is past in which the model of the disposable seems applicable to architecture as a means of freeing it from the monumental as well as from falsifying and mystifying "edifying values." The disposable is not the same thing as the ephemeral, for the former presupposes the object while the latter concerns the domain of events, and, if we think of the arts, refers to the register of the spectacle of the world of objects (to everything that must be played and performed). In the 1960s, the disposable was valorized over and against the monumental and permanent qualities of the sacralized object; it appeared as liberation with respect to things; a new lightening and the benefit of mobility. As the word suggests, one could freely dispose of things, use them and easily separate from them. One was no longer attached. In the domain of culture, the journal, as distinguished from the book, was the first "example," in the sense of both instance and lesson, of this promotion of the throwaway object associated in the present case with the quotidian and the ephemeral character of actuality. Printed matter was the initial domain of social experiment with the relation between the acceleration of time and the constitutive obsolescence of the modern. But the triumph of the disposable corresponded, in the 1960s, to the empire of another material: that of plastic.

This triumph has long since lost the appeal of newness (save for a few who remain nostalgic). For architects such as Herzog & de Meuron who associate forms and materials strictly as part of a practice of experimental research, there are no privileged materials; all are worthy of consideration, and chemistry is as significant as computation. But the rupture in the hierarchy of materials is not (necessarily) synonymous with a rejection of the durability of forms or a condemnation of the

Jean-François Chevrier

monumental. In 1978, the conceptual artist Dan Graham, who had opted in the late 1960s for ephemeral interventions in the media, set the concepts of permanence, transhistoricism, and monument over and against the disposable. Graham was inspired by Aldo Rossi's theories of architecture. This return to the monument was not, or not yet, a return to nature or a return of nature. By the same token, in the practice of Jacques Herzog and Pierre de Meuron, which began in that same year, 1978, monument and nature were initially linked.

The concept of the monumental work is itself ambiguous; monumentality and large dimensions—the expression of collective memory and the demonstration of power—are too often conflated. Confused with the habitual technological waste created by high-rise constructions and other pachyderms of productivist engineering, the monument can with great difficulty be held up as a paragon of ecological responsibility; the latter is, rather, associated with the principle of respect for the environment and an attitude of minimal intervention. Incidentally, let me add that the relation of the monumental to nature implies the question of the norms of historical intelligibility without which the idea of a communal, habitable, and transmissible earth is unthinkable.

In the history of art, there has always been a double reference: the reference to nature and the reference to exemplary works (or monuments) of the past. Indeed, the reference to nature has often stood against the cult of the past. In the sixteenth century, the requirement of realism appeared at the edges of the Baroque age as a refutation of Mannerism. The model of nature was then constantly evoked along these lines, against "manner" or against the stale norms of a classicizing ideal. In the nineteenth century, the requirement of realism was bolstered by the study of facts advocated by positivism; it yielded the programmatic enunciations of an art whose duty it was to privilege actual and real subjects all the while avoiding the mannered quality of studio productions. The "return to nature" was evoked in this context. According to Francis Wey, an art critic close to Gustave Courbet, painters had better look at photography in order to acquire for themselves the criteria of the truth and to disengage from the "system of the cliché," in other words, from the domination of ready-made formulas.

In truth, the model of nature has always been conceived of as a stance either for or against the idea of system. Ever since the foundation of academies in the Italy of the High Renaissance, the idea and the ideal of nature, that is to say, idealized nature, was the foundation of a system of fine arts that perpetuated itself through academic pedagogy until the end of the nineteenth century. In 1867, the first edition of the ultimate exposition of this system was published under the title *Grammaire des arts du dessin*. Its author, Charles Blanc, reexamined the three "arts of drawing": architecture, sculpture, and painting. In the exposition of "Principles" with which the treatise begins, Blanc recalled that architecture, the "older sister" of painting and sculpture, "had encompassed and dominated all the arts."[1]

It has been proposed that architecture ultimately disengaged itself from the Beaux-Arts system at precisely the moment when structures—what we might call "constructed performances"—designed without direct artistic intention (the architecture of engineers) had reached a critical mass. Yet we know today that the so-called conflict between the Beaux-Arts and the Modernist movement involved a far more complex network of interferences. The technical talents of masters, at all levels of a given undertaking, often inscribed themselves in a continuation of vernacular knowledge. The Modernist movement itself did not systematically repress this form of knowledge, despite the overwhelming impact of the rationalization of labor. In the wake of the Beaux-Arts system or, rather, through its "modern" transpositions, the model of nature was essentially transmitted as a diffuse norm allowing adaptation to geographical specificities. But the notion of adaptation itself is perhaps restrictive. The model of complexity provided by nature is tied to a vivid combination of forms and materials, which is rooted in the structure of bodies (including that of the human body).

Of Herzog & de Meuron's early projects, the *Steinhaus* or Stone House in Tavole, Italy, which was designed in 1982 and built between 1985 and 1988, was among the most significant in terms of the extraordinary attention to materials that was for so long the mark of their practice (Figure 9.1). The apparatus of stonework combined with concrete beams materializes itself as an open structure (extending beyond the closed zone of the edifice) inscribed in the site. In 1982, positing the model of nature in architecture (as in art) was not an obvious move. In the 1960s, what was termed the "linguistic turn" had substituted language for nature. A commonplace semiology associated with Pop imagery was spreading like wildfire. For Herzog & de Meuron, the model of nature was not a rigorously moralized principle but, rather, a matter of perception, the phenomenological reference to the

9.1
Herzog & de Meuron, Stone House, Tavole, Italy, 1982–1988 (Photo: © Margherita Spiluttini).

Jean-François Chevrier

pre-linguistic experience of the world. The model of nature was a means of keeping at bay rhetoric, verbal eloquence and, even, the verbal identification of discrete and discontinuous things in order to favor the structure and silent metaphor inscribed in the fabric or "flesh of the world" (to use one of the philosopher Maurice Merleau-Ponty's expressions).[2]

Fabric and texture are, for Herzog & de Meuron, a matter of density (the notion of the "urban fabric" stems exactly from this criterion). The building of the TEA in Santa Cruz de Tenerife is a long hermetic form, spread out over 160 meters and encompassing nearly 9,000 square meters of space: a volume carved out of concrete with nuanced grey tones, which could have emerged from a lava flow, that of the Teide, the volcano dominating the island. The building presents a rough, even brutal, aspect, which condenses and exalts the power of the site. Its placement corresponds to a deep urban trench defined by the bed of a canal evacuating rainwater: the Barranco de Santos, which is dry most of the year but which can often transform itself into a veritable torrent. The orographic definition of the site thereby engages with the site's physical and geographical conditions, which seem today to intrude into the urban fabric. The landscape expresses danger, a risk, a form of pathos. The building distributes itself horizontally like a large ramp that reaches from a monumental bridge built in 1943 spanning over the Barranco and that follows the incline of the terrain down to match the level of the port. Because the building extends outwards instead of rising upwards, it tends to melt into the urban landscape (Figure 9.2).

The building acts as a transition between two levels of the city. Not only does internal circulation cross through the building, as can be seen in many other

9.2
North façade of the TEA along the Barranco de Santos (view to the east) (Photo: © J.-F. Chevrier and Élia Pijollet, 2010).

contemporary constructions to an almost caricatural degree, but more importantly, the building is itself a crossing. The path through the interior was conceived in such a way as to preserve its autonomy vis-à-vis other programmatic functions; the visitor can engage it without necessarily having to enter into the various closed spaces that the building offers. By the same token, this path organizes the building, since all other spaces communicate with it and by means of it (Figure 9.3). Here, the urban dimension orchestrates a clear distribution of the elements of an otherwise complex program.[3]

As one enters the building at the upper level, the first impression is that of an extraordinary overture bolstered by a rush of openness and clarity particularly tangible when the blinding light and full heat of summer render forms hazy. At the outlet of a zigzagging entryway, the view unfolds onto a large, slanted interior courtyard, whose openness is protected from the sun by the ripples of moveable fabric and whose triangular format is glassed in on the three sides. This opening onto urban emptiness (a square, a patio) on the inside of the building is spectacular; it offers a strong contrast to the hermetic aspect of the exterior. Before leading to a ramp ensuring the ultimate junction with a street to the lower part of the city, the patio functions as a gallery or a large footbridge overlooking the spaces of the library that occupy the entire height of the building; the interior traversing path dissects the volume of the library, which deploys itself below on both sides. Between paned bays, the gaze plunges into large spaces illuminated by a host of chandeliers in the shape of large bulbs suspended from long transparent tubes (Figure 9.4).[4]

The urban emptiness around which the building organizes itself strikes a contrast with the surrounding urban confusion, as is the case with the several

Jean-François Chevrier

earlier attempts at localized organization that manifestly did not yield coherent circulation in the area. Cities today are continually being undone by fragmentation, dispersion, the scattering of public spaces—this as much because of the effects of persistent zoning practices as because of the poverty of functional connections in the urban fabric. Here, to the contrary, the idea was to give a monumental quality to an urban connection; it is realized as such without its effects being overworked. While the lower section of the TEA neighbors one of the most beautiful structures in the city, the Church of the Concepción, the upper section clings to the municipal square (Figure 9.5).

As is the case with other contemporary edifices, the building brings together concrete, aluminum, and glass, yet this combination of materials is not rhetorical;

9.5
The TEA seen from the
General Serrador Bridge
(with the entrance to the
Mercado de Nuestra Señora
de África in the background)
(Photo: © J.-F. Chevrier and
Élia Pijollet, 2010).

the building inscribes itself in a landscape and interprets its insular and volcanic character (the island surged out of the ocean with the volcano). Stone is transposed into the treatment of the concrete, water is discovered in the play of reflections in the glass, vegetation shows itself in the ornament and in filtered light effects.[5] This interpretation of the natural compositional elements of the urban landscape (of the built environment) is affirmed by the layout of the nearby Plaza de España. The project here rests on a simple and efficient concept: to rediscover the commingling of sea and city proper to a port site. These two disjointed elements—the square (projecting slightly over the port) and the TEA (descending along the Barranco)—create an ideal urbanity, which is deliberately ruptured from the arrogance of edifices and monuments related to the Franco era.[6] Until the transformation made by Herzog & de Meuron, the square was a large congested rotary. At its center stood the gigantic Cross erected in 1944 as the culminating point of the monument to the Fallen of the Spanish Civil War (*Los Caídos*). The monument, which revels in the grandiloquent Neoclassicism of a bellicose heroism and the victory of a martial and Catholic Spain, is today marginalized thanks to the re-centering of the square to the north and the raising of the ground level, which now covers the statue pedestals.

The materials seem extracted from the island landscape (a coating sewn with light stones, clay earth, white concrete, and black concrete eliciting a lava flow). The most spectacular gesture of the new layout is the design of the basin conceived as an immersed square or shallow pond (Figure 9.6). Lighting is furnished by glass bubbles suspended like large droplets from an aleatory network of lines stretched between inclined poles. The planting of slow-growing trees projects this artificial microcosm into a temporal duration that cannot be reduced to touristic consumption. Nature as model plays itself out at all levels—from the design of the site to the details of the urban furnishing—without in fact excluding artifice and the spectacular.

The TEA is an example of what one might term *challenged brutalism*. From the outside, the edifice presents an austere aspect, denuded of any theatrical or

9.6
View of the Plaza de España
(Photo: © J.-F. Chevrier and
Élia Pijollet, 2010).

decorative appeal; without evoking a strictly functional structure, such as a hangar or a depot, it gives the impression of an altogether slow if not amorphous expansion, thereby avoiding the effect of Brutalist shock; it stands as neutral as opposed to provocative. But neutral does not mean prosaic or commonplace; the volumetric of the cut-plane design of the roof appears both massive and rigorously ordered as if it were itself one whole face of the building (Figure 9.7); a similar treatment of the roof

9.7
North façade of
the TEA along the
Barranco de Santos
(Photo: © J.-F. Chevrier and
Élia Pijollet, 2010).

Nature, Model of Complexity

is found in the de Young Museum project. As for the interior, aluminum and glass produce an acceleration and euphoria of perception; the hardness of architectural profiles, in particular the pointed overhangs—one of the Neoexpressionist clichés of contemporary architecture—is softened by the play of reflections and the nuanced work of the restricted palette of colors. The aluminum framing and the shimmering glass counteract the matt textured concrete. The building commingles cold and hot, slowness and speed.

The project is thus the result of a combination of a totalizing formal stance, which allows the clear articulation of a programmatic complexity, and of extremely sophisticated details of construction. One relevant detail along the lines with which I began, in relation to the envelope and the image of the body, is the perforation of the three concrete walls that scan the radiating expansion of the building in its parcel of land (the climate of the island made it possible to dispense with the insulation lining). While small rectangular openings, uniformly dispersed in an apparently aleatory pattern, create the shimmering effect of the long wall of the north façade (externally the most visible part of the building), inside, in the library, the angles are rounded and produce a sequence of irregular portholes carved out of the thickness of the envelope (Figure 9.8).[7] These piercings in the concrete partitions bear a resemblance to those punctuating the metallic envelope of the de Young Museum. The two patterns issue from the same process: the screening process applied to photographic motifs such as foliage at the de Young Museum and the rippling sea at the TEA, both of which disappear as motifs in their architectural transposition. The translation of the photographic motif into geometric cuts retains only the contrast between black and white, void and solid; it renders abstract a reference to the

9.8
Library of the TEA (north wall) (Photo: © J.-F. Chevrier and Élia Pijollet, 2010).

Jean-François Chevrier

natural world all the while reifying a mobility of perception in the physical reality of the building.[8] Such mobility refers backs to the experience of one's own body— interior and exterior—in all its postural variety.

What I term "challenged brutalism" refers very precisely to what Paul Ferdinand Schilder, in his foundational book *Image and Appearance of the Human Body* (1935), called a "constructive life energy." The point is to give to a building the flexibility of anatomical and psychic structures as these are lived and constructed from the interior to the exterior and vice versa. Opticality is one of the vectors of a multi-sensorial experimentation with the image of the body. As Schilder put it:

> We expand and we contract the postural model of the body; we take parts away and we add parts; we rebuild it; we melt the details in, we create new details; we do this with our body, and with the expression of the body itself. We experiment continually with it. . . . One should not speak so much about growth and evolution, when one means by it something passive and automatic. One should emphasize the continual activity, the trying out. One may speak of growth and passing of shapes, "*Gestalten.*" But here again one should be aware that one is not dealing with automatic development but with a tendency of the constructive life energy. . . . In the phases of construction and destruction, two principal human tendencies come out. One is the tendency to crystallize units, to secure points of rest, definiteness, and absence of change. The other is the tendency to obtain a continual flow, a continuous change.[9]

This reference to experimentation with the image of the body has the immense merit, if applied to architecture, of rejecting the static model of the iconic image.

At Tenerife, Herzog & de Meuron have avoided, as they always do, paying allegiance to a historical norm that has been associated with recognizable procedures, typical forms or formulas of construction. They have pushed aside the categories and labels of architectural criticism in order to aim at an empirical response to a specific situation. One thinks of the example of Le Corbusier as interpreted by the promoters of the New Brutalism in the early 1950s. But the differences are obvious as much in the materials (in the treatment of concrete, in particular) as in the cladding of the building punctuated by cubes with a minimalist aspect covering the ducts. Today the team of Herzog & de Meuron has at its disposal a vast array of possibilities, which the architects deploy and elaborate in view of the particular circumstances; what remains at stake always, in the play of forms and materials, of scales and orientations, is the optimal interaction between site and program.

Programmatic complexity (the diversity of functions assembled under the same roof, as it were) instigates today a *monumental flexibility*; the latter is made manifest simultaneously in the plan of the urban conception, in the treatment of the landscape—this term is preferable to the idea of context, which leads to the centrality of an object with autarchic tendencies—and in the modeling of interior volumes. In several projects by Herzog & de Meuron, this flexibility is immediately discernible in the effect of the multiplication of the façades and in superimposed, embedded volumes that are also dislocated in relation to the building's axis of stability (the spinal column). In the composition of the VitraHaus, multiplied façades seem to extend to the point of producing the centrifugal impression of the building's limitlessness; one is reminded of the faceted compositions of Cubist or Cubo-Futurist painting. The idea is to encourage visitors mentally to displace themselves in the building interior even before having crossed the threshold, as if in a picturesque landscape.

Another recent project along these lines is the parking structure erected in Miami; a building without an interior, it is entirely open and presents itself as an irregular pile of seven strata made out of naked concrete (Figure 9.9). Rhythm is the determining factor here: vertically, in the variation of distance between strata (approximately between 2.5 to 10 meters); and horizontally, in the overflow of the strata in relation to each other. This, in fact, is a transposition of the "dislocations" (the dislodged boxes) of VitraHaus. The building resists the constitution of a unitary form; it seems instead to be issued from a game of folds whose sculptural quality is unveiled as one moves nearer. Seen from afar, at the scale of the landscape, the concrete envelope seems lightened, as if this were a house of cards. In the interior,

9.9
Herzog & de Meuron, 1111 Lincoln Road, Miami Beach, Florida, USA, 2005–2010 (Photo: © 2009, Iwan Baan and MBEACH1, LLLP).

Jean-François Chevrier

the inclined pillars, the stairs and the ramps form a spider-like network deploying and linking together the seven levels of the building. As with the train station signal box in Basel and the Ricola warehouses in Mulhouse, Herzog & de Meuron have given to a functional edifice the ambiguous charm of a structure both brutal and precious.

The most complex, ambitious, and risky at all levels (including the economic one) remains the Elbphilharmonie in Hamburg. Already now, the building, which is in construction, fulfills its role as an urban stimulus in a sumptuous but unfortunately ravaged estuary—parceled out and rendered prosaic by the negligence of functionaries and the mediocrity of recent architectural innovations and renovations. From afar, the building rises, immense, like a new landmark around which the landscape of the Hanseatic metropole tends to be reshaped. Up close, it strikes to the contrary as surprisingly modest, intimate, and welcoming. The logic of the carefully integrated landscape respected at Tenerife is here translated into the vertical dimensions of an enormous optical machine. The design of the exterior volume is reflected and unfolded in the interior by the play of sculpted forms, carved whole cloth from the edifice block where spaces are most vast and, elsewhere, cut out or modeled. The most significant space is undoubtedly the foyer, defined by staircases between five levels and open to the landscape. This intimate monumentality at the territorial scale is, in the end, the very emblem of nature as model of complexity, as it comes to be associated with programmatic complexity.

Notes

1. Charles Blanc, *Grammaire des arts du dessin*, int. Claire Barbillon (1880 ed.; Paris, École nationale supérieure des beaux-arts, 2000), 89, voiced regret that the relation of architecture to the other visual arts had been overturned over the course of history. Architecture "in turn was subjected to their influence; it became *sculptural* under Paganism and *picturesque* under Christianity."

2. During an interview (unpublished) in 2008, Jacques Herzog explained to me that: "One cannot escape nature, for nothing, including language itself, can be extracted from this system. This is our attitude, and it isn't a nostalgic idea. Romantic, maybe, but in the nineteenth-century sense, in the sense that things form an ensemble from which they really can't be separated. The successful projects are the ones that reveal complexity, that are capable of reuniting very different elements, and not those architectures that guarantee function, that answer a demand in a strictly functional manner. This is the case with the Beijing stadium, we made an Olympic stadium but its real meaning lies elsewhere. I have never given symbolic meaning to a tree, but a tree is system of great complexity nonetheless, and this becomes interesting when one considers its different aspects. I have always been fascinated by research; before architecture, I had started studies in chemistry and biology at Basel. We have always been interested in the invisible phenomena that determine the visible."

3. The program is complex since it required assembling under a single roof: a large municipal library; exhibition spaces for a collection based around the local Surrealist

artist Oscar Dominguez as well as for other exhibits and a center of photography; an auditorium, a cafeteria, a rather vast ensemble of offices for the cultural department of the Council of Tenerife.

4   Open round the clock, the extensive library gives the building its amplitude and its interior life. It includes spaces for children in the basement, which open onto an interior courtyard along the south wall. On the first floor, the library communicates with the exhibition spaces, which are distributed on three levels and which have their principal access in the central court. A third triangular court separates the exhibition zone from the cultural administration offices. This configuration of three courtyards cut out into an expanding interior volume recalls one of the characteristics of the de Young Museum.

5   The vegetation also appears as such in the courtyards planted with trees.

6   The project of the Plaza de España (which originally dates from 1908) is bordered on the south by the Council of the Canary Islands, the central post office, and the casino. The construction of the buildings began in 1934 when General Franco was military governor of the island. Laid out in the 1940s, the square was inaugurated in 1950.

7   On both sides of the museum, the wall that borders the church square as well as the wall that opens onto the interior court shared with the offices of the cultural department of Tenerife are similarly pierced, but without the effect of rounding off the angles toward the interior.

8   The process of transformation of motifs is documented in Gerhard Mack, ed., *Herzog & de Meuron, 1997–2001. The Complete Works* (Basel: Birkhäuser, 2009), vol. 4, 58, 92.

9   Paul Ferdinand Schilder, *The Image and Appearance of the Human Body* (1935; London: Routledge, 1999), 210–211.

Case Study III

Steven Holl Architects, Sliced Porosity Block, Chengdu, China (2007–2012)

The Sliced Porosity Block is a hybrid of different functions, like a giant chunk of a metropolis. The program calls for five towers with offices, serviced apartments, retail space, a hotel, cafés and restaurants. It is located just south of the intersection of the First Ring Road and Ren Min Nan Road in Chengdu. Its sun-sliced geometry results from required minimum sunlight exposures to the surrounding urban fabric, prescribed by code and calculated by the precise geometry of sun angles.

The large public space framed by the block is formed into three valleys, inspired by the poem "Prelude" by Tu Fu (AD 712–770):

> This fugitive between the earth and the sky, from the northeast
> storm-tossed to the southwest, time has left stranded in three
> valleys . . .

In some of the porous openings, chunks of different buildings are inserted.

Our micro-urban strategy will create a new terrain of public space: an urban terrace on the metropolitan scale of Rockefeller Center. This new terrain is sculpted by stone steps and ramps, with large pools that spill into stepped fountains. Trees, plantings, and benches are flanked with cafés and escalators soaring up to suspended pavilions. Roof gardens are cultivated through their individual connections to condominiums or hotel cafés.

At the shop fronts there will be luminous color, neon, backlit color transparency—like the wash of color that suddenly appears in the great black and white films of Andrei Tarkovsky. The six design strategies are worked out in the concept watercolor sketches as follows:

1. Integral urban functions shape urban space
2. Porosity
3. Micro-urbanism
4. Super-green architecture
5. "Three valleys" inner garden
6. Spatial geometry lit via pond skylights

The aim for the Sliced Porosity Block is to form new public space and to realize new levels of green construction in Chengdu. The complex is heated and cooled geothermally by 480 wells. The large podium ponds harvest recycled rainwater with natural grasses and lily pads creating a cooling effect.

Construction period:	October 2008–November 2012
Project type:	direct commission
Building area (square):	3,336,812 sq. ft. / 310,000 sq. m
Site area:	57,415 ft. / 17,500 m
Floor area (square) above:	2,098,963 sq. ft. / 195,000 sq. m
Floor area (square) below:	1,237,850 sq. ft. / 115,000 sq. m

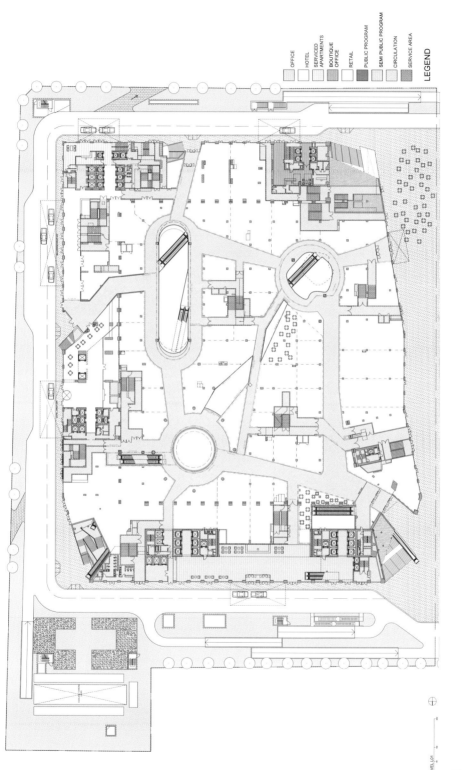

LEGEND

OFFICE
HOTEL
SERVICED APARTMENTS
BOUTIQUE OFFICE
RETAIL
PUBLIC PROGRAM
SEMI PUBLIC PROGRAM
CIRCULATION
SERVICE AREA

LEVEL L01

1

Level 1 floor plan (© Steven Holl Architects).

Sliced Porosity Block, Chengdu, China (2007–2012)

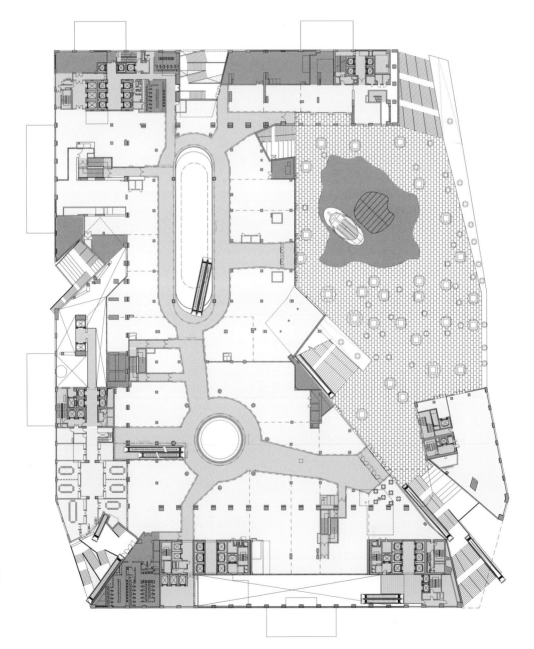

OFFICE

HOTEL

SERVICED
APARTMENTS

SOHO
OFFICE / RES

RETAIL

PUBLIC PROGRAM

SEMI PUBLIC PROGRAM

CIRCULATION

SERVICE AREA

LEGEND

LEVEL 02

Level 2 floor plan © Steven Holl Architects

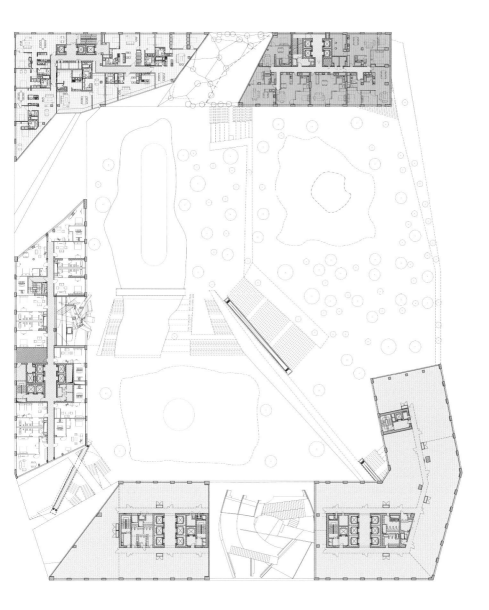

LEVEL 11

3   Level 11 floor plan (© Steven Holl Architects).

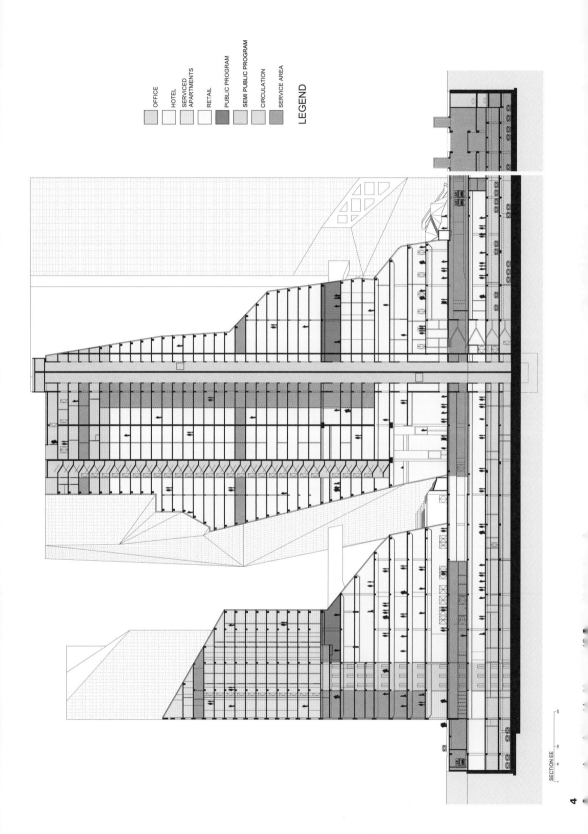

LEGEND

OFFICE
HOTEL
SERVICED APARTMENTS
RETAIL
PUBLIC PROGRAM
SEMI PUBLIC PROGRAM
CIRCULATION
SERVICE AREA

SECTION EE

Case Study III: Steven Holl Architects

01 LOCATION PLAN   SCALE: 1/500

5   Site plan (© Steven Holl Architects).

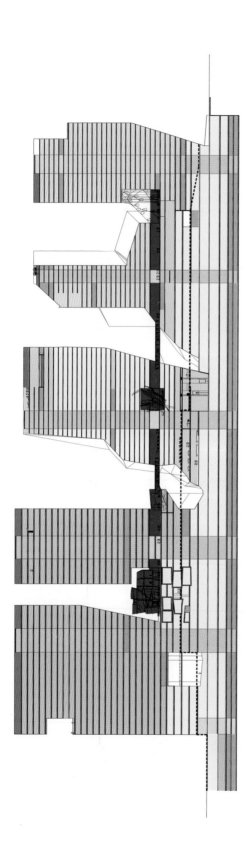

6   Unfolded section showing public loop in red (© Steven Holl Architects).

Case Study III: Steven Holl Architects

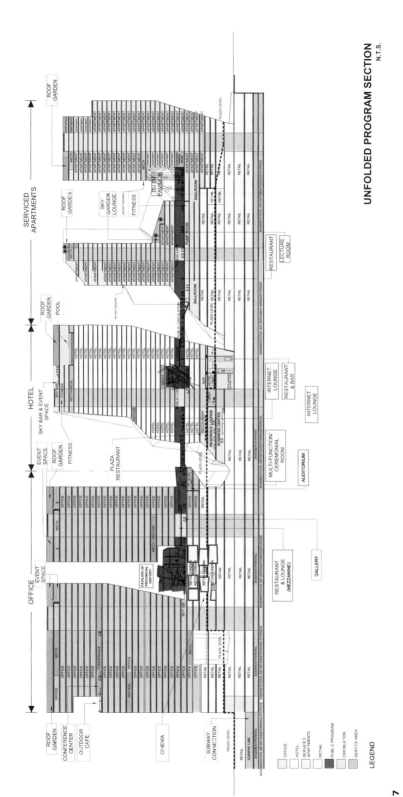

7

Unfolded section showing public loop in red (with text) (© Steven Holl Architects).

Sliced Porosity Block, Chengdu, China (2007–2012)

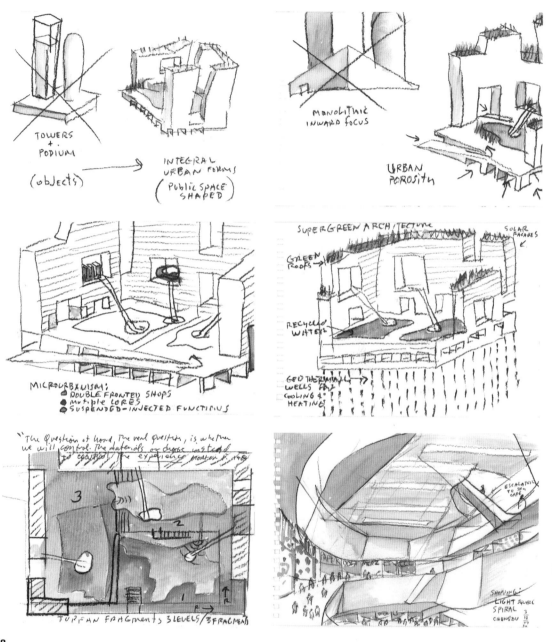

8

Concept watercolor sketches (© Steven Holl Architects).

Case Study III: Steven Holl Architects

9
SH Raffles City model (© Iwan Baan).

10
SH Raffles City model
(© Iwan Baan).

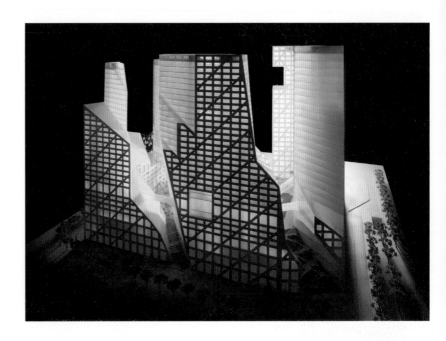

11
Work site photograph
(© Nathan Willock).

Case Study III: Steven Holl Architects

12
Work site photograph (© Nathan Willock).

Part IV

The Nature of Infrastructure

10

Agri-tecture
Elizabeth Diller

Since its completion, the High Line has passed through the filter of countless post-rationalizations.[1] However, little time has been spent discussing a pre-theorized High Line—that is, a High Line understood in the context of our own work and trajectory. The High Line is the culmination and continuation of a body of work that has spanned more than three decades, with projects that range from the environmental scale of the Blur Building to the urban guerrilla installation of Soft Sell. This body of work was integral to establishing the High Line's conceptual foundations and represents a number of our obsessions through the years—spectatorship, the urban, rethinking the natural, the relationship between "smart" and "dumb" technologies, uncertainty and the unexpected.

Constructed in Yverdon-les-Bains, Switzerland, for the 2002 Swiss Expo, the Blur Building was our first project at an environmental scale (Figures 10.1–10.3). During the development of the pavilion, the nature of nature was questioned by asking "What is the weather?" and "How does one work with natural phenomena of fog and with a natural material like water?" The site—the water of Lake Neuchâtel—was taken as a touristic backdrop, as the primary building material, and as a static interference with vision and sound.

At a time when there was widespread and devoted interest in high-definition simulation, Blur worked to obliterate high-fidelity vision and make a low-definition, low-resolution space. It was a habitable medium that was form-less, feature-less, depth-less, scale-less, mass-less, surface-less, and dimension-less. This is why it is called *Blur* and not *Cloud* (although this has not prevented the project from being interpreted as a cloud).

In order to produce this low-definition, low-resolution effect, it was necessary for the Blur Building to function as a real-time weather station capable of reading

10.1
Blur, 2002 (Photo: © Beat Widmer).

10.2
Approaching Blur, 2002 (Photo: Courtesy of Diller Scofidio + Renfro).

Elizabeth Diller

the natural conditions as they were occurring—the wind speed, the humidity, the temperature, and the dew point among others. The project employed smart system technology that constantly fought to think on its own. The system had to be trained to become intelligent about how to act in given scenarios. It took over six months of development before the system could fully understand and compensate for the specific environmental conditions in order to successfully and consistently produce the cloud-like effect.

10.3
Inside Blur, 2002 (Photo: Courtesy of Diller Scofidio + Renfro).

Ultimately, the goal of the Blur Building was very dumb: to make an exhibition pavilion where there was absolutely nothing to see and nothing to do except to think about our dependence on vision itself. Ironically, it required a tremendous amount of smart technology to achieve this dumb goal.

In 2004 and 2008, we were presented with opportunities to further explore the idea of "assisted nature" through our work on the Pure Mix and Arbores Laetae projects, respectively (Figures 10.4 and 10.5). Pure Mix was an exhibition in Kemi, Finland, and Arbores Laetae was designed for Liverpool's Biennial. Both projects served as platforms from which to critique, investigate, and reveal the arbitrary distinctions that society has drawn between the natural and the man-made.

Pure Mix was an installation that took place in the dead of the winter on an iced-over section of a Finish harbor. By infiltrating the existing eco-system with alien water prepackaged and imported from various parts of the world, Pure Mix investigated the idea of "assisted nature." A network of apertures were carved into the ice and filled with different brands of bottled water, with the respective logos engraved onto the top layer of ice. In the spring, the "pure" frozen bottled water would melt and mix with the "natural" harbor water.

With Arbores Laetae, we were most interested in playing with the expectation that a natural material has a predetermined and predictable relationship to its surroundings. We selected a brownfield site occupied by a grove of new Hornbeam trees. The exaggerated height of the trees produced a surreal and eerie distortion of scale when juxtaposed to the scale of the human body. Three of the trees on the site were planted on a bias in buried turntables that were synchronized to rotate slowly at slightly different speeds, thereby upturning the expectation that the natural material—a tree—is stably connected to the ground. The rotations were timed to cause the trees to occasionally brush against one another or, at other moments, open up a wide void in the grove, producing a constant play of light and

Agri-tecture

10.4
Pure Mix, 2004 (Photo:
© Jeffrey Debany. Courtesy
of Diller Scofidio + Renfro,
John Roloff, and The Snow
Show).

10.4
Pure Mix, 2004 (Photo:
© Jeffrey Debany. Courtesy
of Diller Scofidio + Renfro,
John Roloff, and The Snow
Show).

shadow. Anyone observing the trees in the middle of the grove could see that a few members of the group were "badly behaved."

Another line of inquiry focused on audience and spectatorship. The projects that emerged from these investigations often took the form of guerrilla interventions at the urban scale.

Soft Sell was a video installation in New York's Times Square and was originally created as part of the 42nd Street Project presented by Creative Time

10.5
Arbores Laetae, 2008 (Photo:
© Jon Barraclough. Courtesy
of Diller Scofidio + Renfro
and the Liverpool Biennial).

10.6
Soft Sell, 1993 (Photo: Courtesy of Diller Scofidio + Renfro).

(Figure 10.6). A red-lipsticked female mouth offered a series of consumerist pleasures in the form of solicitations made to people on the street. The lips were projected on the doors of an abandoned pornographic theater and engaged a Times Square that had not yet been Disney-fied. Soft Sell came at a time when people were used to talking back to screens and large crowds would gather and talk back to the projected lips. The solicitations of Soft Sell were not sexual, but were all kinds of impossible, unfulfillable dreams.

> Hey you, wanna buy a one-way ticket outta here?
> Hey you, wanna buy a hot tip?
> Hey you, wanna buy the latest sensation?
> Hey you, wanna buy a new body?
> Hey you, wanna buy some fatherly advice?
> Hey you, wanna buy a building permit?
> Hey you, wanna buy a piece of the American dream?
> Hey you, wanna buy a souvenir to show your friends and family?
> Hey you, wanna buy the mayor's ear?
> Hey you, wanna buy a deluxe Hoover upright?
> Hey you, wanna buy a get-out-of-jail-free card?
> Hey you, wanna buy your way up the ladder?
> Hey you, wanna buy a new lifestyle?
> Hey you, wanna buy a place in history?
> Hey you, wanna buy a three-carat diamond pinky ring?
> Hey you, wanna buy a condo with an all-night doorman?
> Hey you, wanna buy a sure thing?
> Hey you, wanna buy a chance to do it all over again?
> Hey you, wanna buy a piece of the action?
> Hey you, wanna buy a place at the head of the line?
> Hey you, wanna buy a winning combination?
> Hey you, wanna buy some good luck?
> Hey you, wanna buy forgiveness for your sins?
> Hey you, wanna buy a good night's sleep?
> Hey you, wanna buy your fifteen minutes in the spotlight?
> Hey you, wanna buy an alibi?
> Hey you, wanna buy a rare opportunity?
> Hey you, wanna buy a left kidney?
> Hey you, wanna buy a judge?

The High Line offered us the opportunity to deploy many of our previous obsessions in a single project (Figures 10.7–10.9).

The High Line was originally constructed in order to save lives. It was designed to supplant the original rail line that ran at street level along 10th Avenue on the western edge of Manhattan and transported goods throughout the Chelsea

Elizabeth Diller

10.7
The High Line, 2009. (Photo: © Iwan Baan. Design by James Corner Field Operations, Diller Scofidio + Renfro, and Piet Oudolf).

10.8
The High Line, 2009. (Photo: © Iwan Baan. Design by James Corner Field Operations, Diller Scofidio + Renfro, and Piet Oudolf).

10.9
The High Line, 2009. (Photo: © Iwan Baan. Design by James Corner Field Operations, Diller Scofidio + Renfro, and Piet Oudolf).

Elizabeth Diller

and Meatpacking neighborhoods. The train was responsible for many pedestrian casualties, so much so that men on horseback—known as "West Side Cowboys"— were commonly seen escorting the train. Efforts to minimize the dangers of the transportation route culminated in the construction of the elevated railway in the 1920s. Over the next 50 years of its use, the character of the surrounding neighborhoods and the primary modes of transportation changed dramatically, and coupled with the region's economic shift from industry to services, the High Line gradually fell into disuse.

When we inherited the High Line, it was an abject leftover of industrial culture, seen by many as a dark scar meandering between buildings and occupying prime real estate. As the Chelsea neighborhood transformed into a burgeoning arts district, new high-end businesses followed the museums, galleries, and boutiques that took root in the neighborhood underneath the High Line. The neighborhood's new constituencies developed detached relationships to the abandoned railway. To the public that was denied access to the rail surface, the High Line was commonly understood as a blight, anything but a resource or a catalyst. Nearby property owners frequently called for the demolition of the railway, as it was perceived to negatively affect property values. Under Rudolph Giuliani's administration, the High Line was slated for demolition.

This quickly changed when Friends of the High Line, a grass-roots organization created to preserve and transform the High Line, commissioned Joel Sternfeld in 2000 to photograph the landscape that took root after the railway fell into ruin. The photography was taken over the course of a year, recording the shifting bio-systems created by the changing seasons. The images revealed an amazing array of vegetation growing on the line—plants that were neither there when the High Line was built nor necessarily native to the area; the seeds had blown in from various places—sea containers, birds, and train wheels, among others. Sternfeld's photographs ignited the public's imagination and, with the political support of the new Bloomberg administration, the High Line was saved from destruction and funds were allocated to transform the railway into a public park and resource.

Sternfeld's photographs uncovered an interesting twist to the project: the conquest of nature over industrial culture. The newly designed High Line had to preserve the perversity of this idea, especially since the plant life that took to the High Line created a series of unique landscapes that were hard to imagine as existing anywhere else. For us, the primary question raised by the competition was, "How do you bring the public up to the High Line so that they can enjoy the landscape, without destroying the beautiful microenvironments that are already established?" The conventional way to enable the public to walk on the High Line would have been to separate the surface of the railway into hardscapes for people and softscapes for plant life. But the existing High Line landscape evaded the normal division between hardscape and softscape; concrete, steel tracks, dirt, and vegetation were deeply intertwined and the distinction between each was blurred.

The High Line design as it exists today takes its cue from the way in which nature inevitably finds its way through the man-made environment. The design digitized the surface into discrete linear planks that were designated as either green or hardscape. This system made it possible to control a gradient from 100 percent solid hardscape to 100 percent solid landscape, or anywhere in between. This technique was called *agri-tecture*: part agriculture, part architecture. The long paving units—or planks—have tapered ends that comb into planting beds to create a textured, "pathless" landscape where the public can meander in unscripted ways. The combed edge of the paving units avoids a harsh border between hard and soft. The entire surface is composed from the planks: they are the language throughout the whole system.

The development of a planking system was paralleled by efforts to catalog the myriad of plants on the High Line. The seeds of these plants were harvested, placed into nurseries to grow, and then replanted and mixed with several other species into various configurations that could be integrated into the planking system on the High Line. Our intent was to translate the biodiversity that took root after the High Line's ruin into a string of site-specific urban microclimates, such that the stretch of railway would include sunny, shady, wet, dry, windy, and sheltered spaces.

The redesigned High Line can also be understood as a series of urban moments: moments of movement and moments of stasis. The entry points were conceived of in terms of speed—there are expeditious ways of transitioning from the City to the High Line, or there are slow ways to access the park by passing through the thickness of the steel structure, which is some six feet thick. The slow access points are durational experiences designed to prolong the transition from the frenetic pace of city streets to the slow, otherworldly landscape above.

The High Line re-purposes service-oriented infrastructure in order to accommodate a culture of leisure at a different pace than other public amenities that occupy linear space. Hudson River Park, running parallel to the High Line and along the edge of the Hudson River, facilitates fast-paced leisure activities— bicycles, rollerblades, and the runner. The opposite is true for the High Line; it is designed for feet, for slowness. As a result, the socialization of the High Line produces a different kind of phenomenon—it self-edits throughout the day. The constituents evolve over the course of the day, from joggers and work commuters in the morning, to the self- or un-employed and nannies during the daytime, to couples and single folk on the prowl in the evening, to cruisers late at night. Spaces were designed to encourage long pauses, offering opportunities to exercise and sharpen voyeuristic tendencies. The 10th Avenue Overlook was developed with a simple sectional move that created a grandstand for people to watch traffic pass underneath and move up 10th Avenue. On the street level, traffic is an obstacle; above, it is a form of entertainment, an everyday event that is transformed into an intense and mesmerizing display of nothingness. The High Line offers a glimpse into an otherwise hidden side of the City—a City off the grid and without spotlights. The backs and tops of buildings are seen in intimately new ways. The insides of

Elizabeth Diller

homes and industrial programs are revealed. Cracks in the urban fabric are blown open and the spaces between buildings are occupied by a new kind of public life.

The High Line was originally sold to the City's administration as a catalyst for economic development. But the extent of the High Line's success and the public's embrace of the project were difficult to predict. The park is credited for the investment of several billion dollars in the surrounding neighborhoods as well as the creation of thousands of new jobs. It has since become a model for the redevelopment of infrastructure in cities around the world.

The scale of the High Line's economic success, however, was not the only unexpected result. When we first began the design process, we were committed to playing the role of the High Line's architects—that is, its cultural guardians. As the project evolved and our understanding of its post-industrial nature deepened, we thought it necessary to protect the High Line from architecture. Eventually, we abandoned the idea of control, both as its architects and its non-architects.

Unplanned social adaptations of the High Line as public space have abounded. Unscripted appropriations included a cabaret singer putting on performances from her fire escape directly adjacent to the High Line and frequent nudity on display at the Standard Hotel hovering above the Park. The cabaret singer invited other artists to join her performances and the collaboration was appropriately called "Renegade Cabaret." Large crowds would gather to watch and a new form of public engagement with the City was created.

Eventually, the studio accepted that many things would exceed or deviate from what we expected to happen on the High Line and that this non-scripted evolution was another kind of nature that had to be attended to—the growth of the City. And so now we embrace what we cannot control; uncertainty produces far more interesting results than anything we could have predicted.

Note

1   This chapter is adapted from Elizabeth Diller's lecture delivered on March 31, 2010, at the Harvard Graduate School of Design.

11

Nature, Infrastructure and Cities

Antoine Picon

11.1
Diller Scofidio + Renfro,
James Corner Field
Operations, The High Line
(Photo: Antoine Picon).

The past decades have been marked by a profound shift in our understanding of the relations between nature, infrastructures and cities. Part of the success with which a project like the New York High Line was met is linked to the fact that it offers a striking expression of this shift (Figure 11.1). Before the rise of the environmental crises we now face, nature served as the support for infrastructures. Roads, bridges and canals were generally located in natural settings. They exploited the productive

11.2
Diller Scofidio + Renfro,
James Corner Field
Operations, The High Line
(Photo: Antoine Picon).

power of nature to the benefit of mankind. In our contemporary technologically driven world, nature increasingly appears as a fragile entity that is itself in need of infrastructural support. This new and ambiguous condition is among the meanings conveyed by the High Line. Nature is literally on its deck like a superficial layer that needs to be tended as if it were some sort of ornament.

At this stage, however, there arises the question of the difference between the situation presented by the High Line and the traditional urban program of the suspended garden (Figure 11.2). From Babylon, eponymous world marvel, to modern and contemporary urban plantations on decks and roofs, this program has always been a constant feature of the city. To what extent are we observing something new with a realization such as the High Line? To answer this, two dimensions must be taken into account. The first involves the symbolic or even fictional character of the relation to nature embodied by the High Line. The second touches upon the notion of "return" that constitutes one of the threads of the collection of essays gathered in this volume. What the High Line seems to epitomize is the "return" of nature in a world that had long taken its presence or absence for granted. Actually, in our contemporary urban environment, nature is often neither present nor absent; it is returning, that is to say, it is dynamically asserting its power to appear and unfold. Another way to put it would be to say that nature appears more than ever as a potentiality, a virtuality.

The dimension of the virtual is inseparable from a series of related themes and notions like emergence, a much-discussed issue in design circles today. Through these themes and notions, what is likewise at stake is the relation between nature and information. Is nature fundamentally informational? By the same token, what can be said about the nature of information? These questions will repeatedly intervene in our attempt to understand what is currently happening regarding the relations between nature, infrastructures and cities.

Nature and Infrastructure

Let me begin by addressing the ongoing shift in the relation between nature and infrastructure. Nature used to surround infrastructures (Figure 11.3). Most bridges, viaducts or dams were located in the countryside, and part of their aesthetic appeal lay in the marked contrast between their generally straightforward and artificial-looking lines and the seemingly spontaneous sinuosity of natural topography.

During the second half of the eighteenth century, this contrast played a decisive role in the emergence of two new aesthetic categories: the sublime and the picturesque. The story of their rise has generally been told in relation to architecture and the art of gardens, but one should not forget the role played by infrastructures in the affair. In the eyes of the engineers in charge of their conception and realization, the sublime epitomized the initial disproportion between nature and human labor as well as the heroic character of the fight necessary to render the two compatible by the end. As for the picturesque, it spoke to the capacity of infrastructure, once built, to complement nature harmoniously all the while revealing some of its hidden features.[1] Understood in this light, an infrastructure was akin to

11.3
Paul Bodin, Viaduct of the Vaur, 1897–1902 (Photo: Antoine Picon).

an event. It dramatized the natural scenery that surrounded it like a fabric designed to enliven a garden. Revealingly, eighteenth-century parks were frequently adorned with bridges, from the Palladian bridge at Stowe to the small-scale replica of the Coalbrookdale Iron Bridge in the Wörlitz gardens.

Now infrastructures were not only found in the countryside. From bridges to sewers, they were also urban. Some of them, like canals, brought natural elements into the city. But the nature that arrived into the middle of the city was often seen as degraded and synonymous with urban squalor. In places such as Manchester, urban waterways seemed, for instance, doomed to waste and pollution. This led urban reformers, architects, landscape architects, and engineers to an innovative answer: to bring nature directly into the city by designing plantations and parks as infrastructures. Indeed, in order to bring an allegedly undamaged nature into the city, many nineteenth-century parks had to be conceived as infrastructures. This approach was especially clear in the case of Haussmannian Paris where the plantations and the parks were interpreted as elements of a complex network covering the entire city. In this network, the trees appeared as an integral part of the infrastructure, just like the sewers running underground or the lampposts regularly disposed between them. A realization like the Park of the Buttes-Chaumont in the northeast of Paris was even designed by an engineer and based on an accumulation of technological tours de force such as the creation of artificial hills on a former quarry. The garden also featured a series of bridges, a railway line and above all a great deal of reinforced cement. Documented by photographer Charles Marville, the construction of the Park of the Buttes-Chaumont was emblematic of what it meant in practice to approach nature in infrastructural terms. Interestingly, despite its artificial character, Parisians consider this park to this day as the most natural of all the gardens of the city.[2]

One could make a similar argument with Central Park, which was designed both as a consummate infrastructure and as a place where untamed nature could survive in the midst of one of the busiest cities in the world. The same line of argumentation applies, of course, to subsequent urban parkways. From the aesthetics of territorial infrastructures, industrial-age urban parks and parkways inherited a propensity to make use of sublime and picturesque effects.

The success of the High Line—the symbolic impact it has had both on its users and on the various design communities interested in the future of urban parks—may very well be related to a series of profound changes in the relations between nature, infrastructures and cities that I have just evoked. To put it simply, one could say that these relations were typical of an industrial context that no longer applies to our world.

These changes are in turn indicative of a shift in our conception of nature, which is linked to its increasingly informational dimension. In contemporary science and philosophy, nature is interpreted as information driven. And since information is fundamentally commensurate with events—a bit is nothing but an elementary occurrence, to paraphrase philosopher Pierre Lévy—nature appears as a complex maze of events ranging from micro unfolding of ordered structures to macro changes.[3] In contemporary design theory, the concept of emergence is often mobilized in order to characterize this new understanding of nature in terms of events that seem to lead to spontaneous phenomena of auto-organization.[4] Contrary to what Mark Jarzombek suggested in the lecture series that gave birth to the present book, today's information-based nature is certainly not dead.[5] If this were the case, we would not be preoccupied by so many natural entities, from rainforests to red tuna, from the polar ice caps to pandas.

Again, whereas the traditional conception cast nature as only marginally a matter of events, it appears now as fundamentally constituted by myriad events. A lot of things happen all the time in the natural realm. There is no need to insist on the connection between this new conception of nature and the importance taken in our contemporary culture by mass media, with the world of information in the journalistic sense. Nature in the age of information is nature as information but also nature as news.

Many pieces of news revolve around the notion that nature is not dead but vulnerable. Rainforests are threatened by human development, ice caps by global warming. Red tuna and pandas are endangered species. This means that nature is in need of support. Its survival has become a scientific and technological challenge. Specialists of science, technology and society studies often refer to that situation by saying that we live in a techno-nature in which the respective roles of the natural and the artificial are often reversed. Science and technology now surround and often support nature instead of the reverse. A number of natural parks in Europe are emblematic of this situation. What they present to their visitors is an artificially maintained nature, a scenery curated like fragile plants in a greenhouse. Put another way, nature is very often now the superficial layer, something akin to software.

In traditional industrial society, nature used to support infrastructures. Now, it is often supported by infrastructures, whether physical or electronic. In other words, the urban park and parkway status, this infrastructure-supported status of nature that used to be an exception motivated by the exceptional character of the urban environment, has become a commonplace situation. This should not come as a surprise given the fact that the urban environment has become more often the norm than the exception. Nature is now typically supported by infrastructures. Our current fascination with vertical gardens might have to do with this fact. To see plants in this way, as a vertical forest stemming out of a wall like an urban ornament, reminds us of the new place of nature in our world. In such a context, nature is no longer a pervasive condition. It happens. The nature of the natural in an information-driven age is to "happen," thus generating an endless stream of news.

It would be tempting to interpret the High Line as the very symbol of this new situation. Yet things are actually not that simple, for let us not forget that suspended gardens are almost as old as the city itself. Could the High Line be just another instance of the old Babylonian marvel?

Antoine Picon

11.4
Diller Scofidio + Renfro,
James Corner Field
Operations, The High Line
(Photo: Antoine Picon).

To take this a step further, one could argue that nature's supported character goes further than its need for technological protection. Nature is also what quite literally returns in the midst of our urban sprawl using infrastructures as its channels much like a radio broadcast is carried by a given wavelength (Figure 11.4). Nature is what haunts the sprawl. In numerous cases, natural life, wildlife even, is to be found alongside technological systems. In Europe, the margins of untended freeways have become, for instance, the dwelling place of various endangered species (like the last slow worms in France). In the United States, coyotes and other wild animals often enter cities following rail tracks (Figure 11.5). Once again, nature is what literally returns in cities, and this return is there again an event. Nature is necessarily something that happens in a profoundly urban world. Cities, just like infrastructures, took place in nature. Now nature takes place in infrastructures and cities.

What seems to be at stake is another inversion, for nature is not only in need of infrastructural support. Contemporary urban infrastructures often represent a means for nature—wild nature, that is—to survive and penetrate the urban environment as a series of occurrences. With some of its plants apparently gone wild, the High Line is all the more fascinating in that it is not an authentic expression of this context. Of course, it conveys the notion of a supported nature and an impression of wilderness at work at the core of the urban fabric and urban infrastructure—something like a return of nature. It conveys this return precisely because it avoids the traditional genres of the sublime and the picturesque, although the case is less clear with the picturesque. One may indeed wonder whether a new type of picturesque is not at work in such a project.

11.5
Diller Scofidio + Renfro,
James Corner Field
Operations, The High Line
(Photo: Antoine Picon).

Yet as soon as one looks more closely at the High Line, one realizes that the nature in question is not wild but carefully tended. It cannot be wild given the number of people that go for a stroll on this elevated promenade. Nature does not really return in the case of the High Line. The pedestrian is in fact confronted with a fiction and so oscillates constantly between the belief in this fiction and the disillusion generated by a reality that is fundamentally different. What appears as a fiction on the High Line actually corresponds to the prevailing state of things almost everywhere else where nature is supported by infrastructure, where all kinds of natural species use these infrastructures to return to cities.

Another fiction that presents itself here is that of a ruined infrastructure colonized by nature. The truth is that the High Line is no longer in ruins despite its staging to the contrary as well as the fact that its natural elements belong to an almost traditional genre of urban parks and gardens. Its ambiance is that of a highly civilized place where the remains of a former railroad vocation are not really ruins but carefully crafted evocations.

There is therefore an almost traditional aspect in the conception of the High Line. Following a long tradition of sophisticated parks and gardens, it situates itself at the threshold of illusion and disillusion, with the additional complication that outside the garden, the illusion is actually a reality whereas the allegedly disillusioned state does not correspond to the prevailing state of affairs. The gardens of André Le Nôtre already functioned in terms of this fragile limit between illusion and disillusion.[6] The same can be said of the aforementioned Park of the Buttes-Chaumont.

One often says that gardens are magic. Actually what they achieve is closer to prestidigitation. A good trick must appear like magic, so that one is almost

Antoine Picon

tempted to believe that there is something supernatural at work in it. But the act of conjuring must simultaneously convey the notion that it is an illusion. Where would be the art otherwise? What happens in reality with these gardens is not nature but, rather, an evocation of nature as something that happens. This transmutation might lead to broader lessons for designers at large. Contemporary garden and landscape architecture have emerged as a potent source of inspiration for architecture and urbanism.[7] What can we learn from the High Line and similar projects of our time?

The answer could very well be that to deal convincingly with nature, design must fictionalize it. At the same time, the fiction must convey something of the new prevailing condition of nature at a scale that is broader than the actual project. It must, among other things, suggest that nature is supported. Last lesson: to fictionalize something today is to make it appear as an occurrence or, better yet, an event.

It is worth noting that the need to fictionalize in order to convey the truth of a higher order used to be characteristic of the relation between architecture and tectonic. One of the best expressions of this relation is perhaps Sullivan's treatment of the high-rise theme at the Wainwright Building in Saint Louis (Figure 11.6). In

11.6
Louis Sullivan, Wainwright Building, 1891
(Photo: Antoine Picon).

Nature, Infrastructure and Cities

order to express the rhythmic dynamism of the steel frame, Sullivan chose to have twice as many vertical pilasters as steel columns. In other words, one pier out of two was actually nonstructural, meaning that something akin to a constructive lie was necessary for conveying the higher order truth of the tectonic order. This could be called the dialectic of tectonic. The first order of structural reality has to be negated so that a higher order of tectonic truth becomes tangible.

With the spectacular development of digital technologies, we may be witnessing the end of tectonic as we knew it.[8] Does this mean that nature is going to replace the tectonic or, rather, play the role the tectonic used to fulfill vis-à-vis architecture? Are we going to see the emergence of a dialectic of nature based on a similar play between reality and truth, disillusion and illusion? By the same token, one is left to wonder whether we are on the verge of witnessing a radical inversion of the categories of the natural and the artificial, meaning that now nature must be fictionalized whereas previously artificial creations like structures were in need of such fictionalizing.

For the architectural disciplines, the big difference between yesterday and today—between the age of the tectonic and the age of nature—is that formerly, fictions used to make present the reassuring coherence of the built object. Sullivan had to lie in order to emphasize such coherence. Today's fictions stage open-ended occurrences, events and processes that do not necessarily possess a human scope. We have not yet succeeded in our attempts to tame the nature of information.

Notes

1   On the rise of the "technological sublime," see Antoine Picon, *French Architects and Engineers in the Age of Enlightenment* (Cambridge: Cambridge University Press, 1992), and David E. Nye, *American Technological Sublime* (Cambridge, MA: MIT Press, 1994).

2   On the Park of the Buttes-Chaumont, see for instance Ann Komara, "Concrete and the Engineered Picturesque: The Parc des Buttes-Chaumont (Paris 1867)," *Journal of Architectural Education* 58 (Sept. 2004): 5–12; Antoine Picon, "Nature et ingénierie: le parc des Buttes-Chaumont," *Romantisme: Revue du dix-neuvième siècle* 150 (2010): 35–49.

3   See Pierre Lévy, *La machine univers: Création, cognition et culture informatique* (Paris: La Découverte, 1987), 124.

4   Cf. Michael Hensel, Achim Menges, Michael Weinstock, eds., "Emergence: Morphogenetic Design Strategies," *Architectural Design* 74/3 (May–June 2004): 48–53.

5   Mark Jarzombek, presentation for the Symposia on Architecture "The Return of Nature: The Apparatus of Sustainability," given at Harvard Graduate School of Design on February 24, 2010; and see Chapter 8 in this volume.

6   On this aspect of Le Nôtre's work, see Georges Farhat, "L'anamorphose du territoire: les fonctions paysagères de la perspective topographique dans l'économie seigneuriale en France, autour de l'oeuvre d'André Le Nôtre (1613–1700)," PhD dissertation defended at Université de Paris I-Sorbonne, 2008.

7   Cf. Jean-Claude Garcias, *Sullivan* (Paris: Hazan, 1997).

8   Cf. Antoine Picon, *Digital Culture in Architecture: An Introduction for the Design Professions* (Basel: Birkhäuser, 2010).

Case Study IV

George L. Legendre, Henderson Waves,
Singapore (2004–2008)

The brief of Henderson Waves bridge is simple enough: to link two ridge summits with a continuous plane. Its site is part of a chain of hills stretching from Mount Faber Park through Telok Blangah Hill and Kent Ridge Park on the southern coast of the Island of Singapore. The proposal implements the vision of the Southern Ridges Master Plan, which calls for people to walk or cycle through nine kilometers of hills and natural parks, blessed with unique panoramic views. The international bridge design consultation launched in 2003 proposed two alternative sites of intervention and called for proposals of drastically different size. Given the extreme relief and dramatic qualities of the setting, we opted for the "big leap" of Henderson Crossing. On the first site visit in July 2004, we discovered a site buried in secondary equatorial undergrowth and marveled at its beauty.

The structure springs from a scenic point off Mount Faber and lands on the southwest side of Telok Blangah Hill, spanning some 700 feet over a four-lane freeway. The location for the springing point maximizes the visual impact of the structure over the gorge, while minimizing its length. On the landing end, the structure bends gently towards the east and wraps around the peak of the hill. It then reconnects with an existing ring road, creating a continuous circulation loop before heading west towards the next milestone of the master plan. At the base of the loop, pedestrians walking across the bridge and carrying on west pass under the deck and have wondrous views of its underside.

Bridges have typically simple briefs, but our own brief was even simpler than most: to leap over the gap with *one* equation only. The mathematical formula at work is a direct application of this office's trademark research, and is summarized in *IJP The Book of Surfaces* where the form of the Henderson Waves, a 3-D surface obtained by composing a linear force with two periodic ones, is described without symbols.[1]

The seemingly idiosyncratic form of Henderson Waves meets several challenges at once: in order to cross the gap between springing point and land without going over the prescribed slope, the bridge bends in plan while rising steadily. It also undulates, deforms and self-intersects to provide adequate egress, shelter and scenic viewing for pedestrians, marathon runners and cyclists. The complex, doubly curved deck forms a delicate tapestry of thousands of modular boards of tropical hardwood, which breaks at regular intervals to allow a wheel-chair to pause and a pedestrian to sit. This "synthetic landscape" is very imposing, with the figures speaking for themselves. It has nine waves, with the longest spanning some 57 meters over the traffic of Henderson Road. Being six meters high at its apex, you could fit a traditional Singapore shop-house under its arch. The developed length of the deck runs over 300 meters, and the difference in elevation between springing and landing points is about the full height of a seven-story housing block.

Henderson Waves opened in 2008. It has since received the Singapore President's Design Award (2009), the Design Award of the Singapore Institute of Architects (SIA) (2011); the Cityscape Award from the Institute for International Research (IIR) Middle East; the Urban Land Institute Award for Excellence in the Asia-Pacific; and the BCA Design & Engineering Safety Excellence Award, Singapore. The project has welcomed 300,000 visitors and is featured on more than two million websites.

Note

1   George Liaropoulos-Legendre, *IJP The Book of Surfaces* (London: AA Publications, 2003), 28.

1
Henderson Waves,
panoramic view from south
(Photography by MHJT).

Case Study IV: George L. Legendre

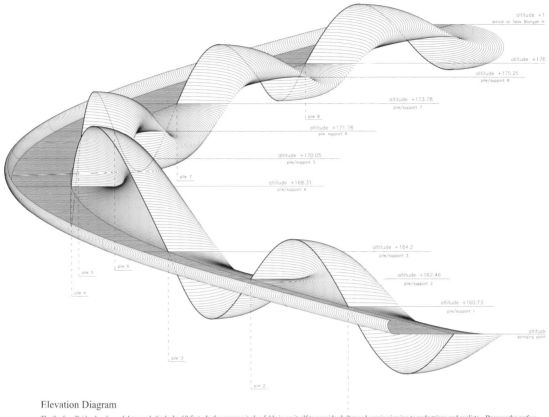

altitude +1
arrival at Telok Blangah H

altitude +176

altitude +175.25
pile/support 8

altitude +173.78
pile/support 7

pile 8

altitude +171.78
pile support 6

altitude +170.05
pile/support 5

pile 7

altitude +168.31
pile/support 4

altitude +164.2
pile/support 3

pile 5   pile 6

altitude +162.46
pile/support 2

pile 4

altitude +160.73
pile/support 1

pile 3

altitude
springing point

pile 2

Elevation Diagram

The Surface Bridge bends, undulates and climbs by 60 feet. In the process it also folds in on itself to provide shelter and scenic viewing to pedestrians and cyclists.   Because the surface rises while sliding in and out of alignment in all 3 dimensions, the drawing above is usually mistaken for as a bird's eye view (in actuality it is an elevation, a facade).
The height difference between springing and landing is the size of a 7-storey housing block, and the deck is 1000 feet long.

2
Henderson Waves, schematic diagram of elevation. The surface bends, undulates and climbs in a single movement. The periodic motions induced by the equations make the form glide out of alignment in all three dimensions at once (Photography by MHJT).

3
End works of bridge near the landing point, Telok Blangah Hill (Photography by MHJT).

4
Master plan of Henderson Waves. Mount Faber Park is on the right, Telok Blangah Hill is on the upper left (Photography by MHJT).

Case Study IV: George L. Legendre

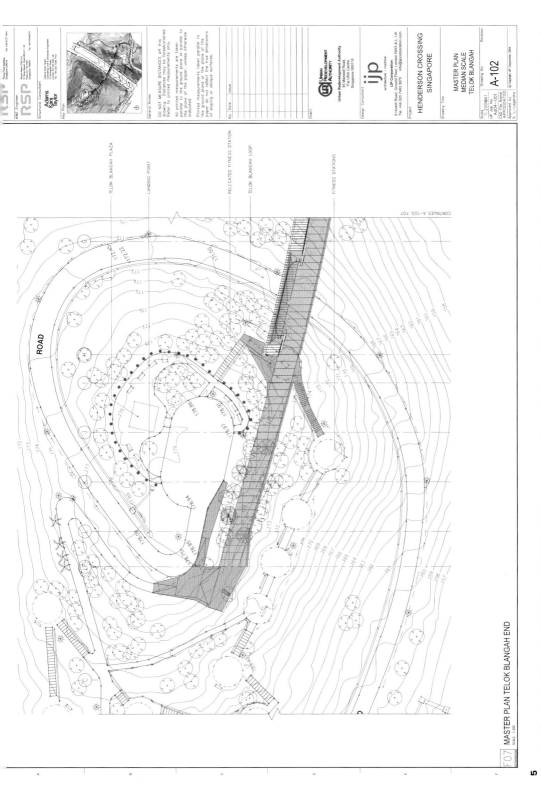

F07 MASTER PLAN TELOK BLANGAH END
SCALE 1:200

5 Plan of end works, landing point, Telok Blangah Hill. The bridge connects to the existing loop, which passes below it and heads west towards Alexandra Link (Photography by MHJT).

6 The bridge slips over the existing loop before reaching the end of the crossing, landing point, Telok Blangah Hill (Photography by MHJT).

Case Study IV: George L. Legendre

7

Plan of end works of bridge, springing point, Mount Faber Park. The bridge connects to the existing ring road via a timber walkway (Photography by MHJT).

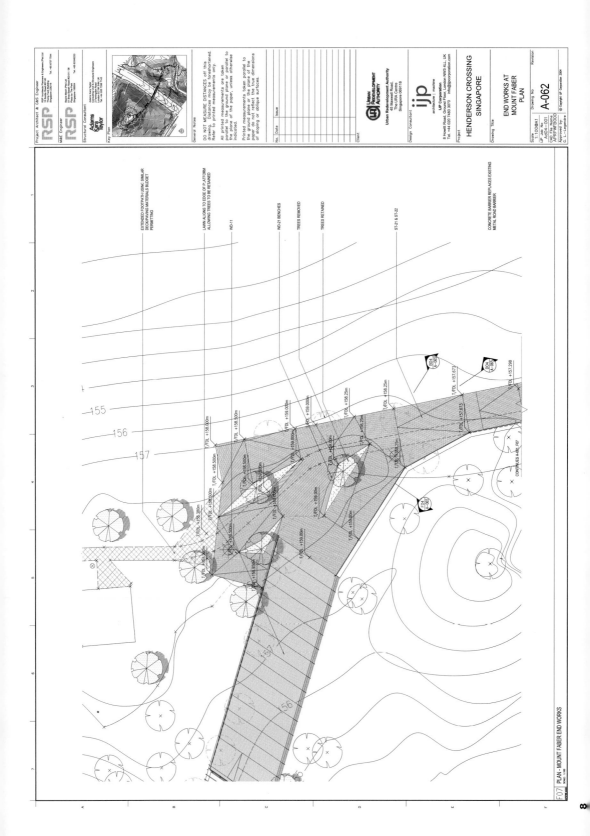

9
View of downside pod from the loop near landing point (span 6, also shown in drawing in Figure 11) (Photography by MHJT).

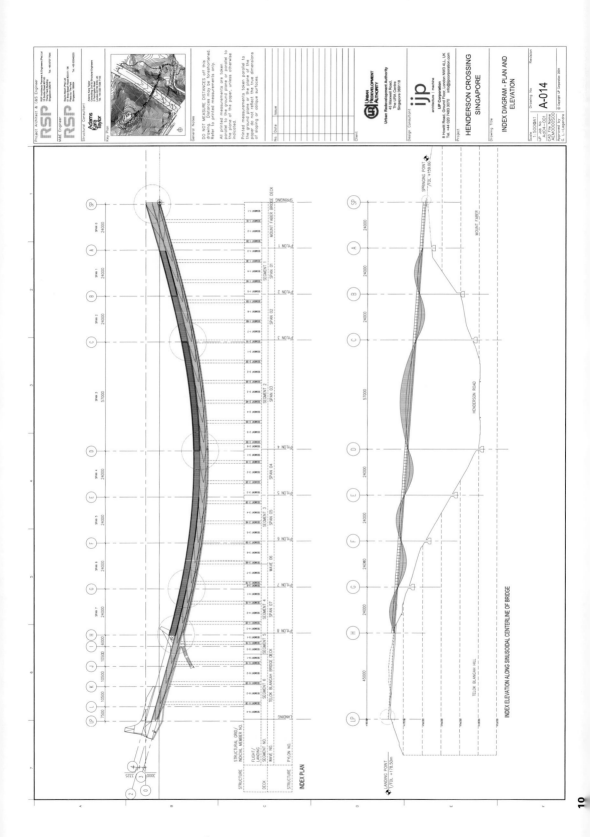

Case Study IV: George L. Legendre

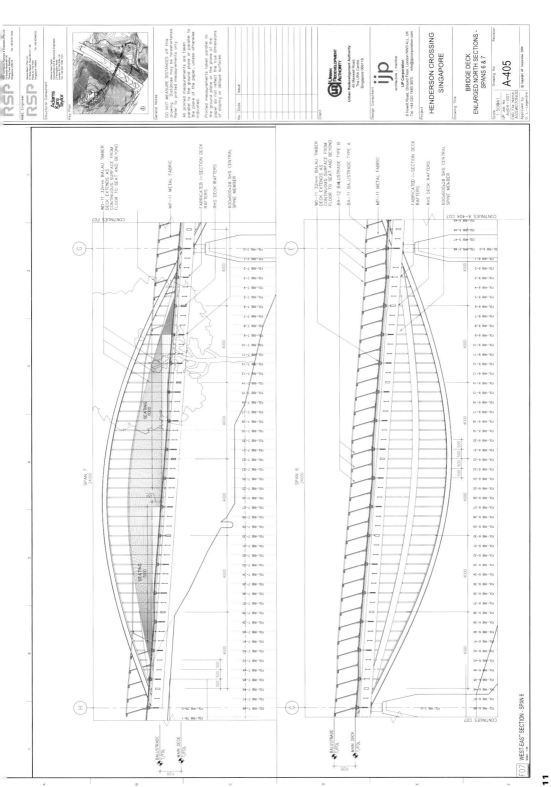

11

Section of spans 6 and 7, near the landing point, Telok Blangah Hill (see Figure 9) (Photography by MHJT).

Central span of bridge, timber deck and seating areas (Photography by MHJT).

12

13
Detail of planting and seating, end works of bridge, Telok Blangah Hill (Photography by MHJT).

Henderson Waves, Singapore (2004–2008)

14
The bridge under construction, summer 2007. Prior to being hauled up into position, the central span of the bridge rests on a makeshift platform at the foot of the tallest concrete pile (Photography by MHJT).

Case Study IV: George L. Legendre

Part V

Nature, Unnaturally

12

Block That Metaphor!

Jorge Silvetti

My chapter finds itself unwittingly, if usefully, framed by the last part of this volume on nature and architecture, and I should say something about this. I always worry that discussions about architecture and sustainability prompt too much talking about Nature and not enough about Architecture—because the problem we have is Architecture: *Nature is; it exists. Architecture we must make.*

This brings me to one of my favorite topics: what architecture looks like these days, and what that tells us about the state of the art as well as the state of architectural education more generally. If we consider the architecture currently on offer in magazines, competitions and graduate theses, then it admittedly looks very much like "Nature." The polemical position I would like to introduce to the discussion, in a nutshell, is this: Architecture should not look like what it is not—a statement that can only be understood in the context of broader reflections on the "Nature of Architecture" and what this means historically as well as currently. I shall address the issue somewhat obliquely by focusing on a few relevant examples of how Nature has entered into the equation of Architecture.

By the same token, and since I am taking my lead from titles, I would like briefly to mention the source of my own. For those not familiar with the expression "Block That Metaphor!," this is the heading for a minuscule and delicious occasional feature published in *The New Yorker*. It showcases independent snippets serving as humorous graphic fillers at the end of full-length articles in which are quoted a host of mixed metaphors and unintended meanings picked up from newspapers, magazines and advertisements—a litany of figures of speech gone wrong. If I appropriate *The New Yorker*'s title, this is because, on the one hand, my essay is only a snippet of a much larger debate on the "Nature of Architecture" and, on the other, we must block not one but many metaphors. For while any moderately educated reader can readily pick up on mixed metaphors or incongruous comparisons in a piece of writing, the task of unlocking such mechanisms of misfired meaning in architecture is not so easy—especially when a confounding literalism seems to be at work. The issue of understanding the efforts of literal bio-mimicry in creating human environments remains a great challenge, since these efforts should arguably be conceived instead to help us *differentiate* our acts from those of nature and, in so doing, to protect us from it. Highlighting this inherent cultural perversion strikes as a way to remind ourselves that even the oft-cited Vitruvian myth of primitive shelter insists on the transition from the human "imitation of the nests of swallows" to building better dwellings by virtue of "the powers of thought and understanding."[1] Literal bio-mimicry, therefore, opens a myriad of doors of inquiry as to what such recourse to natural imagery stands for at this particular moment.[2]

Out of all this, it is the process of architectural creativity on which I want specifically to focus. Let us not despair at the surprising recurrence of literalism, for its formal repertoire and image sources per se do not really threaten architecture. Mostly, the repertoire points to naïveté, as such visual operations bring the design process and architectural efficiency lamentably close to the role of magic in early human societies. These were societies in which formal similarities, say, the visual affinity between a garlic clove and a human tooth—a forceful example of the "going together" of things that Claude Lévi-Strauss identified as the intellectual basis of magic—imparts to the garlic clove the power to cure a tooth in pain.[3] Naturally, this curative power was due to its chemical composition and not its form (which is why Hippocrates, for one, prescribed garlic as a cure for any number of ailments).

Such "sympathy" between analogous forms is not what worries me—think of Leonardo da Vinci's drawing juxtaposing the layers of an onion with the dissected human brain—although its recurrence today points to intellectual poverty rather than to scientific discovery.[4] As with all formal trends to which we inevitably fall victim to some degree, their longevity is necessarily curtailed and, indeed, we are already witnessing the fading away of naive naturalism. But if the latter is fading, just as the invasion of blobs receded almost a decade ago, what they threaten to leave in their wake is an invisible and insidious metaphorical transformation—insofar as their ostensive claim to being "natural" is transposed from palpable images and transformed into intangible processes.

The Natural Process

Forms, like metaphors, are never innocent. Their appearances have consequences—particularly if they lie—and while one may tire of naturalized aesthetics, the literal message of "Architecture as Nature" seems to have emerged with increasing efficiency as it has migrated from the visual analogue to the less tangible domain of beliefs. In other words, the exercise of producing the visual metaphor of nature

Jorge Silvetti

in architecture has resulted in a silent, undetected reverse transfer of what these sympathetic forms suggest: namely that in addition to looking like nature, they are seen as being the result of a "natural" process of production, the very process of design.

Hence at the moment when the forms themselves are gradually being discarded, they are not falling into oblivion without leaving their mark. All to the contrary, they are leaving behind their baggage—transferring their meaning, so to speak, by following a process typical of a contemporary culture prone to peripatetic semantics: from one practice to another, from one medium to another, from forms and images to processes of making. As Kenneth Burke once wrote, such slipperiness is constitutive of the metaphor, "a device for seeing something in terms of something else. It brings out the thisness of a that, or the thatness of a this."[5] By the same token, metamorphic slipperiness is what some of the most exciting digital techniques of computation, in their ability to manipulate, coordinate and relate multiple variables and parameters, have enabled. The mesmerizing, almost sublime and confusing sight of printers spitting hitherto sleek and unimagined images, as well as 3-D models of a representation of an architecture that looks like nature, seduces the mind. It induces us to believe that a process of creation in which seemingly so little human intervention occurs is also natural, with this frightening corollary: that the state of mind that has allowed architecture to think about itself as the result of a "natural" process so precise—so seemingly outside our hands, so abandoned to invisible controls—cannot help but see the results (formal, organizational, structural, etc.) not only as inevitable but, worse yet, as a manifestation of *truth*. And if the whole process produces truth—here is the real problem—there is no need to assess the resulting form. Judging form is no longer important. Critical thinking has become moot.

Small wonder, then, that what has seemingly vanished is the discourse of ideas, which good architectural form had always conveyed to us and by means of which it had always provoked us. Instead, there are conversations about how and what scripting programs were used, and to what purpose, or what the appropriate algorithmic relationships of parameters were—as if sorting out programs, verifying algorithms and counting constraints were akin to checking with the technical crew at an airport to make sure that all controls are in working order before a departure for a successful trip.

The Relationship between Architecture and Nature

Revivals may be retrograde, but when they are intentional, at least their purposes can be argued. Yet if they are the product of lamentable ignorance or the wholesale dismissal of their own history, then conditions for disaster abound. Current discourses that claim possession of the keys to an unimpeachably legitimizing process, that consider the status of architectural form as insignificant and irrelevant, and that emphasize presumably measurable performance parameters, are all commonplaces we've visited before—in fact, quite recently.

Personally, I have already been through one such fallacious condition of which I was a willing victim. In the 1970s, when I was working on my Master's of Architecture at the University of California, Berkeley, one thing that was all the rage (besides Christopher Alexander's pattern language, which fortunately never seduced me) was General Systems Theory: a totalizing, synthesizing and multidisciplinary undertaking mostly promoted by behavioral scientists but happily and enthusiastically embraced by architects.[6] General Systems Theory or GST attempted to describe and put into operation deeply complex social and ecological systems by means of sophisticated mathematical and statistical simulation models. Interestingly, the cognitive scientist, sociologist and economist Herbert A. Simon's foundational article, "The Architecture of Complexity," begins with a word of warning:

> A number of proposals have been advanced in recent years for the development of "general systems theory" which, abstracting from properties peculiar to physical, biological, or social systems, would be applicable to all of them. We might feel that, while the goal is laudable, systems of such diverse kinds could hardly be expected to have nontrivial properties in common. Metaphor and analogy can be helpful, or they can be misleading. All depends on whether the similarities the metaphor captures are significant or superficial.[7]

Needless to say, when applied to architecture and design, these models cum metaphors simply fell apart in the face of the intrinsic resistance of any cultural practice to yield to technocratic manipulation—and I found myself, after having written a rather boring thesis in that vein, forever inoculated against all the viruses of Nature (if it can be believed, me, writing about my findings based on an statistical regression model that analyzed social networks in an urban area alongside the moose populations of the Lake Michigan islands).

Soon architecture fought back with productive vengeance, giving us simultaneously the best theory and design that we had experienced in generations and the worst excesses of Postmodernism. At its best, the critique acted as an inspiration stemming from cultural studies, literary criticism, history, anthropology; in short, all the humanities and sciences came to architecture as well-formulated perspectives whose imports could prompt the creation of new architectural products. At its worst, architecture was used to illustrate concepts from those fields without any transformative effect whatsoever; that is, we were left with another form of literalism.

We do not yet know where we stand in the life cycle of these current trends, but it is beginning to be apparent that there are just too many illusions and mirages, too much magical thinking, too much infantilism around to be sustainable. So if

Jorge Silvetti

there exists a willingness to learn from history, recent and less recent, then a serious attempt to alter course would be desirable and, even, imperative.

The Perfect Storm

Here is a brief sketch of the script on how we got here. At least three conditions, all valuable and positive in their own right, have converged to produce an "atmosphere" prone to producing wreckage: first, the environmental crisis and its consequences for architecture introduced the reign of sustainability, second, the availability of sophisticated computational techniques allowed hitherto impossible formal explorations to be generated; and third, the lack of clear formal norms, patterns and standards in architecture resulted in the liberating and energizing sense that all was possible in the ensuing torrent of formal possibilities.

Taken individually, each of these significant ingredients is good and welcome. However their commingling has emerged as toxic and devastating. The confluence of digital technology and formal liberation encouraged experimentation and, conversely, created an immense vacuum in architectural discourse; as the architect was confronted with an infinite number of unexpected formal possibilities, there was not much to say about them. How to discourse about forms that are coming from scripted programs? That was the failure of the first wave of blobs as nobody, save for Greg Lynn who originated the idea with great eloquence in 1995, knew what to say about them. Then, the entrance made by, on the one hand, sustainability, which carried with it the unshakable authority of "Nature" (as if this were some sort of a priori truth and not a changing political and cultural construct), and, on the other, the ineffable and acute ability of architects to analogize forms and construct metaphors: the passage from those mute, smooth and rounded blobs with no story to tell yet imploring us for meaning—the passage from those suggestive, yearning silences—to loud metaphors screaming "I am nature!" was seamless. Now, these metaphors can everywhere be seen as bones, muscles, trees, glands or geographies assuming the authority with which their condition endows them. Next step: the belief that they can perform the task implied by means of their metaphorical forms "naturally," with the requisite verbs attached to them for describing the actions performed. We act as if the process by which such forms were generated is not simply "like" a natural process, but actually *is* one— and because of this, can claim definitive and objective authority. End of discussion. End of Architecture.

Romantic Exemplars

I would like to end on a more optimistic note by turning to history—this in order to give a few examples of the productive, positive and immensely creative relations between the arts, sciences and nature or, more specifically, the *knowledge of nature*—the format in which nature should be brought into architecture (as opposed to as trees, waves, clouds, knolls, tentacles, glands or mollusks). These examples stem from the notably effervescent decades around the turn of the nineteenth century, which witnessed the passage from the Enlightenment to Romanticism. This period could be thought to be, if not similar to our own, at least comparable, presenting us with characteristics resembling some current predicaments and sensibilities (as the literary critic Edward Larrissy says, "the persistence of Romanticism in the present").[8] This was an era "when the arts were increasingly turning away from the frigid idea of Enlightenment aesthetics and towards a new stress on imagination and feeling."[9] This was also an era of major discoveries in which the emergent discipline of science (in the modern sense) referred to the activities of its practitioners as "experimental philosophy"—a characterization falling much closer to the idea of the "knowledge of nature" to which I alluded earlier. According to the historian of science Elizabeth Garber, "natural philosophy and philosophy could not be separated. This was partly because of the belief that the study of experimental phenomena could uncover the actual workings and structures of nature. The findings of experimental philosophers and interpretations of the meanings of their results contained within them metaphysical and philosophical implications no philosopher could ignore."[10]

It is interesting that in such productive decades, both artists and experimental philosophers enjoyed intense personal and professional relationships with each other, a guarantor of the interaction between their respective disciplines. Thus the founder of modern astronomy, Friedrich Wilhelm Herschel was a first-class musician, performer and composer of some 24 symphonies who went on to devote his life to the major discoveries that would change our understanding of the nature of the universe, shatter theological tenets and illustrate the philosophical concept of the infinite and the sublime.[11] Thus Johann Wolfgang von Goethe could navigate between writing paradigmatic Romantic novels and plays such as *The Sorrows of Young Werther* (1774) and *Faust* (a life-long project), studying botany, and developing a theory of color, which not only served as basis for Arthur Schopenhauer's *On Vision and Color* (1816) but also prompted a complex response in the painted works of the English painter J. M. W. Turner (Figures 12.1 and 12.2);[12] all the while, he absorbed the art and architecture of the ancients during his Grand Tour of Italy, over the course of which he collected stone samples, investigated the formation of clouds and experienced on Vesuvius "a hill of ash which had been recently thrown up and was emitting fumes everywhere."[13] And thus Sir Humphry Davy, one of the founders of modern chemistry, penned some of his discoveries in verse because he was a gifted amateur poet encouraged by his close friend Samuel Taylor Coleridge.[14] In all these cases and countless others, the knowledge of nature was central to the dialogue between the sciences and the arts. As Robert J. Richards reminds us, Goethe, in an essay penned in 1789 and entitled "Simple Imitation of Nature, Manner, Style," distinguished between moderate talents "who

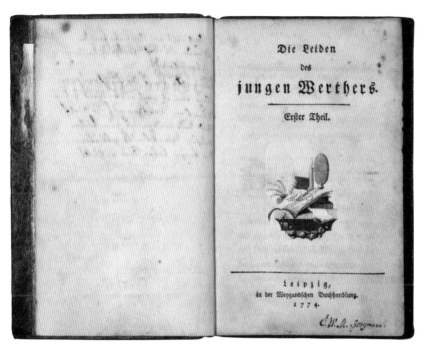

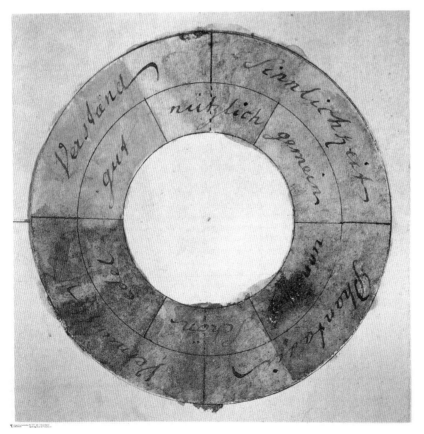

Block That Metaphor!

would imitate nature very precisely in their simple compositions, from those of greater talent, who would discover within themselves a language, a manner, by which to express more complex subjects."[15]

Now to turn to two non-architectural examples in which such expression emerges: The first involves the great Austrian composer Joseph Haydn, the inventor of the "Symphony" form and a man of the Enlightenment living the last chapter of his life by straddling the century. Over the course of his travels to England in the early 1790s—he had accepted the invitation made by the German impresario Johann Peter Salomon to produce and conduct new symphonies in London—he took it upon himself to visit none other than Herschel in his observatory in Slough. Herschel gave him a demonstration of his extraordinary telescope, 40 feet long and 5 inches in diameter, which struck Haydn, so he noted in his travel notebooks, as "so ingenious that a single man can put it in motion with the greatest ease."[16] That glimpse of the universe, and the idea that the cosmos could have evolved out of chaos, undoubtedly came to mark his monumental oratorio *The Creation*, which premiered at the Schwarzenberg Palace in Vienna in 1798.[17] This was Haydn's first attempt at composing in a genre known for centuries in England. And in the musical introduction, subtitled "The Representation of Chaos," he played with receding and assertive tonalities in unprecedented ways in order to convey how, as Richard Taruskin puts it, "inchoate matter strives . . . toward shape and differentiation."[18]

The second example involves the English novelist Mary Shelley: that a woman in that period should have been interested in writing was already somewhat unusual; that she should have been, in addition, seriously interested in "experimental philosophy" was almost unconceivable. Yet, she religiously attended Sir Humphry Davy's lectures on chemistry at the Royal Society, read his *Discourse, Introductory to a Course of Lectures on Chemistry* (1802) and corresponded with scientists of the day. She was especially interested in the discovery of electricity and associated phenomena (something comparable with our excitement with things digital), which had been observed but still largely unexplained. All of this helped her to shape *Frankenstein, or the Modern Prometheus* (1818), which was unmistakably founded on the scientific and philosophical discourses of the time.[19] Her interest in electricity, which at the time was thought potentially to hold the definitive explanation of the origins of life, sits at the core of her disquisition about the nature of man, his ambitions and his conflicted desire to know and to produce (Figures 12.3 and 12.4).

My point, in closing, is perhaps not as apparent as one might think; these artists were serious about learning about nature. If they went through the pains of acquiring a substantive knowledge of nature, when they came back to produce, they did so with the tools of their *métier* (which they never confused for the things they had learned). Mary Shelley wrote the consummate Romantic novel, created a new genre—that of science fiction—and thereby not only reaffirmed her vocation but advanced its capacities. She directed her knowledge of chemistry, electricity, voltaic arcs, etc. at the construction of a story about scientific hubris. *She had a*

Jorge Silvetti

12.3
William Chevalier after Theodor M. von Holst, "Frankenstein and his Monster," frontispiece steel engraving for the revised
1831 edition of Mary Shelley's *Frankenstein, or the Modern Prometheus* (Photo: Courtesy of Getty Images, The Bridgman Art
Collection #80584504).

12.4
Tesla Coil Sparks 4KVA with Corona on Wire, 15 March 2007 (Photo: Arne Groh. Licensed under the Creative Commons Attribution 3.0 Unported License).

literary idea not an electrical idea. For his part, Haydn did the same. He encountered theories about the formation of the universe, then sought out a musical form—the oratory—that would allow him to narrate a sublime story by means of an acoustic marvel evoking the creation of space. However exciting or foreboding, scientific knowledge never kept them away from their respective crafts nor did they ever confuse nature with what they were making: no naive magic here, instead intellectual rigor and artistic integrity. *We should regain that dominion of our own doings, the nature of what we do, i.e. the Nature of Architecture, before we venture to bring nature into the equation.*

To end on a high note (no pun intended), imagine yourself listening to Haydn's *The Creation*, all the while picturing the galaxies alongside the manuscript page containing the notations of what you are hearing: image–music–text (*pace* Roland Barthes). These would be three representations of the same thing in different media: the photographic image; the sound of the music itself; and the sheet of paper whose vertical axis represents the space of the orchestra and whose horizontal axis indicates the rhythmic passage of time (Figures 12.5 and 12.6). They all address spatial infinity within their own substance and without betraying their own nature. No mixing, no blurring, no subsuming, no confusion.

Jorge Silvetti

12.5
Joseph Haydn, score, "The Representation of Chaos" from *The Creation* (1796–1798) (Photo: Courtesy of Music Division, The New York Public Library for the Performing Arts, Astor, Lenox and Tilden Foundation).

12.6
Portrait of Barnard's Galaxy, October 15, 2009, taken using the Wide Field Imager attached to the 2.2-meter MPG/ESO telescope at ESO's La Silla Observatory, Chile (Photograph by the European Southern Observatory. Licensed under the Creative Commons Attribution 3.0 Unported License).

Block That Metaphor!

Postscript: New Rules for Architecture

Rule #1: Architectural projects should not resemble natural forms, irrespective of whether they are good natural forms (such as fruits, flowers, pandas, etc.) or bad-natured natural forms (such as rotten eggs, tumors, arthrosis, swarming killer bees, etc.). Any forms that recall matter in a smelly state of decomposition should be banished.

Rule #2: Discourse on architecture should never refer to the design process as if it were a digestive, meteorological or oceanographic phenomenon. It is not. It is an architectural process. Learn the differences. Starting now, there will be a five-year moratorium on the following terms: propagate, infestate, parasitic, embryonic, harvested, mining, grafting, and so on.

Rule #3: Presentations should not imply that nature is good and architecture is bad. Be an educated person and learn, once and for all, that architecture was invented to protect us from nature. *Nature can kill you.*

Rule #4: Be serious and learn from history. Marc-Antoine Laugier's representation of the primitive hut does not offer historical proof that architecture is the result of a natural process because it shows the natural source of some of its structural components. This is a record of precisely the opposite: the moment at which architecture emerges and distances itself from nature by transforming organic matter into architectural matter.

Notes

1   Vitruvius, *The Ten Books of Architecture*, trans. Morris Hicky Morgan (New York: Dover Publications, 1960), 35, 37. As William A. McClung, *The Architecture of Paradise: Survivals of Eden and Jerusalem* (Berkeley and Los Angeles: University of California Press, 1983), 93, has noted: "It is less in the identification of architecture with nature . . . than in the redefinition of nature itself that Vitruvius laid the basis for the Renaissance glory of the craft."

2   So often at issue is the gloss of scientific authority that references to nature in architecture seemingly want to evoke. As Esa Väliverronen, who has considered the simultaneously communicative and obfuscatory power of metaphor in the environmental sciences in "Biodiversity and the Power of Metaphor in Environmental Discourse," *Science Studies* 11/1 (June 1998), 19–34, emphasizes: "[B]iodiversity is not just a normal scientific concept. It is often used as an all-encompassing term, a 'scientized synonym for nature'. . . . Biodiversity is about almost anything that is good and under threat in our natural environment. The power of biodiversity as a metaphor in semiprofessional and popular discourses is linked to its origin as a scientific concept" (31).

3   Claude Lévi-Strauss, *The Savage Mind* (French ed. 1962; Chicago, IL: University of Chicago Press, 1966), 9.

4   Leonardo da Vinci, *Leonardo on the Human Body* (New York: Dover Publications, 1983), 330.

5   Kenneth Burke, *A Grammar of Motives* (Berkeley and Los Angeles: University of California Press, 1969), 503.

Jorge Silvetti

6 See, for instance, Ludwig von Bertalanffy, *General System Theory: Foundations, Development, Applications* (New York: George Braziller, 1969).

7 Herbert A. Simon, "The Architecture of Complexity," *Proceedings of the American Philosophical Society* 106/6 (Dec. 1962), 467.

8 Edward Larrissy, ed., *Romanticism and Postmodernism* (Cambridge: Cambridge University Press, 1999), 1.

9 Andreas Friesenhagen, "Let there be light," liner notes for the Harmonia Mundi HMC 992039 recording of Joseph Haydn's "Die Schöpfung," performed by the Freiburger Barockorchester directed by René Jacobs (2009).

10 Elizabeth Garber, *The Language of Physics: The Calculus and the Development of Theoretical Physics in Europe, 1750–1914* (Boston, MA: Birkhäuser, 1999), 140.

11 For a recent history of Romantic science in England organized around the biographies of prominent scientists and artists of the period, see Richard Holmes, *The Age of Wonder: How the Romantic Generation Discovered the Beauty and Terror of Science* (New York: Pantheon Books, 2008).

12 On this, see for example Gerald Finley, "Pigment into Light: Turner, and Goethe's 'Theory of Colours'," in Frederick Burwick, Jürgen Klein, eds., *The Romantic Imagination: Literature and Art in England and Germany* (Amsterdam: Rodopi B.V., 1996), 357–376.

13 Johann Wolfgang von Goethe, *Italian Journey, 1786–1788*, trans. W.H. Auden and Elizabeth Mayer (London: Penguin Classics, 1970), 189. See David Seamon, Arthur Zajonc, eds., *Goethe's Way of Science: A Phenomenology of Nature* (Albany: SUNY Press, 1998).

14 Roger Sharrock, "The Chemist and the Poet: Sir Humphry Davy and the Preface to Lyrical Ballads," *Notes and Records of the Royal Society of London* 17/1 (May 1962): 57 76.

15 Robert J. Richards, *The Romantic Conception of Life: Science and Philosophy in the Age of Goethe* (Chicago, IL: University of Chicago Press, 2002), 402.

16 Norman Lebrecht, ed., *The Book of Musical Anecdotes* (New York: Simon & Schuster, 1985), 51.

17 Karl Geiringer, *Haydn: A Creative Life in Music* (Berkeley and Los Angeles: University of California Press, 1982), 356.

18 Richard Taruskin, *Oxford History of Western Music* (Oxford: Oxford University Press, 2009), ex. 11–10a.

19 I find it interesting that the feminist interpretation likewise pushes back against the metaphor. Anne K. Mellor, *Mary Shelley: Her Life, Her Fictions, Her Monsters* (London: Routledge, 1988), 89, writes: "The explanatory models of science, like the plots of literary works, depend on linguistic structures which are shaped by metaphor and image. When Francis Bacon announced, 'I am come in very truth leading to you Nature with all her children to bind her to your service and make her your slave,' he identified the pursuit of modern science with the practice of sexual politics: the aggressive, virile male scientist legitimately captures and enslaves a fertile but passive female nature. Mary Shelley was one of the first to comprehend and illustrate the dangers inherent in the use of such gendered metaphors in the seventeenth-century scientific revolution."

Case Study V

Preston Scott Cohen, Inc., Fahmy House, Los Gatos, CA (2007–2014)

The Fahmy House appears at once to be derived from an exceptionally wide gable and a simple linear shed building. Designed for a site that is so exceedingly steep and populated by native oak trees as to be almost impossible to develop, the primary goal was to minimize the environmental impact of new construction while integrating interior and exterior spaces with a coherent form. The house, both in plan and section, conforms to the topography, avoids disturbing the root-protection zones of the trees and stays under a strict height limitation.

The earthen materials and tectonic expression of the façade contradict the implicit elasticity of the overall shape of the house, which seems to be projected onto the site. The chevron provisionally defines half of an exterior courtyard that has a tenuous relationship with the interior of the house. The tension becomes most acute at the vertex of the chevron where the interior space, descending from the front of the house, extends below a green roof. Owing to the emphatic correlation between the sloped site and the overall form of the chevron, this subterranean space is unsuspected from the exterior.

At the beginning of the design process, in accordance with rules imposed by the town of Los Gatos, California, an arborist was hired to produce a tree inventory and to rate all of the trees from good to poor condition. The root zones of the trees were projected onto a three-dimensional computer model of the topography. The difficulty was to maintain the integrity of the chevron form while dodging the roots and keeping the building below the height limit (18 ft.) and below the cumulative height limit, from the lowest point on the site to the highest point on the roof (35 ft.). In order not to require significant cutting and filling, to control erosion and run-off, the house had to run parallel to the topographic slope, which is skewed relative to the street. This demand as well as the driveway forced the house to be located near the street, the area with the most trees. The driveway is the minimum area that can approximate a hyperbolic parabola and thus not exceed the maximum allowable slope; it slopes 15 percent downhill and at its right edge, 14.6 percent uphill on its left. Given the narrowness of the house, its position on the site and the angle between its two wings, it was possible to save five out of the six trees deemed to be in 'good' condition and two of the three deemed to be 'fair.' The chevron gable-form, bending in plan and sloping with the hill, with one end near the street extended to accommodate a garage, coincides with generative processes initiated by site constraints and environmental imperatives.

Client: Stewart and Colette Fahmy
Program: 4,785 sq. ft. residence
Project Team: Preston Scott Cohen (Design); Gilles Quintal (Project Architect); Hang Cheng, Matthew Allen, David Saladik, Matt Storus, Ashley Merchant, Dan Sullivan (Project Assistants).
Schedule: 2007–2008 and 2010–2011, design; 2014, construction.

1
Prospect (Courtesy of Preston Scott Cohen).

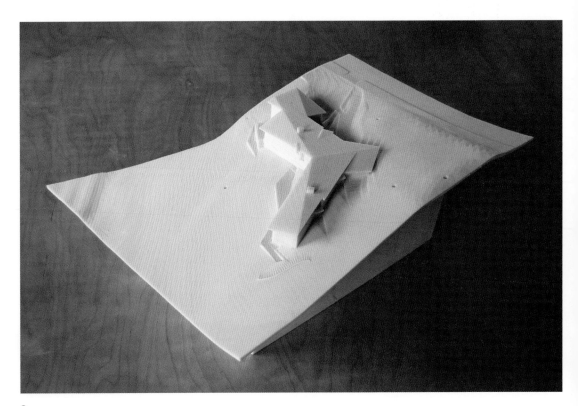

2
Model (Courtesy of Preston Scott Cohen).

Case Study V: Preston Scott Cohen, Inc.

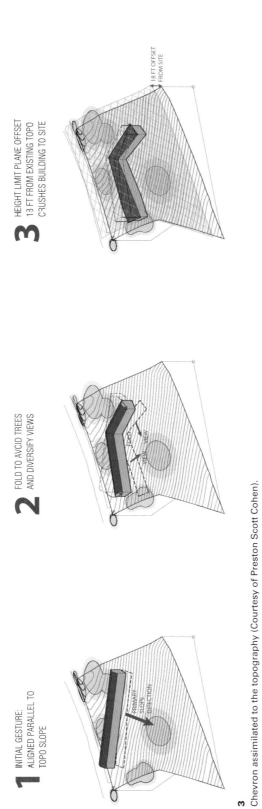

1 INITIAL GESTURE: ALIGNED PARALLEL TO TOPO SLOPE

2 FOLD TO AVOID TREES AND DIVERSIFY VIEWS

3 HEIGHT LIMIT PLANE OFFSET 13 FT FROM EXISTING TOPO CRUSHES BUILDING TO SITE

3
Chevron assimilated to the topography (Courtesy of Preston Scott Cohen).

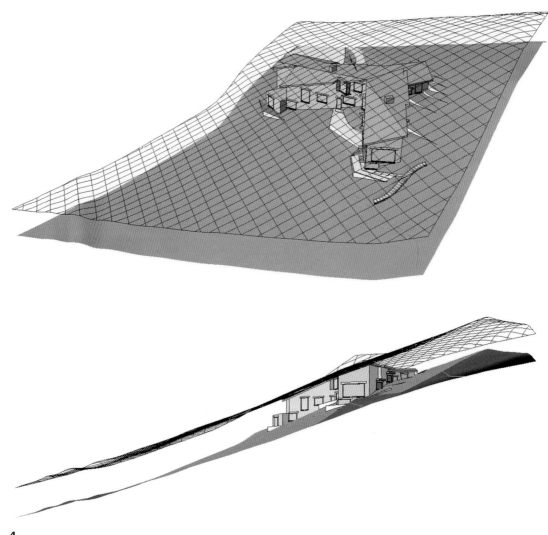

4
Height limit (Courtesy of Preston Scott Cohen).

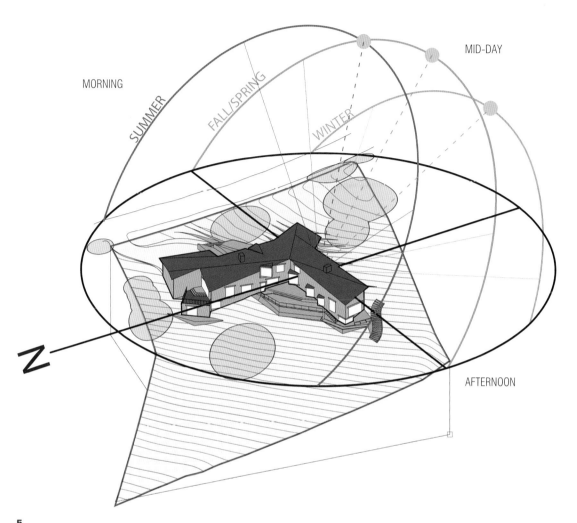

MORNING

SUMMER

FALL/SPRING

WINTER

MID-DAY

AFTERNOON

N

5
Solar diagram (Courtesy of Preston Scott Cohen).

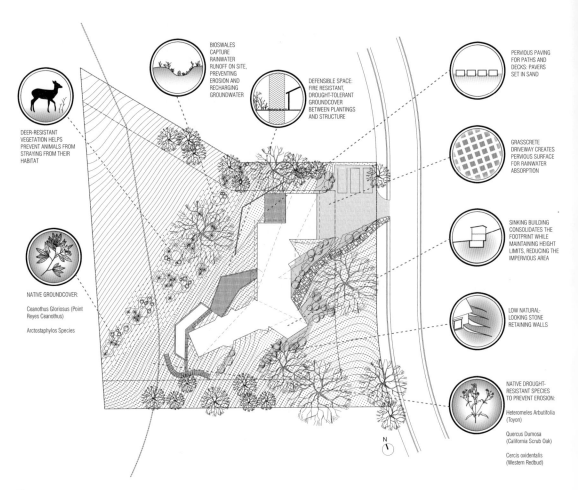

BIOSWALES CAPTURE RAINWATER RUNOFF ON SITE, PREVENTING EROSION AND RECHARGING GROUNDWATER

DEFENSIBLE SPACE: FIRE RESISTANT, DROUGHT-TOLERANT GROUNDCOVER BETWEEN PLANTINGS AND STRUCTURE

PERVIOUS PAVING FOR PATHS AND DECKS: PAVERS SET IN SAND

DEER-RESISTANT VEGETATION HELPS PREVENT ANIMALS FROM STRAYING FROM THEIR HABITAT

GRASSCRETE DRIVEWAY CREATES PERVIOUS SURFACE FOR RAINWATER ABSORPTION

SINKING BUILDING CONSOLIDATES THE FOOTPRINT WHILE MAINTAINING HEIGHT LIMITS, REDUCING THE IMPERVIOUS AREA

NATIVE GROUNDCOVER:

Ceanothus Gloriosus (Point Reyes Ceanothus)

Arctostaphylos Species

LOW NATURAL-LOOKING STONE RETAINING WALLS

NATIVE DROUGHT-RESISTANT SPECIES TO PREVENT EROSION:

Heteromeles Arbutifolia (Toyon)

Quercus Dumosa (California Scrub Oak)

Cercis oxidentalis (Western Redbud)

N

6
Site plan (Courtesy of Preston Scott Cohen).

Case Study V: Preston Scott Cohen, Inc.

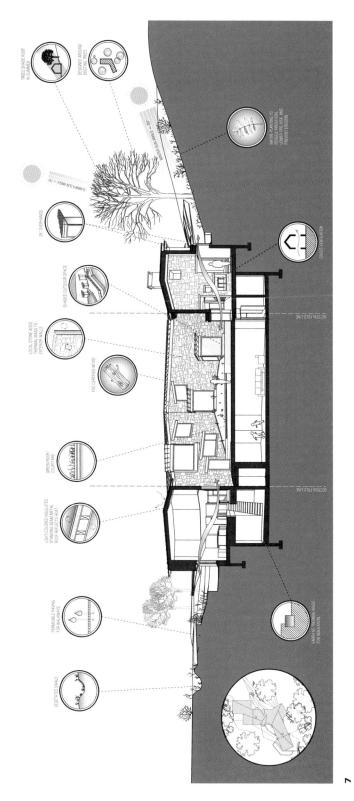

7

Site section (Courtesy of Preston Scott Cohen).

Fahmy House, Los Gatos, CA (2007–2014)

8
Chevron façade (Courtesy of Preston Scott Cohen).

9
Green roof at vertex (Courtesy of Preston Scott Cohen).

Case Study V: Preston Scott Cohen, Inc.

10
Behind and below the vertex (Courtesy of Preston Scott Cohen).

11
Living room (Courtesy of
Preston Scott Cohen).

Fahmy House, Los Gatos, CA (2007–2014)

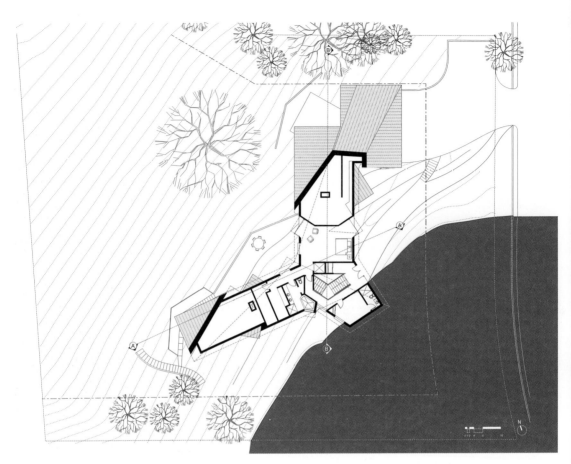

12
Entrance plan (Courtesy of Preston Scott Cohen).

Case Study V: Preston Scott Cohen, Inc.

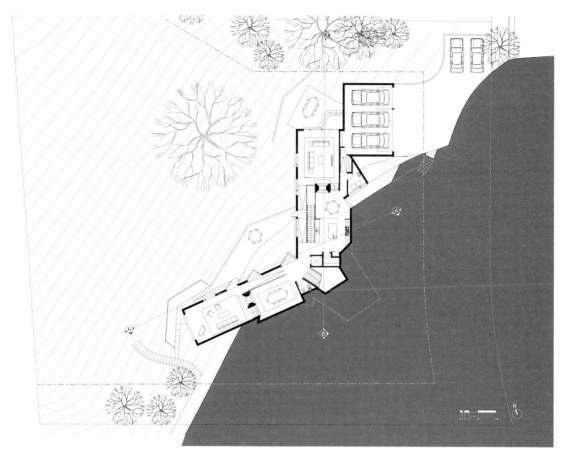

13
Main plan (Courtesy of Preston Scott Cohen).

Fahmy House, Los Gatos, CA (2007–2014)

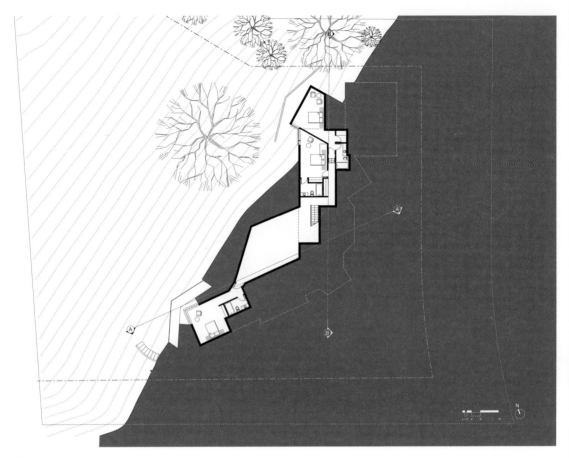

14
Lower plan (Courtesy of Preston Scott Cohen).

Case Study V: Preston Scott Cohen, Inc.

Index